HUMAN CHEAT CODE™

HUMAN CHEAT CODE™

UNLOCK YOUR CORE VALUES FOR PERSONAL AND PROFESSIONAL SUCCESS

RODNEY LEE MILLS

1012 SOLUTIONS LLC™

TABLE OF CONTENTS

INTRODUCTION

There comes a point when the surface-level routines of life stop being enough, and something deeper begins to stir, a quiet but persistent urge to uncover the truth behind the most essential questions a person can ask: *Who am I?* and *What is my purpose?* It's a longing that feels both ancient and intensely personal, as if some hidden part of you already knows there is more beneath the layers you've accumulated over the years. You start to sense that your identity isn't just a collection of roles, expectations, or memories, but something more fluid, more profound, waiting to be understood. And purpose, once thought to be a destination, reveals itself as a journey, a process of aligning your actions with the deeper currents of your values, passions, and inner drive. The search becomes a kind of awakening, a willingness to question everything you've been told, everything you've assumed, and everything you've avoided. It's not about finding quick answers but about embracing the exploration itself, trusting that each step inward brings you closer to a truth that feels authentically your own.

I personally believe every person carries a distinct inner design, a blend of abilities, instincts, perspectives, and creative impulses that no one else on earth possesses in quite the same way. I believe that uniqueness isn't accidental. I believe it's directly connected to a purpose that is just as singular. I personally believe when you begin to understand the way you're *wired* and recognize that your design is pointing you toward the work, relationships, and contributions you're meant to make, something powerful happens. I believe your purpose stops feeling abstract and starts feeling aligned with who you truly are. I believe that when your unique design and unique purpose finally meet, the world receives the fullest expression of you. Your clarity, your energy, your creativity, your presence. In that alignment, I believe your contribution becomes not only more impactful but deeply fulfilling, because you're no longer offering a version of yourself shaped by expectation or comparison. You're offering the world the one thing only you can give: **your whole authentic self**.

Imagine arriving at a moment in your life when you sense that the real journey ahead isn't about mastering the world around you, but about awakening to the person you were intentionally created to be. You begin to wonder what it would feel like to truly know yourself beneath the habits, the roles, and the stories you've carried for years, to uncover the unique design woven into you from the beginning. What if you could see how you lead, how you communicate, how you respond under pressure, and how you move through conflict with a clarity that feels almost like rediscovering something placed in your core on purpose? And what if that same insight helped you understand the people around you with equal depth, so your relationships, your decisions, your leadership, and even the way you shape your life begin to align with something greater than yourself? As you move forward and continue to read this book, you're opening yourself to that possibility. You're entering a framework that doesn't just describe behavior but reveals the deeper motivations and patterns that hint at a thoughtful, intentional design. It helps you see why certain interactions feel natural while others feel strained, and how you can use that awareness to build a life that reflects the purpose you were meant to live out. This isn't just information, it's a new lens for seeing yourself and others with clarity, compassion, and a sense of divine intentionality. And stepping into that alignment has the potential to change everything that comes next.

The Core Values Index™ (CVI™)

What if I told you there is an assessment capable of revealing the stable, unchanging motivations that drive a person at their core, rather than the shifting traits most assessments measure? What if I told you, it can do this with a level of accuracy and repeatability that far exceeds the tools most organizations rely on today?

The CVI™ created by Lynn Ellsworth Taylor, is not a personality test. It is a psychometric assessment designed to measure the stable and unchanging core motivations that shape human behavior. Instead of capturing shifting preferences or situational traits, the CVI™ focuses on the deeper motivational energies that remain consistent across time and circumstance.

I was told that Taylor's work began with a search for the forces that drive human motivation at its most fundamental level. This exploration led to the identification of four core value energies: *Merchant, Innovator, Banker,* and *Builder.* I learned that these values describe how individuals are naturally wired to contribute and that these core values offer a framework for understanding a person's most authentic patterns of decision making, problem solving, and interpersonal engagement. After using the CVI™ for years now, I believe it provides a way to see this deeper structure so people and organizations can align roles and environments with an individual's innate core values.

For readers who want empirical validation, the CVI™ stands out because of its unusually high resistance to manipulation. In psychometric science, tools that are easy to fake typically show lower test–retest reliability because altered responses produce inconsistent scores. The CVI™ has demonstrated exceptional stability over time. Independent research, including a longitudinal study conducted by *Seattle Research Partners* in 2014, reported a **97.7 percent test–retest reliability rate**. This level of consistency exceeds the reliability benchmarks of many widely used organizational assessments and suggests that the CVI™ measures something deeply rooted rather than something influenced by mood, context, or strategic answering. I have personally seen this reliability firsthand with hundreds of individuals I have professionaly consulted, worked with, and given advice to. The CVI™ has time and time again, proven its reliability in my numerous encounters.

I learned that a major reason for this stability is the CVI™ forced choice format. Instead of asking respondents to rate behaviors or preferences, the assessment presents sets of equally positive descriptors and requires instinctive selection. Because there is no obvious ideal answer, respondents cannot easily tailor their responses to produce a desired outcome. This structure minimizes social desirability bias and reduces the likelihood of conscious manipulation, allowing the assessment to capture a person's true motivational core rather than a curated self-presentation.

Over decades of use in hiring, team development, and organizational design, the CVI™ has earned a reputation for reliability because it measures something more stable than personality traits or behavioral tendencies. Many popular assessments show reliability ranges between 60 percent and 80 percent. The CVI™ consistently performs far above that range. For organizations seeking a tool that remains accurate over time, and for individuals who want an assessment grounded in empirical consistency, the CVI™ offers a level of repeatability and predictive clarity that is rare in the field. Because core values do not change, the CVI™ only needs to be taken once, and its insights remain valid for years, and in my opinion, for life.

Unlike assessments that evaluate performance, aptitude, or personality, the CVI™ deliberately avoids measuring strengths and weaknesses, learned skills, accumulated knowledge, past experiences, IQ, or behavioral style. These qualities can shift over time as people grow, adapt, or encounter new environments, making them unreliable indicators of a person's enduring nature. By excluding these fluctuating factors, the CVI™ isolates the deeper value-based drivers that remain constant throughout life. This distinction is crucial because it prevents temporary circumstances or external achievements from distorting the results. The clarity that emerges allows individuals and organizations to make decisions rooted in long-term alignment rather than short-term capability. In doing so, the CVI™ helps ensure that roles, collaborations, and expectations are built on who a person is at their core, not merely what they have learned or how they are performing at a given moment.

While the CVI™ is the foundational framework woven throughout this book, it's important to note that *The Human Cheat Code*™ isn't a technical manual about the CVI™ itself. Instead, it is a consolidation of my personal understanding of the CVI™, how I have used it, and approaches I think would be value added to readers. If you're looking for a comprehensive exploration of the CVI™ assessment, its origins, methodology, scoring system, and theoretical underpinnings, then Taylor's *The Core Values Handbook* published by Elliot Bay Publishing is the definitive resource. The *Core Values Handbook* offers a deep dive into the original mechanics of the CVI™ and is ideal for those who want to understand the tool in its purest form. The *Human Operating System*™ (*HOS*™) *Manual* is another reference to explore. HOS™ contains the basic construct, theory, and validations of the CVI™ along with a facilitator's glossary, manual, and detailed logic and descriptions of operating modalities of all the core values, natures, and participatory types of contributing individuals. I recommend visiting *Taylor Protocols*™ web site as they have a plethora of services you will find beneficial for your personal and professional growth as well as that of your organization.

The Human Cheat Code™ takes a different approach. Its focus is on concepts I have learned, observed, and developed while using the CVI™. This book is my interpretation of the CVI™. I have taken these lessons and experiences and captured them in this book. I purposely broke out *The Human Cheat Code*™ in a way that helps you to continue your learning of the CVI™ and its multiple uses. You will notice that in some places, there is a repetitive explanation of the four core values themselves throughout the book for the various topic areas. This is deliberate because I expect you to go back and reference sections of this book and not have to review all the material. This approach is taken so you can leverage the insights from your CVI™ profile and this book to transform your personal and professional life.

In *The Human Cheat Code*™, I will take steps like breaking up the CVI™ capacity scores into four distinct labeled categories that adds utility in a way a single composite score simply can't. This is important because through my use of the CVI™, to separate a broad idea like *capacity* into its component parts and make it useable day-to-day, you have to see the underlying patterns broken up that reveal who a person really is and how much they bring into the world. Instead of categorizing someone into one core value or number, you get in my opinion a multi-dimensional, more definitive, and explanatory profile that describes and highlights an individual's core values, capacity within each core value, and their tendencies.

A crucial part of this book is learning to recognize the *dark side* of a person's CVI™ profile and the aggravating factors that can distort or mask their results. These elements add depth, accuracy, and honesty to the CVI™ by revealing not just who someone is at their best, but also how their core values can shift under pressure.

While the CVI™ identifies a person's innate capacities, the core values that feel natural, energizing, and effortless, each of those capacities has a *dark side*. This darker expression isn't about diagnosing flaws. It's about understanding how core values can become liabilities when they're overused or triggered. The *Innovator* who normally brings clarity and solutions may become impulsive or dismissive under stress. The *Merchant* who thrives on connection may slip into avoidance or emotional manipulation. The *Banker* who ensures accuracy may turn rigid or withholding when overwhelmed. The *Builder* who drives action may become controlling or aggressive when threatened. Recognizing these patterns matter because it gives people the self-awareness to interrupt them before they erode trust, credibility, or performance. Understanding *going dark* and the factors that aggravate core value capacity scores allows individuals to avoid or transition from their dark side to their core values that are meant to bring contribution into the world, ensuring their natural core values remain assets rather than unintended liabilities in every area of life. I again will repeat these *dark* observations repeatedly throughout the book for later reference purposes.

Although Taylor doesn't specifically use the exact phrase *going dark*, Taylor states that our deepest fears (the opposite of that core value) emerge when a core value is stressed, overextended, or misapplied and the individual's *dark side* comes out. In essence, when an individual loses their sense of contributing in positive ways they are *going dark*. *The Human Cheat Code*™ seeks to introduce terms and descriptors that are practical and can be used in everyday language when you can spot these patterns in real time (both in yourself and others). Being able to say, "You're going dark right now" gives everyone a shared vocabulary for understanding what's happening beneath the surface and why performance may suddenly dip or relationships become strained.

By the time you finish this book, you'll find yourself returning to this book again and again as a practical reference guide. Its structure is intentionally designed so you can quickly locate the insights, strategies, and recommendations you need for any individual or situation, organized clearly by CVI™ type.

My goal is not to replace Taylor's decades of work, but to honor it by offering another perspective and resource that shares his foundational framework alongside my own observations and learned lessons. As a Value-Added Reseller (VAR) for the CVI™ and certified practitioner in several well-known human assessments, and having worked with thousands of individuals on personal and professional development, I've come to view the CVI™ as the essential starting point for every individual *needs* assessment discussion. The CVI™ in my opinion provides a clear baseline for understanding the person I'm engaging with, allowing me to see their core motivations before exploring anything further. From that foundation, I can conduct a needs assessment to determine whether additional tools or assessments are appropriate.

Whether you are navigating a difficult conversation or relationship, preparing for an important decision, or simply trying to understand what drives you or others, the CVI™ in my opinion serves as the most reliable entry point for meaningful discovery.

As you move through this book, you'll learn how to apply insights in real, tangible ways; shaping your decisions, improving your interactions, and aligning your daily actions with who you are at your core. It's not just about self-awareness. It's about using that awareness to create meaningful traction in every part of your life.

Before we dive into the lessons of this book, it's important that you've taken the CVI™, ideally before learning too much about how it works. The assessment is intentionally designed to be difficult to "game," but approaching it with a fresh, unprimed mindset ensures the most accurate reflection of your innate core values. Information on how to take the CVI™ can be found on page 267 of this book.

With that said, if you are ready, let's step into the essential principles of the CVI™ and begin your journey of discovery.

CHAPTER 1
YOUR INNER DRIVE
AND PURPOSE

nner purpose also known as *Drive* is the deeply rooted sense of meaning that guides a person's actions, decisions, and aspirations. Unlike external achievements or societal expectations, it stems from an internal compass that reflects our truest selves and the contributions we feel called to make. This compass is innate, forming a quiet yet powerful force that makes certain goals feel more fulfilling than others. When we are aligned with our drive, we gain clarity and direction, even amid uncertainty. It's what turns effort into passion and routine into impact. And unlike fleeting motivation, drive endures. It doesn't merely push us forward; it pulls us toward something that feels deeply and authentically ours.

This enduring pull toward authenticity is not something we stumble upon by chance. It's something we uncover through introspection and connection to our values and lived experiences. Often, I believe it begins as a subtle but persistent feeling that our lives are meant to serve something greater than ourselves. As we explore this feeling, we begin to recognize the intersection of our natural abilities, the activities that energize us, and the impact we yearn to make. Drive isn't just about proficiency, it's about meaning. For some, it's sparked by service, creativity, leadership, conserving, or problem-solving. For others, it's rooted in relationships, learning, enhancing, or building something lasting. What makes this sense of drive so powerful is its ability to guide decisions, fuel resilience, and anchor us through life's uncertainties. When our actions align with this internal compass, life transforms from a checklist of tasks into a mission. We stop chasing external validation and begin pursuing genuine fulfillment. And the more we live in harmony with that drive, the more clarity, confidence, and momentum we gain. Not by following a script, but by finally honoring the drive that's always been within us.

Purpose is the quiet force that gives shape to our days, the inner compass that points us toward meaning rather than mere motion. I personally believe that *greater purpose* goes beyond personal gain or momentary satisfaction. It is the deeper calling that connects our individual lives to something larger, something that contributes to the well-being, growth, or transformation of the world around us. I believe every person carries such a calling, even if it reveals itself slowly. I personally believe that we are not here by accident. Each of us has a way of contributing that no one else can replicate, because our experiences, talents, perspectives, and passions form a combination that exists nowhere else in the world. That uniqueness is not a flaw but a design, ensuring that the world receives a rich tapestry of contributions rather than a single repeated pattern. And when we take the inner drive that stirs within us, the desire to create, to help, to build, to heal, to inspire, and pair it with consistent, courageous action; we unlock the ability to fulfill the purpose that has been waiting for us all along.

This alignment between inner drive, outward action, and serving a greater purpose doesn't just bring fulfillment, it also unlocks performance. A person's ability to excel is often rooted not in raw talent or external pressure, but in the clarity and conviction of their drive. When someone is deeply connected to what drives them, whether it's a mission, a value, or a vision, they tap into a reservoir of energy that others may never access. Drive transforms effort into devotion and turns obstacles into fuel. While many are motivated by competition or recognition, those guided by drive are propelled by meaning. This alignment creates a flow state where performance feels natural, even inevitable. They're not just working harder, they're working from a place of authenticity, which sharpens focus, deepens resilience, and amplifies results. In this way, drive becomes the ultimate performance enhancer, not because it pushes someone to outdo others, but because it pulls them to become the best version of themselves.

The drive to grow into our fullest selves often springs from something deeper than ambition. I personally believe it comes from an inner pull toward the purpose we were created to fulfill. Rather than trying to prove our worth, we're really seeking harmony between the truth within us and the impact we're meant to make in the world. When a goal reflects that deeper calling, whether it's to lead, to create, to uplift, or to solve meaningful problems, it becomes more than an achievement. It becomes an expression of who we are. That sense of alignment fuels a rare kind of determination, propelling us past limitations and into the unique contribution only we can offer. People who operate at their highest level aren't simply striving for success, they're responding to the purpose woven into their identity. And when their inner drive meets intentional action, it reveals a purpose and clarity that no external reward can match. It's the shift from effort to purpose-driven momentum.

To bridge the gap between this abstract sense of drive and the clarity needed to act on it, the CVI™ offers a transformative solution. While drive is often described as a quiet force or internal compass, the CVI™ gives it language, structure, and visibility. By identifying a person's dominant core values: *Merchant, Innovator, Banker,* and *Builder,* the CVI™ reveals the unique energies that shape how we naturally contribute, make decisions, and find fulfillment. It doesn't prescribe a path, it illuminates why certain paths feel more aligned than others. Understanding one's CVI™ profile brings to light motivations that may have always been present but never fully articulated. This awareness accelerates the journey toward purpose-driven living, enabling individuals to pursue goals that resonate with their deepest sense of self. In essence, the CVI™ transforms drive from a vague intuition into a strategic advantage, one that unlocks a flow state where performance, passion, and authenticity converge.

Beyond individual insight, the CVI™ also offers profound utility in understanding group dynamics. When CVI™ results are aggregated across a team, organization, or community, they form a behavioral blueprint that can predict how that group will respond to challenges, opportunities, and interpersonal interactions. Even without direct engagement, the CVI™ provides insight into collective team preferences, blind spots, and decision-making tendencies. It's like having a psychological map that forecasts outcomes before they unfold. Whether assembling a project team, navigating a negotiation, or preparing for a leadership transition, the CVI™ allows leaders to anticipate responses and tailor strategies accordingly. In this way, it becomes a predictive engine, one that transforms human complexity into actionable clarity.

We've explored how drive fuels performance, shape's identity, and anchors fulfillment, but now we turn to the framework that makes this invisible force visible. The CVI™ doesn't just name our motivations. It quantifies them through four core energies that, together, form the architecture of human contribution. But this raises compelling questions, "Why these four?" Why *Builder*, *Merchant*, *Innovator*, and *Banker*? Where did these archetypes originate, and how can they possibly describe the full spectrum of human nature across cultures, generations, and personalities? In the next chapter, we'll dive into the origin and meaning of each core value, unpack the logic behind their naming, and explore how their unique combinations, measured in precise capacities, create a personalized yet universal blueprint of who we are. This is where the CVI™ begins to reveal its true depth. Not as a static label, but as a *Human Cheat Code*™. A dynamic lens through which we can understand every person we encounter and for us to understand the life we ourselves are meant to live.

CHAPTER 2
THE FOUR CORE VALUES

Where did the four core values of the CVI™ (*Merchant, Innovator, Banker,* and *Builder*) originate, and why do their names resonate so deeply? These energies weren't plucked from thin air. They emerged from Lynn Taylor's profound exploration into the timeless forces that drive human behavior. To learn more about these core values in their purest form, I encourage you to read Taylor's *The Core Values Handbook* where he dives deep into each core value.

Taylor's work wasn't just about categorizing human behavior; it was about uncovering the elemental patterns of contribution that have endured across centuries and civilizations. *Merchant, Innovator, Banker,* and *Builder* are not personality types. They are echoes of ancient archetypes that have shaped the trajectory of human progress. *Builders* like Alexander the Great, embody the primal force of creation and protection, reminiscent of warriors, craftsmen, and pioneers who laid the foundations of nations and society. *Merchants* like Catherine the Great, channel the connective energy of relationship and exchange, akin to the diplomats and traders who bridged cultures and fostered trust. *Innovators* like Leonardo Da Vinci, reflect the restless curiosity of philosophers, inventors, and scientists. Those who challenged norms and envisioned new futures. *Bankers* like Socrates and Plato, represent the guardians of continuity, mirroring the scribes, stewards, and scholars who safeguarded knowledge and ensured stability.

These archetypes endure because they reflect universal modes of human contribution, distinct yet interdependent energies that have always been essential to collective survival and flourishing. By distilling them into a measurable framework, the CVI™ doesn't just offer insight into our innate self. It offers a lens into the architecture of civilization. Each name is more than a label. It's a metaphor for a way of being.

When it comes to drive, *Builder* signifies the drive to act and achieve. *Merchant* embodies the drive to connect and inspire. *Innovator* channels the drive to solve and refine. *Banker* reflects the drive to preserve and protect. Together, they form a dynamic system that transcends time, culture, and context, revealing that our deepest motivations are not random, but rooted in the very fabric of what it means to be human.

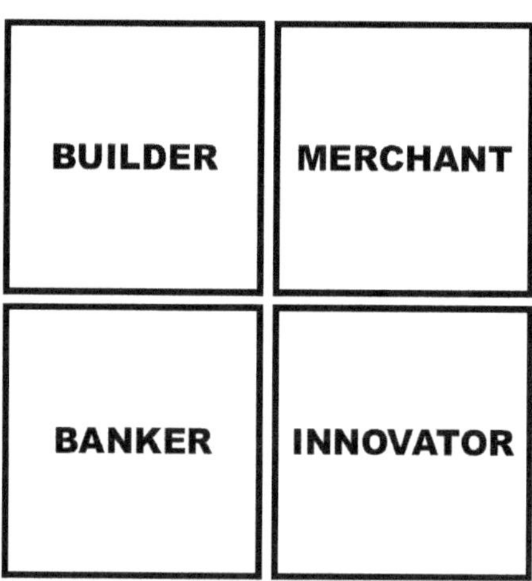

Figure 1. Four Core Values

Builder

Builders bring a sense of urgency, efficiency, and decisiveness that keeps teams focused and moving forward. *Builders'* energy and drive are contagious, pushing teams to stay engaged, productive, and committed to excellence. *Builders* turn ideas into reality. They ensure strategies aren't just theoretical, they translate into measurable results.

The *Builder* is defined by a powerful drive to take action and make things happen, often moving with a speed and certainty that sets them apart.

Builders are naturally:

- Action-oriented
- Step forward and engage quickly
- Start with a decision
- Operate from a "decide and do" mindset
- Bring a strong, assertive presence
- Unafraid to take charge
- Voice a direction
- Push through obstacles when others might stall

Much of their effectiveness comes from their intuition. *Builders* trust their gut, sensing the right move even when data is incomplete, and acting with confidence that inspires others. Their focus on impressive and lasting results means they aren't satisfied with activity alone. They want outcomes that matter, solutions that endure, and achievements that leave a mark. *Builders* also carry a natural leadership moxie, a boldness and resilience that helps them rally people, navigate pressure, and stay steady when stakes are high. Above all, they are bottom-line thinkers, cutting through complexity to identify what truly needs to be done and driving relentlessly toward the most efficient, impactful path forward. This combination of decisiveness, instinct, and results-driven energy makes the *Builder* a force of momentum in any environment.

When a *Builder* "goes dark," the same drive that normally fuels action, clarity, and progress can flip into intensity, pressure, and domination.

When *dark*:

- Their natural decisiveness becomes rigid insistence
- Leave little room for discussion or other viewpoints
- They bulldoze ahead
- Convinced speed matters more than collaboration

In real-world situations, this can look like a manager who dismisses team input because "we don't have time," or a parent who becomes overly controlling when stressed, making every decision unilaterally. Their instinct to take charge may escalate into micromanaging, issuing commands rather than guidance. The *Builder's* focus on results can also turn into impatience, snapping at delays, pushing others beyond reasonable limits, or showing frustration when people don't move as quickly as they do. In group settings, a dark *Builder* might dominate conversations, shut down brainstorming, or label others as "too slow" or "too soft." Under pressure, they may rely solely on gut instinct without considering consequences, leading to impulsive decisions that create more problems than they solve. At their darkest, *Builders* can appear intimidating, forceful, or dismissive, sometimes not out of malice but because their internal urgency overwhelms their awareness of impact. These moments highlight the dark side of their capacity. The same energy that drives progress can, when unchecked, create tension, fear, or burnout in the people around them.

A *Builder* begins to "go dark" when the following occurs:

- Environment that consistently blocks their drive for action
- When action is not taken leaving them stuck in stagnation
- Lack of momentum that feels suffocating
- Failing to empower them by limiting their authority
- Ignoring recommendations/requiring constant permission
- Endless collaboration when every decision requires multiple meetings, consensus, or prolonged discussion

- If leaders or teammates change course frequently, appearing indecisive or inconsistent
- Withholding resources, whether budget, tools, or personnel
- A culture that is risk-averse. One that avoids bold moves, innovation, or decisive action

When these conditions stack up, a *Builder's* contribution twist into their dark side: impatience, forcefulness, or explosive frustration. What was once a powerful engine for progress becomes a source of tension, and the very person who could have driven success ends up feeling alienated, underutilized, and ultimately pushed into their dark side.

A *Builder* reaches their highest capacity when the environment around them matches their natural drive for action, ownership, and forward momentum.

The best way to activate a *Builder* is to:

- Take action. Where progress matters more than perfection
- Allow them to learn by doing, experimenting, adjusting, and gaining insight through real-world engagement rather than theoretical planning
- Give them opportunities to take the lead
- Allow them to make decisions
- Get out of their way, removing unnecessary oversight and trusting their ability to drive measurable results: clear targets, visible progress, and tangible outcomes
- Hold to the course decided upon, maintaining consistency and commitment rather than shifting direction mid-stream

When these conditions are in place, a *Builder* becomes a force of momentum, delivering decisive action, strong leadership, and meaningful results that elevate the entire team.

Merchant

Merchants create a compelling future and rally people around it.

They don't just set goals. They make people feel connected to a bigger purpose. *Merchants* understand that great achievements come from collective effort. They break down silos, encourage open communication, and foster trust among team members. *Merchants* ensure different perspectives are valued and leveraged for better decision-making and innovation.

The *Merchant* embodies the pulse of connection, persuasion, and emotional intelligence, bringing a unique ability to open others to new visions and possibilities.

Merchants are naturally:

- Deeply intuitive with people
- Sense emotions, motivations, and unspoken needs with remarkable clarity
- See individuals not as roles or resources, but as rich stories waiting to be understood
- Develop and foster meaningful relationships
- Love storytelling. Communicate with warmth
- Inspire, unite, and move others toward shared purpose
- Decisions by consensus, valuing harmony / collective input

Merchants excel at fostering collaboration by ensuring every voice feels heard and appreciated. Their commitment to others runs deep, they give themselves totally, investing their energy, empathy, and heart into the people and causes they believe in. Driven not by romantic love but by a profound desire to uplift and connect, *Merchants* thrive in environments that call for vision, influence, and emotional resonance. While their longing for unity can sometimes lead them to sidestep conflict, at their best, *Merchants* are the soul of collaboration, bringing people together and creating the relational glue that allows teams and communities to flourish.

When a *Merchant* "goes dark," their normally charismatic, connective energy twists into something far more chaotic and self-protective, creating a ripple effect that everyone around them can feel.

. . .

When *dark*, the *Merchant*:

- Becomes manipulative
- Use charm to control outcomes or people
- Create stovepipes or cliques, pulling a few trusted allies close while shutting others out
- Over-promise. Make commitments they can't possibly keep
- Clingy, seeking constant reassurance, attention, or validation

When conversations get uncomfortable or accountability looms, *Merchants* change the subject, dodging responsibility with humor, distraction, or sudden shifts in focus. If they feel unappreciated or misunderstood, they may whine and pout, slipping into a victim mindset that drains energy from the room. And as stress mounts, they become forgetful, not because they lack ability, but because their emotional bandwidth is overloaded and their attention is scattered across too many self-created fires. In the real world, this looks like missed deadlines, fractured communication, drama pockets forming in the workplace, and a once-engaging person becoming unpredictable, reactive, and difficult to rely on, leaving others confused about what happened to the *Merchant* they thought they knew.

A *Merchant* begins to "go dark" when:

- Emotional connection and trust is shaken
- People disregard their feelings or feelings of others
- Others don't value their relationship
- Someone's behavior negatively affects their relationships
- People move forward without them
- Someone becomes confrontational and burns bridges
- Someone lies to them, even about small things

Out in the world, this can look like a coworker brushing off their concerns in a meeting as "too emotional," or friends planning an outing and forgetting to include them. It might show up as a colleague spreading gossip that damages their reputation, or a manager asking for their input but consistently talking over them. It could be a project team making major decisions without looping them in, or a partner confronting them harshly in public and leaving them feeling exposed. Even something as simple as a friend lying about why they canceled plans can hit harder than expected. These moments accumulate, each one chipping away at the *Merchant's* sense of belonging until they slip into that darker, manipulative, more defensive version of themselves.

A *Merchant* comes alive, truly alive, when:

- The environment around them taps into their natural gifts for connection, enthusiasm, and relational leadership
- Others lead through inspiration, painting a vision that stirs imagination and gives something meaningful to rally around
- When you show that you trust them, not just with words but with real responsibility
- Give them space to talk freely allowing their ideas, creativity, and emotional intelligence to flow
- You genuinely listen to them

Merchants thrive when they are included in efforts, especially those that involve people working together toward a shared goal, because collaboration is their natural habitat. When you collaborate with them to make decisions, they feel like true partners rather than sidelined contributors, and their buy-in becomes wholehearted. And perhaps most importantly, when you provide opportunities for them to connect with teammates, clients, friends, or communities, they step into their highest expression: the warm, magnetic, relationship-driven leader who brings people together, builds momentum, and infuses the environment with optimism and unity.

A *Merchant* at their best is unmistakable. They become the emotional engine of a team, a family, or a community. You see it when a *Merchant* leader kicks off a project with a compelling vision, offering inspirational ideas, stories, and energy that pull everyone in. It shows up when someone hands them real responsibility and says, "I trust you with this," and the *Merchant* responds by going above and beyond because they feel genuinely valued. In meetings, they thrive when they're given room to talk through their thoughts, and you can feel the shift when people actually listen, nodding, asking questions, engaging with what they're saying. They flourish when they're included in planning sessions, brainstorming groups, or collaborative efforts, because being part of a shared mission fuels their motivation. When decisions are made with them rather than around them, they become deeply invested and bring their natural enthusiasm to the table. And when they're given opportunities to connect: team lunches, client conversations, community events, or even informal check-ins, they become the warm, magnetic presence who builds bridges, strengthens relationships, and elevates the entire environment simply by being fully engaged and fully themselves.

Innovator

Innovators streamline workflows, optimize processes, and ensure the organization runs like a well-oiled machine. Their ability to create effective systems minimizes errors and improves productivity. *Innovators* design scalable frameworks and forward-thinking strategies. They position the organization for long-term success rather than short-lived gains. *Innovators* anticipate challenges, devise contingency plans, and respond to crises with level-headed and logical solutions.

Innovators are naturally:

- Spark of insight, strategy, and elegant problem-solving
- Feel compelled to understand, refine, and improve everything they touch
- Ask the hard questions
- Notice patterns others overlook
- Naturally thrive in complexity
- Process and systems-oriented

Calm under pressure, *Innovators* can detach emotionally to assess situations with clarity and precision, making them exceptional strategic thinkers and architects of better systems. Their process and system-oriented mindset allow them to assess and develop effective courses of action, experiment thoughtfully, and enhance outcomes through continuous improvement. They excel at improving systems and processes, often serving as the steady mind behind the mission. While their gift is discernment, they may wrestle with indecision or over-analysis, especially when the stakes are high. Yet when empowered, *Innovators* bring depth, clarity, and transformation to any endeavor, unafraid to stay in conflict long enough to uncover the most elegant and effective solution.

When *Innovators* "go dark," the very contributions that make them insightful and strategic can twist into their *dark* expressions.

When *dark*, the *Innovator*:

- Is an unrelenting interrogator
- Collapses into analysis paralysis
- Emotionally withdraws creating distance than perspective
- Micro-manages
- Weaponizes wisdom that is not generic but precise leaving deep cuts to the recipient
- Uses complex information to confuse and regain control

Out in the world, this *dark side* shows up in ways that can be both subtle and deeply disruptive. An *Innovator* might pepper teammates with endless questions that feel less like curiosity and more like cross-examination. They may stall decisions, insisting they need just one more piece of information, causing projects to lose momentum. Their desire for things to be done "perfectly" can lead them to hover over others' work, correcting, tweaking, and tightening until collaboration feels impossible. In meetings, they might withhold key insights or drop overly technical explanations that leave others feeling disoriented or inadequate. Their stubbornness can surface as an unyielding attachment to their own logic, even when it slows progress. And when frustration builds, they may retreat into a simmering silence that no one fully understands until, seemingly out of nowhere, they resign from a task, a team, or even a relationship. These behaviors don't always come from malice. They can come from an *Innovator* who feels unsafe, unheard, or unable to bring their gifts forward constructively.

When *Innovators* begin to *go dark*, it is often triggered by:

- Questioning their wisdom
- Embarrassing or humiliating them (publicly or subtly)
- Refusing to innovate or insist on maintaining the status quo
- Rushing them or denying the time they need to think deeply
- People who ignore the pros and cons or fail to evaluate decisions with nuance
- A team that gets caught up in ineffective behavior: reactivity, drama, shortcuts, or emotional chaos

These conditions can push them into their dark side: interrogating others, over-analyzing, withdrawing, becoming stubborn, or slipping into retaliatory swipes. Ultimately, *Innovators* go dark when their wisdom is dismissed, their process is disrupted, or their environment refuses to evolve.

Innovators perform at their best when:

- Given uninterrupted time to think and explore
- They are allowed to strategize freely and take things apart
- Others welcome their questions rather than rush them
- Alternative solutions are genuinely considered and not dismissed for convenience
- People around them remain curious, engage with their ideas, and challenge assumptions thoughtfully

When these conditions are met, *Innovators* shift from cautious observers to powerful architects of transformation. Out in the world, supporting an *Innovator* looks like giving them breathing room before demanding decisions, trusting them to explore the mechanics of a problem, and inviting them into early conversations rather than presenting them with a finished plan. It means letting them sketch diagrams on whiteboards, dismantle processes to see what's underneath, and ask questions that may seem tangential but ultimately reveal the heart of the issue. Teams that work well with *Innovators* don't rush brainstorming sessions. They pause to weigh pros and cons, explore multiple pathways, provide time for quiet reflection, and treat complexity as an asset rather than a burden. Including them in version development might look like looping them into prototype reviews, asking for their input on system improvements, or letting them refine workflows before rollout. When these behaviors are present, *Innovators* feel valued, engaged, and empowered, and their contributions elevate the entire team, organization, or effort.

Banker

Bankers methodical approach ensures that decisions are backed by evidence and risks are carefully mitigated. *Bankers* rely on data, research, and facts rather than assumptions, leading to more accurate and strategic choices. By identifying potential pitfalls before they occur, they protect the team or organization from unnecessary setbacks, financial losses, and reputational damage. *Bankers'* attention to detail minimizes errors, enhances efficiency, and ensures that processes are executed flawlessly.

Bankers naturally:

- Embody the foundation of stability, precision, and stewardship
- Depend on consistency and trust
- Are driven by a deep commitment to knowledge
- Gather the kind of detailed, factual insight that preserves, protects, and ensures continuity over time
- Make data-driven decisions that minimize risk and maximize long-term success
- Value accountability and doing things the right way
- Guard the relationship or group by conserving and managing resources wisely
- Naturally risk-averse

When fully expressed, *Bankers* are the quiet force that holds everything together, ensuring efficiency, continuity, and a stable foundation upon which others can build.

Out in the world, a *Banker's* contributions show up in steady, practical, quietly powerful ways that keep teams and organizations grounded. You'll see them asking thoughtful questions to gather the full picture before moving forward, reviewing documents carefully, and double-checking details others might overlook. They're the ones who build spreadsheets to track resources, create step-by-step processes to ensure continuity, and rely on data rather than gut feelings when making decisions. In meetings, they often bring the conversation back to facts, risks, and long-term implications, helping balance out more impulsive voices. Their risk-averse nature means they naturally look for potential pitfalls and work to prevent problems before they happen. While others may chase big ideas, *Bankers* make sure those ideas are feasible, sustainable, and responsibly managed. They are the people who keep systems running smoothly, protect organizational memory, and ensure that nothing important slips through the cracks.

When *Bankers* "go dark," their natural contribution of stability, precision, and stewardship can shift into rigid, protective, and distancing behaviors.

When *dark*, the *Banker*:

- Becomes aloof in judgment
- Create emotional barrier keeping others at a distance
- Undermines decisions in secret
- Withholds information
- Quietly resists direction
- Uses "No" as their default response
- Withholds resources: time, information, access, or support
- Pretends capitulation. They nod along in agreement but have no intention of following through
- Fixates on flaws rather than possibilities

Out in the world, this dark behavior shows up in subtle but impactful ways. A *Banker* might sit silently in a meeting, offering little input but radiating disapproval through tone or body language.

They may agree to a plan publicly, then quietly slow it down behind the scenes by withholding data, delaying approvals, or insisting on more documentation. When presented with new ideas, they might immediately list every reason it won't work, shutting down momentum before it begins. Their emails may become curt, overly formal, or laced with passive-aggressive undertones. They might refuse to share resources: budgets, tools, or information, claiming it's "not the right time" or "needs more review." Their change aversion can stall projects, frustrate teammates, and create an atmosphere of stagnation. Over time, their overly critical lens can erode trust, making others feel scrutinized rather than supported. These behaviors don't stem from ill intent. They arise when a *Banker* feels unsafe, rushed, or excluded from the process. But without awareness, their protective instincts can unintentionally undermine the very stability they value.

Bankers can slip into their "dark" expression when:

- Accuracy and stewardship are undervalued
- Their research is ignored or dismissed
- They are called out on the spot
- They are excluded from discussions, particularly those involving planning, resources, or long-term implications
- Wastefulness of any kind (time, money, or effort)
- Efforts moved forward without facts/based on guesswork
- Acts of injustice: unfairness, favoritism, unethical behavior
- Leaders or teammates lack credibility

These conditions don't just frustrate them, they threaten the stability they work so hard to maintain, pushing them into the very behaviors that define their darker side.

Bankers perform at their best when:

- Environment supports thoroughness, stewardship, and a deep respect for accuracy
- Have time to research, gather facts, and verify details
- They are allowed to show their work

- Resources and institutional knowledge are preserved rather than wasted or ignored
- Decisions are made based on data instead of impulse
- Established routines ensure consistency/reliability
- Included in discussions. Particularly those involving planning, resources, or long-term implications.

When these conditions are present, *Bankers* become the quiet but powerful backbone of any team or organization.

Out in the world, supporting a *Banker* looks like giving them space to dig into research before expecting answers, and inviting them to walk the team through their spreadsheets, documentation, or analysis. It means respecting their instinct to conserve resources by avoiding unnecessary spending, redundant work, or rushed decisions. You'll see them thrive when meetings include time for reviewing data, weighing risks, and discussing long-term implications rather than jumping straight to action. Letting them establish routines might look like standardized workflows, checklists, or consistent reporting structures that help everyone stay aligned. Including them in discussions ensures they feel connected to the process rather than blindsided by decisions made without their input. And when they are encouraged to inform others, whether through training, documentation, or sharing insights; they become trusted guides who elevate the entire team's clarity and competence.

A Complex Nature

You should have felt an immediate pull toward one or two of the core value energies, maybe the clarity-seeking *Innovator*, the purpose-driven *Merchant*, the steady *Banker*, or the action-oriented *Builder*. Keep in mind that your inner drive is rarely powered by a single core value. It's a more intricate blend of these core value energies, with different capacities, shaped by your innate instincts and the deeper motivations you still may be uncovering.

Whether you're communicating with greater clarity, navigating conflict with less friction, or optimizing team dynamics so people can operate in their natural core values, the CVI™ becomes far more than an assessment. It becomes a strategic advantage. There's a reason I refer to it as The *Human Cheat Code*™. When used well, the CVI™ unlocks a deeper understanding of how people think, act, and thrive. In the next sections, we'll expand on exactly why the nickname the *Human Cheat Code*™ is so fitting and how you can leverage your CVI™ results to elevate relationships, performance, and collaboration across every area of work and life.

Closing Thoughts

Can a person's unchanging nature truly be explained by just four core energies (*Builder, Merchant, Innovator, and Banker*)? At first glance, it might seem overly simplistic to distill the complexity of human motivation into four categories. After diving into the four core values individually, it becomes clear that the CVI™ is far more nuanced than simply placing people into four distinct categories. The CVI™ doesn't stop at identifying a person's dominant value, it goes deeper by measuring core value capacities, revealing how strongly each value shows up and how they interact within an individual. This layered insight helps us see that people aren't one-dimensional. They are a blend of core values, instincts, and internal drivers that shape how they think, decide, and contribute. By exploring these capacities, we gain a richer, more accurate picture of how someone is wired, how they naturally operate under pressure, and how they bring their best to the world. This deeper understanding sets the stage for more meaningful development, collaboration, and self-awareness.

The strength of the CVI™ is that it doesn't stop at naming four core energies, it also measures the capacity of each core value within a person, ranging from 0 to 36 with a total capacity for all four core values at 72 per individual. This numerical depth transforms a simple framework into a highly personalized map of human capacity. Two people may share the same dominant core value, but their unique blend of capacities creates entirely different expressions of that core value. It's this granularity that makes the CVI™ so powerful. It reveals how we are uniquely wired, yet universally connected through these shared archetypes.

This capacity-based approach allows for extraordinary accuracy, making every CVI™ report deeply personalized. It's this layered understanding that reveals how we are both profoundly unique and inherently connected. The CVI™ doesn't box people in, it opens a window into the subtle interplay of motivations that shape who we are and how we show up in the world.

CHAPTER 3
CAPACITY

apacity as a general definition refers to the maximum potential or ability of a person, system, or organization to perform, produce, or hold something. It encompasses both tangible limits like physical space or energy, and intangible ones like with the CVI™, such as resilience, bandwidth, or creative output. When we talk about capacity in relation to CVI™ *fulfillment*, we're exploring how one's ability to create, connect, improve, or stabilize directly influences their sense of purpose and satisfaction. Fulfillment arises when we operate near the edge of our capacity, not in burnout, but in meaningful engagement.

A person's CVI™ capacity number (numbers identified inside each quadrant of the CVI™ chart) reflects their innate, hard-wired potential, but it doesn't guarantee they are operating anywhere near that level in real life. Capacity becomes especially revealing when you look closely at the capacity scores. At the highest end of the scale, capacity shows up in unmistakable ways. People operate with what feels like endless energy, sustained effort, and an almost instinctive ability to perform tasks aligned with that value. Their contribution looks effortless from the outside because they're working from a deep internal reservoir. On the opposite end, extremely low capacity is just as visible. It often appears as low performance, minimal effort, or a lack of energy, not because the person is unwilling, but because that particular value simply isn't a natural engine for them. Understanding where someone falls on each core value capacity range isn't about judgment. It's about clarity. When you know a person's capacity and natural limits, you can temper expectations, avoid misalignment, and place them in roles or situations where their innate energy will actually work for them. It also allows you to call upon the right individuals at the right moments, maximizing both their contribution and their sense of fulfillment. In this way, the CVI™ becomes not just an assessment tool but a practical guide for getting the very best out of every individual by honoring how they are wired.

It's important to note that capacity can be suppressed or distorted by many factors: immaturity, "going dark" under stress, working in a toxic culture, or being assigned to responsibilities that don't align with their core values. When these conditions are present, even someone with a high CVI™ capacity score in a particular core value may show inconsistent behavior, low engagement, or reduced effectiveness. In other words, the number represents what is possible, but the person's current context determines what is accessible. Understanding this gap is essential for accurate coaching, development, and role alignment. I will go into more detail on aggravating factors in Chapter 6 of this book.

Here's an analogy on capacity that I will continually use throughout the book. A person's CVI™ capacity is like a high-performance engine built into a car. The engine may be capable of incredible speed, power, and efficiency. That's the design. It's capacity. But the car won't perform anywhere near its potential if the tires are under inflated, the fuel is low-grade, the alignment is off, the driver is inexperienced, or the road conditions are poor. None of those issues change the engine's inherent capability (capacity). These things simply limit how much of that capability can be accessed. In the same way, a person's CVI™ score reflects their built-in capacity, but immaturity, stress, unhealthy environments, misaligned roles, or "going dark" can keep that natural power from showing up in their daily performance.

• • •

Builder Capacity

Builder capacity expresses itself through decisive action, forward momentum, and the ability to turn intention into tangible results. For a *Builder*, capacity is measured not just in physical stamina or productivity, but in the inner drive to take charge, make things happen, and push through obstacles with determination. When *Builders* are operating near the edge of their capacity, they feel alive, fully engaged in challenges that require courage, quick judgment, and a willingness to take risks. Their fulfillment comes from seeing progress, protecting what matters, and stepping into roles where their core values and resolve are needed. When their capacity is underutilized, *Builders* may feel restless or constrained, as though their natural force is being bottled up. Conversely, when they exceed their capacity, they may slip into over-control or impatience. Healthy *Builder* capacity is about channeling their power into purposeful action, choosing battles wisely, pacing their intensity, and recognizing that their greatest impact comes when they balance force with focus.

Merchant Capacity

Merchant capacity is rooted in emotional connection, relational energy, and the ability to inspire, uplift, and build trust. For *Merchants*, capacity is less about physical limits and more about the depth of presence they can offer others. Their bandwidth is tied to empathy, enthusiasm, and the desire to create meaningful bonds. When *Merchants* operate near the edge of their capacity, they are fully engaged in relationships, listening deeply, encouraging others, and weaving together shared purpose. They thrive when they can influence through vision and passion, and they feel fulfilled when their generosity of spirit leads to genuine connection. Underutilized capacity leaves them feeling disconnected or unappreciated, while exceeding capacity can lead to emotional exhaustion or overextension in trying to meet everyone's needs. Healthy *Merchant* capacity involves honoring their relational gifts while also protecting their emotional reserves, recognizing that their influence is strongest when they are grounded, authentic, and not spread too thin to have meaningful engagement with others.

Innovator Capacity

Innovator capacity is expressed through problem-solving, creativity, and the ability to synthesize ideas into elegant solutions. For *Innovators*, capacity is measured in mental space, curiosity, and the freedom to explore possibilities. Their bandwidth expands when they have time to think, experiment, and refine. It contracts when they are rushed, micromanaged, or forced into rigid structures. Operating near the edge of their capacity feels like being in a state of flow, where complexity becomes exciting, insights emerge naturally, and their unique perspective adds value. *Innovators* feel fulfilled when they can improve systems, design better approaches, or bring clarity to confusion. When their capacity is underused, they may feel bored or stifled. When exceeded, they may become overly analytical, detached, or perfectionistic. Healthy *Innovator* capacity is about creating the conditions for their mind to work at its best: space, autonomy, and the freedom to iterate, so their creativity becomes a source of contribution rather than pressure.

Banker Capacity

Banker capacity is grounded in knowledge, structure, and the ability to bring order and stability to the world around them. For *Bankers*, capacity is measured in clarity, information, and the time needed to process details thoroughly. Their fulfillment comes from being the steady anchor, ensuring accuracy, preserving resources, and providing dependable insight. When operating near the edge of their capacity, *Bankers* are deeply engaged in analysis, organization, and thoughtful planning. They thrive when they can bring coherence to chaos and ensure that decisions are grounded in facts rather than impulse. Underutilized capacity leaves them feeling overlooked or under-informed, while exceeding capacity can lead to overwhelming rigidity or withdrawal. Healthy *Banker* capacity involves honoring their need for preparation and precision while also recognizing that their value lies not just in what they know, but in how they apply that knowledge to support long-term stability and wise decision-making.

Numerical Capacity Ranges

Since the *The Core Values Handbook* doesn't use specific numerical capacity ranges to describe how strongly a person is wired to express each of the four core value energies, to help you better utilize capacity and make it easier to understand the degree to which an individual operates in each core value, I will share the capacity breakout I learned from Justin Erickson who is the Founder of Hardwired Coaching LLC. He broke up the four numerical ranges this way: *Profound, Proficient, Possible, and Painful.* After a short discussion with him, *Proficient* was changed to *Pronounced* to more accurately reflect that level of capacity. I also modified my *Possible/Painful* ranges slightly from his version. These named capacity ranges represent the degree of natural, intrinsic motivation a person has in each quadrant giving language you can use when discussing capacity.

Capacity in the CVI™ is not about skill or personality. It is about innate drive and the internal "fuel tank" available for a particular type of contribution and these ranges will provide granularity and uniqueness of individual CVI™ results. A *Builder* with a capacity score of 18 operates at a completely different level of a *Builder* with a capacity score of 28. A core value with high capacity in a quadrant has a deep well of energy for that type of activity, while someone with low capacity may find the same activity draining, frustrating, or unsustainable. These categories reveal where someone is most likely to thrive, where they may struggle, and how they can best structure their life and work to operate near the edge of meaningful engagement rather than burnout. These categories compliment Lynn Taylor's work where a numerical category range within Taylor's established core values categories allow individuals to better understand why they flourish and struggle in a core value quadrant.

Most people have one dominant score (Profound or Pronounced), one secondary score in the mid-range (Pronounced or Possible), and two scores in the middle to lower ranges (Possible or Painful) so with this in mind, capacity scores are broken up this way:

Category	Score Range	Interpretation
Profound (Core)	**26–36**	Deep, natural, effortless capacity. This is where someone performs with the highest ease, energy, and consistency.
Pronounced (Functional)	**19–25**	Strong, reliable, and clearly observable capacity. The person can perform well here with consistency.
Possible (Adaptive)	**10–18**	Situational or developing capacity. The person *can* operate here, but it requires intention, support, or structure.
Painful (Fragile)	**0–9**	Draining, costly, or unsustainable capacity. Operating here for long periods leads to stress, burnout, or disengagement.

Figure 2. Capacity ranges measure the *energy* available

Profound Capacity

Profound Capacity (26–36): Core values flow naturally. Their core value capacity represents a person's deepest, most natural source of power, an area where they are intrinsically driven, highly resilient, and capable of sustained contribution without feeling depleted. Someone with profound capacity in a quadrant doesn't just perform well there. They need to operate in that space to feel fulfilled. Out in the world, this looks like the *Builder* who instinctively takes charge and feels alive when making decisions, the *Merchant* who effortlessly builds relationships and inspires others, the *Innovator* who thrives on solving complex problems, or the *Banker* who finds comfort and satisfaction in organizing, analyzing, and ensuring accuracy. When someone has profound capacity, they often underestimate how exceptional their natural ability is because it feels so intuitive. They also experience the most intense "dark side" in this quadrant when overstressed, because the same energy that fuels their brilliance can become overextended or distorted. Profound capacity is both a gift and a responsibility. It shows where someone is built to lead, contribute, and create their greatest impact.

Behavioral signature:

- Acts with ease, confidence, and consistency
- Performs at a high level with minimal stress
- Feels energized by tasks in this range
- Shows mastery without needing external motivation

What it looks like in action:

- "This is where I do my best work."
- Flow state, natural positive contributions, high engagement

Best roles:

- Strategic leadership
- High-impact decision-making
- Roles requiring mastery and autonomy

Pronounced Capacity

Pronounced Capacity (19–25): Core values flow with little effort. It reflects a strong, reliable, and consistently accessible energy. An area where a person can perform well, contribute meaningfully, and feel aligned, though it may not be as essential to their identity if they have a profound capacity. In everyday life, someone with pronounced capacity can step into these roles with confidence and competence, often serving as a stabilizing force or complementary force to their primary core value. A pronounced *Innovator* may not crave problem-solving the way a profound *Innovator* does, but they can still generate creative solutions when needed and with little effort. A pronounced *Merchant* may not require constant connection, but they can build rapport and influence effectively. This range represents a healthy, sustainable level of capacity, strong enough to rely on, but not so dominant that it overshadows other core values. When someone goes dark in a pronounced quadrant, the behavior tends to be noticeable but not overwhelming. It shows up as stress behavior rather than identity-level distortion. Pronounced capacity is often where people find balance and versatility.

Behavioral signature:

- Reliable and steady performance
- Skills are visible and repeatable
- Comfortable operating here for long periods

What it looks like in action:

- "I can do this well and consistently."
- Strong but not signature contributions

Best Roles:

- Operational leadership
- Project management/Consistent execution roles
- Team coordination

Possible Capacity

Possible Capacity (10–18): Core value must be summoned. Indicates an area where a person can operate, but doing so requires conscious effort, intentional focus, and often more recovery time. This is the range where people may develop skills or perform competently, but the work does not feel natural or energizing. In everyday life, a person with possible *Banker* capacity may be able to manage details or maintain structure, but it will feel like work rather than instinct. A possible *Builder* may take action when necessary but they will not naturally seek out decisive or forceful roles. People with possible capacity often describe these activities as "fine," "doable," or "something I can handle in small doses." When they go dark in this quadrant, it usually shows up as avoidance, frustration, or self-doubt because they are pushing against their natural wiring. Possible capacity is not a weakness. It simply marks the boundary between what is sustainable and what requires conscious energy management.

Behavioral signature:

- Requires planning, structure, or support
- Energy dips if used too long
- Performance varies depending on context

What it looks like in action:

- "I can do this, but it takes effort."
- Good for stretch assignments or development

Best roles:

- Support roles
- Temporary assignments
- Developmental opportunities

Painful Capacity

Painful Capacity (9 and below): Core values deplete immediately.

Represents the area where a person has the least natural drive, the lowest intrinsic motivation, and the smallest internal fuel tank. Tasks in this quadrant often feel draining, confusing, or misaligned, even if the person has learned to perform them well. Out in the world, someone with painful *Merchant* capacity may struggle with relationship-heavy labor or collaborative environments, while someone with painful *Innovator* capacity may feel overwhelmed by ambiguity or problem-solving demands. Painful capacity does not mean incompetence. It means the activity requires disproportionate effort and offers little internal reward. When someone is forced to operate here for extended periods, they may experience stress, burnout, or a sense of being "not themselves." The dark side in this quadrant tends to show up as shutdown, withdrawal, or reactive behavior because the person is functioning far outside their natural design. Understanding painful capacity helps people set boundaries, communicate needs, and avoid environments that chronically drain their energy.

Behavioral signature:

- Draining, stressful, or frustrating
- Performance is inconsistent or unsustainable
- Often avoided or procrastinated
- Leads to burnout quickly

What it looks like in action:

- "I can do this… but I really shouldn't."
- Red flags for role misalignment

Best roles:

- Avoid primary responsibility
- Use only for short-term needs
- Delegate to others with higher capacity
- Automate, outsource, or redesign

. . .

Proximity Rule

While people can access all four core value energies, Lynn Taylor's framework focuses on the idea that one or two of these energies feel the most natural and sustainable. While he does not specifically claim that scores within close proximity of each other allow a person to easily transition between those energies, I learned that Taylor stresses that the highest score (dominant core value) reflects the person's most effortless mode of operation, while the lower scores represent energies that require more conscious effort and may be less reliable under stress.

Even though Taylor doesn't state a "Proximity Rule," as I coin it, it is reasonable to interpret close scores as indicating that a person has more balanced access to multiple energies. This is important because you can only operate in one core value at a time. A transition occurs when a person shifts from one core value energy to another. When the gap between core value scores is small, the individual may find it easier to shift between different modes of thinking or behaving, though this still requires more effort than operating from their dominant core value.

The CVI™ is designed to highlight where someone performs at their best, where they feel most aligned, and where they may experience friction or fatigue when pushed too far outside their natural capacities. This uncomfortableness causes the individual to shift to their dominant core value and in many cases, this shift causes a misalignment of necessary core value energy required and what is actually presented if the individual acts out of innate instinct rather than assessed value needed in that moment.

Think of the CVI™ as describing the engine configuration of a person's internal "performance vehicle." Everyone has all four cylinders: *Merchant, Innovator, Banker,* and *Builder* but the horsepower distribution is different for each person.

When one score is clearly highest, this is like having a primary engine mode, a turbocharged cylinder that delivers the most power with the least fuel. When you operate in this mode, you accelerate effortlessly, maintain speed easily, and perform at your peak without burning out.

When the CVI™ scores are close together, this is where the car analogy gets interesting. If your CVI™ scores sit within a few points of each other, your internal engine is more like a balanced, multi-mode performance car. You can shift between gears more fluidly because none of the cylinders are dramatically underpowered. You still have a dominant mode, but the other modes are strong enough that switching between them doesn't feel like grinding gears.

However, even in a balanced engine, each mode still has a different fuel cost:

- Your highest score = sport mode (maximum performance)
- Your secondary scores = touring mode (good performance)
- Your lowest score = off-road mode (possibly do it, but it's not where the car shines)

What this means in real-world behavior (CVI™ scores are close):

- Adapt more easily to different people and environments
- Can shift between task types without losing momentum
- May appear more versatile or multi-talented
- Can "rev" different energies without stalling out
- May also struggle to identify a single, dominant identity because multiple modes feel accessible

When scores are far apart, this is like having one extremely powerful cylinder and three smaller ones. You can still use the others, but it takes more fuel, more effort, and more conscious control. If you stay in those modes too long, the engine overheats. This is the CVI™ version of stress, fatigue, or disengagement. But even with close scores, the highest one still represents the smoothest ride. That's where your natural torque lives. That's where you get the best mileage. That's where you perform without burning extra fuel.

In the same way capacity is broken up into four categories:

Profound, Pronounced, Possible, and *Painful* to give you more granularity and nuance in understanding how you naturally operate, I want to share a concept I learned that has consistently helped clients make sense of their CVI™ results. The idea of a *Proximity Rule* is simple: whenever a person's CVI™ capacity scores are within three points of each other, they tend to shift between those core values with relative ease. Using the car analogy, this is like having gears that sit close together on the transmission. The engine doesn't strain, the RPMs stay smooth, and the driver can glide from one gear to the next without grinding or losing momentum. But when the gap widens, scores separated by four points or more, the experience changes dramatically. Now the person is trying to jump from third gear to sixth in one motion, and the engine protests. The car can technically do it, but it lurches, hesitates, and burns far more fuel. In CVI™ terms, a capacity gap of four or higher means the individual can still access that lower-scoring core value, but it feels unnatural, effortful, and sometimes downright exhausting. The farther apart the scores, the more the person experiences that shift as a strain on their internal engine, which is why understanding the *Proximity Rule* gives people a clearer sense of where they can move fluidly and where they're likely to feel resistance or performance drag.

Another way to visualize this dynamic is with the image of a beach ball being pushed underwater. Imagine that each point of CVI™ capacity represents one foot below the surface. A core value with a profound capacity score is like holding the beach ball several feet underwater. It's packed with potential energy, pressure, and force. The moment you release it, the beach ball rockets upward with speed and height because the gap between where it was held and the surface is so great. Now compare that to a core value sitting in the "painful" range. It's only a foot or two underwater, so when you let go, it rises, but it doesn't explode out of the water with the same power or urgency. This is why someone with a *profound* core value and remaining *possible* core values will almost always prefer to operate from that profound value. Even though the other values are accessible, the feel is different. The profound one launches with natural momentum, efficiency, and force, while the others drift upward more slowly and require more deliberate effort to use. The greater the gap between capacities, the more dramatic the difference in how each core value behaves when released, and the more instinctively a person gravitates toward the one that shoots out of the water with the most energy.

Squarish Capacities

What happens when someone's CVI™ profile shows all four core values: *Merchant, Innovator, Banker,* and *Builder* clustered tightly together within just a few points? These individuals are what I call *Squarish* CVI™ profiles, and while they are not as statistically rare as the mythical "18-18-18-18 unicorn," they share a similar kind of versatility. Squarish profiles can shift from one capacity to another with remarkable ease, often feeling comfortable and natural in any of the four core values. They don't experience the same internal friction most people feel when moving from one motivational energy to another because their capacities sit in close proximity to one another. However, this balance comes with a trade-off. All four capacities sit in the Possible/Low Pronounced range rather than the Middle-High Pronounced or Profound ranges. This means that when surrounded by people with higher capacities, *Squarish* individuals may feel underpowered or overshadowed, even though they are highly adaptable. Another challenge is that they can "go dark" in any of the four values with equal ease. Most people only go visibly dark in one or two values with significant impact, while the others more softly. But a squarish profile can go dark across all four values with surprising speed, sometimes experiencing an internal collapse that feels more disorienting than what most individuals ever encounter.

The upside, however, is exceptional. When a *Squarish* CVI™ profile is mature, grounded, and not operating from insecurity, they can lead, communicate, and collaborate with virtually anyone. Their balanced capacities allow them to understand and resonate with every core value type, making them natural bridges in teams, families, and organizations. For these individuals, the key is learning to read the moment, recognizing which core value the situation calls for and stepping into that value with intention rather than impulse. When they do this well, they become the connective tissue that helps groups transition smoothly from one stage of the process to the next, ensuring that the right core value shows up at the right time. They may not have the extreme contributions of pronounced or profound profiles, but when healthy and self-aware, they are among the most versatile, stabilizing, and quietly impactful contributors in any environment.

The Unicorn

What about the mythical unicorn, a perfect *18-18-18-18* in all four core value categories: *Merchant, Innovator, Banker,* and *Builder*? The title *unicorn* is the term often used when an individual who scores a perfect 18 in all four core values. Out of more than 1.3 million assessments completed at the date of this writing, I was told that fewer than two dozen people fall into this profile, which makes this profile statistically astonishing. Much like individuals with a squarish CVI™ profile, these unicorns can shift from one capacity to another with remarkable ease, feeling comfortable and natural in every core value. They don't experience the same internal friction most people feel when moving from one motivational energy to another because their capacities sit in perfect balance. However, like squarish CVI™ profiles, this balance comes with a trade-off. All four capacities sit in the possible range. This means that when surrounded by people with pronounced or profound capacities, unicorns may feel inadequate or underpowered, even though they are highly adaptable and not beholden to one or two core values.

When a unicorn is centered, confident, and grounded in who they are, they have an extraordinary ability to lead, communicate, and collaborate with anyone. Their perfectly balanced capacities allow them to connect with every core value type, giving them a unique gift for bringing people together and helping groups function as a cohesive whole. For these individuals, the real opportunity lies in learning to sense *what the moment calls for,* recognizing which core value will serve best, and stepping into that space with clarity and purpose. Because their capacity ends at 18, they need to remember to hand it off to those individuals who have a greater capacity than them. When they do this, they become the steady thread that helps teams move gracefully from vision to strategy to structure to action, ensuring that each stage receives exactly the energy it requires. Though uncommon, unicorns who are self-aware and operating with humility are among the most adaptable, unifying, and quietly powerful contributors in any environment or on any team.

Closing Thoughts on Capacity

Ultimately, CVI™ capacity scores represent the fixed limits of how much of a person's innate core value energy they can consistently bring into real-world performance. It's important to remember that you don't have to have a greater capacity than those you lead. You just have to have the humility to know who to hand it off to and when. Capacity is not something people can increase. It is a stable measurement, which is why the CVI™ maintains its exceptionally high reliability rating above 97%. What individuals can do, however, is develop workarounds, compensating strategies, or learned behaviors that help them function more effectively in areas where their natural capacity is lower. These adaptations do not change the underlying capacity score itself, they simply help a person navigate tasks that fall outside their strongest core value energies. Understanding this distinction is essential for applying CVI™ results accurately. The CVI™ reveals the unchanging innate nature, while capacity scores clarify the consistent limits of how fully that nature can be expressed. This ensures that interpretations of the CVI™ remain grounded, realistic, and true to the instrument's design.

CHAPTER 4
CONTRIBUTION TYPES™

Understanding Lynn Taylor's CVI™ *Contribution Types™* is essential because, although a person can only express one core value at any given moment, the two top values in a Contribution Type™ create a kind of internal ecosystem.

A person's Contribution Type™ offers a far more descriptive and nuanced picture of who they are because it reflects the dynamic way their two highest core values shape real-world behavior. Lynn Taylor's work emphasizes that while each core value has its own distinct energy, people don't operate in isolated compartments, our values interact, influence one another, and create recognizable patterns in how we contribute. The Contribution Type™ captures this interplay by showing how one value drives action while the second value colors the style, tone, and intention behind that action. It explains why two people with the same dominant value can look completely different in practice. The secondary value can affect how the primary one is expressed, and the individual's capacity scores determine the level of contribution and clarity of that expression. Instead of describing a person through a single lens, the Contribution Type™ reveals the blend of motivations, instincts, and behaviors that consistently show up when they engage with the world. It becomes a more complete portrait. One that reflects not just what a person does, but how and why they do it, making it one of the most accurate and practical ways to understand someone's natural contribution.

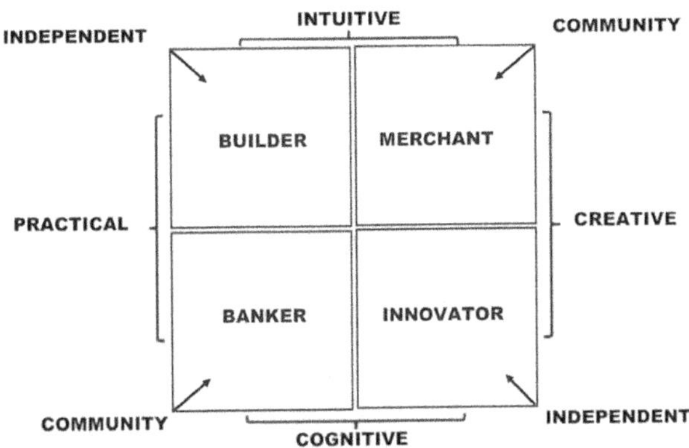

Figure 3. Contribution Type™ reflects two highest values.

CVI™ Contribution Types™:

- Intuitive (*Builder/Merchant*)
- Cognitive (*Banker/Innovator*)
- Creative (*Merchant/Innovator*)
- Practical (*Builder/Banker*)
- Community (*Merchant/Banker*)
- Independent (*Builder/Innovator*)

A *Builder* with a high *Merchant* score may act decisively, but their decisions often carry a relational sensitivity that wouldn't appear in a *Builder* with a low *Merchant* score. Likewise, an *Innovator* with strong *Banker* capacity may solve problems with more structure and caution than an *Innovator* whose *Banker* score is minimal. To an observer, these differences can be dramatic. Two people with the same dominant value may look nothing alike because their secondary value and the capacity of both values, shapes the style of their behavior. Recognizing how Contribution Type™ capacity scores influence expression helps us interpret others more accurately, avoid misreading their intentions, and appreciate the subtle ways their core values interact to create their unique contribution to the world.

In the following paragraphs, I will provide examples of individuals throughout history who I believe represent each Contribution Type™. While these individuals did not take the CVI™ assessment, I use these individuals as people who I believe best represent the assigned core values and Contribution Types™ to help you better visualize the core values and Contribution Types™ in action.

Intuitive Contribution Type™ (Builder/Merchant)

The *Intuitive* Contribution Type™ blends the *Builder's* decisive, action-oriented drive with the *Merchant's* relational insight and emotional intelligence. People with this combination tend to "feel" the right move before they can fully explain it. The *Builder* side gives them a grounded sense of direction, a natural confidence in taking charge, and an instinct for what needs to happen next. The *Merchant* core value adds empathy, persuasion, and the ability to read people quickly and accurately. Together, these values create someone who navigates both tasks and relationships with a kind of internal compass, able to sense opportunities, anticipate reactions, and move forward with conviction. Their intuition isn't mystical. It's the result of combining practical decisiveness with deep interpersonal awareness, allowing them to make rapid judgments that often prove correct.

People with this combination tend to be:

- Visionary yet practical
- Relationship-driven but decisive
- Builders of systems, alliances, and enterprises
- Natural negotiators who also take action
- Loyal, strategic, and entrepreneurial

Out in the world, intuitive contributors show up as leaders who can walk into a room and immediately sense the emotional temperature, then take action that aligns everyone around a shared goal. A sales manager might instinctively know which client is ready to close and which one needs reassurance. A small-business owner might feel when it's time to expand, even before the data fully confirms it. A teacher with this combination may intuitively adjust their lesson plan based on the mood and energy of the class. These individuals excel in roles where quick decisions and human understanding intersect: entrepreneurship, sales, coaching, emergency response leadership, or any environment where reading people and acting decisively creates momentum.

In my opinion, George Washington, Catherine the Great, and Marcus Aurelius each exemplify the Intuitive Contribution Type™ in strikingly different yet deeply consistent ways, blending decisive, *Builder*-style action, with the *Merchant's* relational insight and emotional intelligence. George Washington demonstrated this combination throughout the American Revolution and his presidency. His *Builder* energy showed in his steady command, willingness to make difficult decisions, and instinct for when to advance or retreat. Yet his *Merchant* side was equally visible. He read the morale of his troops with remarkable sensitivity, understood the symbolic power of his actions, created America's first cabinet to help with decision making, and navigated political factions with a calm, unifying presence. He often acted on a felt sense of timing and human dynamics, making choices that balanced firmness with empathy. Catherine the Great displayed the same intuitive blend on an imperial scale. Her *Builder* decisiveness drove sweeping reforms, territorial expansion, and bold administrative changes, while her *Merchant* relational intelligence allowed her to cultivate alliances, charm foreign diplomats, and maintain loyalty among nobles who could easily have turned against her. She had a keen sense for people, their motivations, fears, and ambitions and used that insight to guide her political strategy. Her ability to "feel" the right moment to act, negotiate, or shift direction reflects the hallmark of this Contribution Type™. Marcus Aurelius, though a philosopher-emperor, also embodied this intuitive pairing. His *Builder* side emerged in his disciplined leadership of the Roman Empire during war and crisis, while his *Merchant* side appeared in his deep empathy, his understanding of human nature, and his ability to connect with others through calm, grounded presence. His decisions often reflected a blend of inner conviction, grand vision, and relational awareness, guided by an intuition shaped by both action and vision.

Together, these figures illustrate how intuitive contributors operate in the real world. They read the emotional landscape quickly, act with conviction, and align people around a shared purpose. Washington sensed when his army needed encouragement rather than orders. Catherine the Great instinctively knew when diplomacy would achieve more than force. Marcus Aurelius could feel when a firm decree was necessary and when a measured, empathetic response would stabilize the empire. Their leadership wasn't based solely on analysis or rigid strategy. It emerged from an internal compass shaped by decisive clarity and human understanding. They excelled in moments where timing, trust, and emotional intelligence mattered just as much as tactical skill, demonstrating how the Intuitive Contribution Type™ can shape not only individual success but the course of history itself.

Cognitive Contribution Type™ (Banker/Innovator)

The Cognitive Contribution Type™ merges the *Banker's* precision, accuracy, and respect for proven information with the *Innovator's* analytical creativity and problem-solving depth. This combination produces individuals who think carefully, reason deeply, and approach challenges with both structure and imagination. The *Banker* side ensures they gather facts, verify details, and maintain a disciplined approach to information. The *Innovator* side pushes them to explore possibilities, question assumptions, and design elegant solutions. Together, they create a mind that is both rigorous and inventive, capable of seeing patterns others miss, diagnosing root causes, and constructing solutions that are both accurate and innovative.

• • •

People with this combination tend to be:

- Highly analytical and data-driven
- Calm, steady, and emotionally-even under pressure
- Excellent at identifying patterns and inconsistencies
- Value fairness, consistency, and rational decision-making
- Strong desire for clarity, accuracy, and logical structure

In practice, cognitive contributors thrive in environments where complex problems require both data and insight. A software architect might blend technical precision with creative system design. A financial analyst may spot trends early because they combine meticulous research with conceptual thinking. A medical researcher might follow strict protocols while also imagining new hypotheses or treatment pathways. Even in everyday life, these individuals are the ones who fix broken processes, redesign workflows, or troubleshoot issues others can't quite articulate. They excel in engineering, analytics, research, architecture, strategic planning, and any field where disciplined thinking meets inventive problem-solving.

The Cognitive Contribution Type™ is beautifully illustrated by historical figures like Isaac Newton, Nikola Tesla, and Florence Nightingale, each of whom blended the *Banker's* precision with the *Innovator's* analytical creativity in ways that reshaped entire fields. Isaac Newton embodied the disciplined, detail-driven side of the *Banker* through his meticulous mathematical proofs, exhaustive experiments, and insistence on empirical verification, yet his *Innovator* energy was equally powerful. He imagined entirely new frameworks for understanding motion, gravity, and light, seeing patterns in the natural world that no one before him had recognized. Nikola Tesla, too, demonstrated this duality. His *Banker* side grounded his work in rigorous engineering principles and careful measurement, while his *Innovator* side fueled his visionary leaps into alternating current, wireless transmission, and technologies far ahead of his time. He questioned assumptions others accepted as fixed and designed solutions that were both elegant and revolutionary. Florence Nightingale expressed the Cognitive Contribution Type™ in a different domain but with the same unmistakable blend of structure and imagination. Her *Banker* energy drove her to collect, analyze, and systematize medical data with unprecedented accuracy, while her *Innovator* side allowed her to reimagine hospital sanitation, nursing practices, and public health systems. She didn't just gather information, she used it to diagnose root causes and redesign entire processes, creating solutions that were both scientifically sound and conceptually transformative. Together, these figures show how cognitive contributors think: they combine disciplined analysis with inventive problem-solving, allowing them to see what others overlook and build solutions that are as reliable as they are groundbreaking.

Creative Contribution Type™ (Merchant/Innovator)

The Creative Contribution Type™ arises from the *Merchant's* relational energy and the *Innovator's* conceptual imagination. This pairing produces individuals who generate ideas that are not only original but also emotionally resonant and human-centered. The *Merchant* side brings empathy, storytelling, and the ability to understand what people value. The *Innovator* side contributes curiosity, pattern recognition, and the drive to improve systems and concepts. Together, they create a person who sees possibilities everywhere, someone who can imagine a better future and inspire others to believe in it. Their creativity is not abstract. It is grounded in human needs, motivations, and experiences.

In real-world settings, creative contributors often become brand strategists, designers, marketers, therapists, product developers, or community innovators. A marketing professional with this combination might craft campaigns that connect deeply with audiences because they understand both the emotional and conceptual dimensions of a message. A UX designer may create intuitive interfaces by blending empathy for users with innovative design thinking. A nonprofit leader might envision new programs that meet unmet needs in ways that feel fresh and meaningful. These individuals excel wherever imagination, empathy, and improvement come together to create something new.

People with this combination tend to be:

- Charismatic but analytical
- Visionary yet grounded in practical solutions
- Skilled at building alliances and inspiring others
- Inventive thinkers who reshape people-centered systems
- Motivated by improving the world through insight and connection

The Creative Contribution Type™ is powerfully reflected in figures like Benjamin Franklin, Frederick Douglass, and Maria Montessori, each of whom blended the *Merchant's* relational insight with the *Innovator's* conceptual imagination to reshape the world in ways that were both visionary and deeply human-centered. Benjamin Franklin embodied this combination through his ability to connect with people across social classes and cultures while simultaneously generating inventive ideas that improved daily life. His *Merchant* energy showed in his diplomacy, humor, and talent for building alliances, while his *Innovator* side fueled his curiosity and pattern-driven creativity, leading to breakthroughs in electricity, civic institutions, and public services. Frederick Douglass demonstrated the Creative Contribution Type™ through his extraordinary ability to translate personal experience into powerful storytelling that awakened the conscience of a nation. His *Merchant* empathy allowed him to understand what would move people emotionally, while his *Innovator* mind crafted arguments, speeches, and narratives that reframed the moral logic of abolition. He didn't just advocate for change, he reshaped how people thought about freedom, dignity, and justice. Maria Montessori expressed this Contribution Type™ through her revolutionary approach to education, which combined a deep understanding of children's emotional and developmental needs with a visionary reimagining of how learning environments could function. Her *Merchant* sensitivity allowed her to see the world through a child's eyes, while her *Innovator* creativity led her to design an entirely new educational system grounded in independence, exploration, and respect for individual growth. Together, these figures show how creative contributors operate. They imagine bold new possibilities, communicate them in ways that resonate emotionally, and build solutions that honor human experience. Their creativity is never detached or theoretical, it is rooted in empathy, insight, and a desire to elevate the lives of others.

Practical Contribution Type™ (Builder/Banker)

The Practical Contribution Type™ combines the *Builder's* drive for action with the *Banker's* commitment to accuracy and structure. This pairing produces individuals who excel at getting things done correctly, efficiently, and reliably. The *Builder* side brings confidence, decisiveness, and a bias toward execution. The *Banker* side ensures that actions are grounded in facts, details, and proven methods. Together, they create someone who is steady, dependable, and highly capable in operational environments. They don't just act. They act with precision. They don't just plan. They plan with realism. Their contribution lies in turning ideas into tangible results through disciplined, well-organized effort.

In the real world, practical contributors shine in roles that require consistency, reliability, and hands-on competence. A project manager might keep a complex initiative on track by combining decisive leadership with meticulous planning. A construction supervisor may ensure that work is done safely, correctly, and on schedule. A logistics coordinator might maintain smooth operations by blending quick decision-making with careful attention to detail. Even in personal life, these individuals are the ones who fix things, organize systems, and keep everything running smoothly. They thrive in operations, project management, quality control, manufacturing, logistics, and any environment where dependable execution is essential.

People with this combination tend to be:

- System builders / Strategic planners
- Guardians of order / Highly disciplined
- Loyal, consistent, and grounded
- Excellent at maintaining institutions and long-term stability

The Practical Contribution Type™ is well illustrated by figures like J.P. Morgan, Thomas Hobbes, and Margaret Thatcher, each of whom demonstrated the *Builder's* decisive, action-oriented drive paired with the *Banker's* commitment to structure, accuracy, and disciplined execution. J.P. Morgan embodied this combination through his ability to stabilize financial systems, reorganize failing industries, and impose order on chaotic markets. His *Builder* energy showed in his willingness to take charge during crises such as coordinating private capital to halt financial panics, while his *Banker* side ensured that every action was grounded in meticulous analysis, contractual clarity, and proven financial principles. Thomas Hobbes, though a philosopher rather than an industrialist, displayed the same practical pattern in his methodical approach to political theory. His *Builder* decisiveness appeared in his firm conclusions about authority and social order, while his *Banker* precision shaped his systematic reasoning, careful definitions, and structured arguments. He didn't speculate loosely. He constructed a detailed, logically organized framework designed to produce stability in the real world. Margaret Thatcher also reflected this Contribution Type™ through her direct, execution-focused leadership style. Her *Builder* side drove her to act boldly and decisively in pursuit of her policy goals, while her *Banker* side grounded those actions in detailed planning, fiscal discipline, and a strong emphasis on structure and accountability. She approached governance with a focus on operational clarity, turning broad ideas into concrete, enforceable policies. Together, these figures demonstrate how practical contributors operate. They combine confidence with precision, action with structure, and vision with disciplined follow-through. They excel not by theorizing or imagining possibilities, but by turning complex challenges into organized, workable systems that produce reliable results.

Community Contribution Type™ (Merchant/Banker)

The Community Contribution Type™ blends the *Merchant's* relational warmth with the *Banker's* structured dependability. This combination produces individuals who support, stabilize, and strengthen groups through both emotional intelligence and practical reliability. The *Merchant* side brings connection, encouragement, and the ability to understand people's needs. The *Banker* side adds consistency, follow-through, and a respect for commitments and processes. Together, they create someone who builds trust, fosters harmony, and ensures that people feel both cared for and supported. Their contribution is often subtle but deeply impactful. They essentially create environments where others can thrive.

In real-world settings, community contributors excel in roles that require both people skills and organizational steadiness. A human-resources professional might combine empathy with policy knowledge to support employees effectively. A school counselor may offer emotional support while also helping students navigate academic requirements. A community organizer might build strong networks by blending relational outreach with structured planning. Even in families or friend groups, these individuals are the ones who remember birthdays, organize gatherings, and check in when someone is struggling. They thrive in HR, counseling, administration, customer service, community development, and any role where people and structure intersect.

People with this combination tend to be:

- Relational, diplomatic, intuitive
- Analytical, structured, fairness-driven
- Calm, steady, and trustworthy
- Excellent negotiators and consensus-builders
- Long-term thinkers who value stability and harmony
- Skilled at balancing people needs with practical realities

The Community Contribution Type™ is vividly reflected in the lives of George Marshall, Clara Barton, and Margaret Mead, each of whom blended the *Merchant's* relational warmth with the *Banker's* structured dependability to strengthen the people and systems around them. George Marshall demonstrated this combination through his calm, steady leadership during World War II and the creation of the Marshall Plan. His *Merchant* side showed in his ability to understand the needs of nations and leaders, earning trust across political and cultural divides, while his *Banker* side grounded his work in disciplined planning, logistical precision, and a deep respect for process. He didn't just rebuild Europe, he rebuilt confidence, stability, and cooperation. Clara Barton, founder of the American Red Cross, embodied the same pattern in humanitarian form. Her *Merchant* energy fueled her compassion, her ability to comfort the wounded, and her instinct for what people needed in moments of crisis. At the same time, her *Banker* contribution allowed her to organize supplies, establish reliable systems of care, and build an institution that could function dependably in the most chaotic conditions. She paired empathy with structure, turning compassion into sustainable action. Margaret Mead, the pioneering cultural anthropologist, also expressed the Community Contribution Type™ through her ability to connect deeply with the people she studied while bringing disciplined methodology to her research. Her *Merchant* warmth helped her build trust within diverse communities, while her *Banker* precision ensured that her observations were systematic, consistent, and grounded in careful documentation. She created understanding between cultures by combining emotional insight with structured analysis. Together, these figures show how community contributors operate. They stabilize, support, and uplift others through a blend of empathy and reliability, creating environments where people feel safe, valued, and able to grow.

Independent Contribution Type™ (Builder/Innovator)

The Independent Contribution Type™ merges the *Builder's* self-directed action with the *Innovator's* analytical autonomy. This combination produces individuals who prefer to think for themselves, act on their own judgment, and pursue solutions without excessive oversight. The *Builder* side gives them confidence, initiative, and a desire to take charge of their own path. The *Innovator* side adds curiosity, problem-solving depth, and a preference for conceptual freedom. Together, they create someone who is resourceful, self-reliant, and capable of navigating ambiguity with both courage and clarity. They don't wait for instructions, they create them. They don't follow existing paths. They carve new ones.

In the real world, independent contributors thrive in roles that reward autonomy, innovation, and self-direction. An entrepreneur might build a business by combining decisive action with inventive strategy. A consultant may diagnose problems and implement solutions with minimal supervision. A field engineer might troubleshoot complex issues on-site, relying on both technical insight and personal initiative. Even in everyday life, these individuals are the ones who figure things out on their own, take on ambitious projects, and push boundaries. They excel in entrepreneurship, consulting, engineering, product development, and any environment where independent thinking and decisive action are essential.

People with this combination tend to be:

- Practical visionaries
- System builders who also redesign systems
- Decisive problem-solvers
- Calm under pressure, strategic, and inventive
- People who turn ideas into durable structures
- Leaders who blend creativity with action

The Independent Contribution Type™ is powerfully illustrated by Alexander the Great, Napoleon Bonaparte, and Cornelius Vanderbilt, each of whom embodied the fusion of the *Builder's* self-directed drive with the *Innovator's* analytical autonomy. Alexander the Great demonstrated this combination through his relentless initiative and refusal to be constrained by traditional military thinking. His *Builder* energy fueled his boldness leading armies across continents, taking decisive action in unfamiliar terrain, and pushing beyond the boundaries of what his advisors believed possible. At the same time, his *Innovator* side showed in his ability to analyze battlefield conditions, adapt tactics on the fly, and integrate new cultural and strategic ideas into his expanding empire. He didn't simply follow established methods. He reinvented them. Napoleon expressed the same independent pattern through his meteoric rise and his revolutionary approach to warfare and governance. His *Builder* decisiveness drove him to seize opportunities quickly and assert control in chaotic political environments, while his *Innovator* mind allowed him to redesign military organization, rethink legal structures, and craft strategies that outmaneuvered larger, more traditional forces. He trusted his own judgment above all, often acting with a clarity and speed that left opponents scrambling to respond. Cornelius Vanderbilt, though operating in the world of business rather than conquest, displayed the same blend of autonomy and inventive problem-solving. His *Builder* side pushed him to take charge of his own destiny from a young age, building transportation empires through sheer will and relentless action. His *Innovator* side emerged in the way he identified inefficiencies, reimagined shipping and rail systems, and created new business models that reshaped American commerce. He didn't wait for permission or follow established paths, he built new ones, often literally. Together, these figures show how independent contributors operate. They rely on their own insight, act with decisive confidence, and navigate uncertainty with a blend of courage and creative intelligence that allows them to forge entirely new directions in history.

Closing Thoughts on Contribution Types™

Understanding an individual's Contribution Type™ offers a far richer and more accurate picture of who they are than simply identifying their dominant core value. Instead of relegating someone to one of four broad categories, the Contribution Type™ reveals how their top two values interact, influence one another, and shape the way they naturally contribute in relationships, teams, and decision-making environments. When we also consider capacity scores, the level of contribution and clarity with which each value is expressed, we gain an even more nuanced understanding of a person's unchanging nature. This allows us to see why two people with the same dominant value can behave very differently. Why certain individuals excel in specific roles, why some interpersonal dynamics feel effortless, while others require more intentional communication. In team settings, this deeper insight helps reduce misunderstandings, improves collaboration, and allows leaders to place people where their natural capacities can shine. Instead of trying to fit individuals into rigid boxes, the CVI™ Contribution Type™ honors the complexity of human motivation and gives us a more complete, respectful, and accurate way to understand how someone shows up in the world.

CHAPTER 5
NATURAL FLOW

Every moment of your life, every decision you make, every problem you solve, and every dream you pursue, unfolds according to a *natural flow*. This flow is not something you were taught, nor is it a technique you picked up along the way. It is something far deeper, something woven into the very structure of how human beings are designed to think, create, and act. Whether you are building a business, navigating a relationship, planning a project, or simply trying to make sense of your next step, the same sequence quietly governs the process: *Vision, Strategy, Structure,* and *Action*. First, you must see what could be. Then you determine how to get there. Next, you gather the resources required. Finally, you take decisive action. This pattern is so universal that it shows up everywhere, from the way organizations innovate to the way individuals grow. And it is no coincidence that this same flow is reflected in the CVI™, where the four core values operate in the same order: *Merchant* (Vision), *Innovator* (Strategy), *Banker* (Structure), and *Builder* (Action). This alignment is not accidental. It is a mirror of human nature itself.

When you begin to see this flow, you start to recognize it in every corner of life. A great leader begins with a compelling vision before crafting a strategy. A skilled architect imagines the structure before drawing the plans. A wise parent envisions the kind of relationship they want with their child before deciding how to guide them. Even the simplest tasks follow this pattern. Before you cook a meal, you imagine what you want to make, decide how to prepare it, gather the ingredients, and then begin cooking. The scale may change, but the order does not. Vision always precedes strategy. Strategy always precedes structure. Structure always precedes action. When this order is honored, life moves with clarity and purpose. When it is ignored, frustration and inefficiency follow.

Figure 4. Natural flow of any effort or project.

If you look closely at the world around you, you'll notice something remarkable. Everything in creation follows a pattern. Seasons unfold in order. Seeds sprout, grow, mature, and bear fruit in order. Even the human heartbeat follows a rhythm that cannot be rearranged without consequence. Order is not a constraint. It is the structure that makes life possible. In the same way, the flow of vision, strategy, structure, and action is not a human invention. It is a reflection of something deeper. Something built into the very architecture of how people think, feel, and create. Once you see it, you begin to understand why efforts or initiatives struggle when these steps are out of order.

From the moment you wake up in the morning, this flow is already at work. Before you move, you imagine what the day could hold. Before you plan, you sense what matters. Before you gather what you need, you decide how to approach your tasks. And before you act, you prepare. This sequence is so natural that you rarely notice it, yet it guides everything from the smallest decisions to the most significant life choices. When you try to reverse it, when you act without clarity, plan without purpose, or prepare without direction, you feel the friction immediately. Confusion rises. Motivation fades. Progress stalls. These breakdowns are not failures of effort. They are failures of process. They reveal that you are working against the grain of the natural flow.

The CVI™ captures this design with striking accuracy. It identifies four core energies: *Merchant, Innovator, Banker*, and *Builder* that mirror the natural flow of human action. The *Merchant's* intuitive vision, the *Innovator's* strategic insight, the *Banker's* structured stewardship, and the *Builder's* decisive action are not random traits. They are expressions of a deeper pattern embedded in human nature. Each value reflects a stage of the creative process, and each stage depends on the one before it. When you honor this sequence, your core values are maximized because timing is just as important as what you bring to that moment. When you ignore it, even your greatest gifts can become sources of frustration. The CVI™ doesn't create the flow, it reveals it.

When you begin to see the flow as predetermined rather than a technique to master, something shifts. You stop trying to force yourself into patterns that don't fit. You stop judging yourself for the way you naturally think or work. You stop comparing your contributions to the contributions of others. Instead, you begin to appreciate your CVI™ wiring. You begin to understand why certain parts of an effort energize you while others drain you. You begin to see how your unique combination of core values points toward a purpose that is uniquely yours. And as you align with that purpose, you experience a sense of clarity, peace, and momentum that feels less like striving and more like stepping into who you were always meant to be and how you are meant to contribute.

. . .

It's Human Nature

Before you can understand how the natural flow of human action expresses itself in your life, you need a way to see your own design clearly. Most people move through life with only a partial understanding of why they think the way they do, why certain tasks energize them while others drain them, or why they naturally excel in some environments but struggle in others. They sense that there is a pattern to their contributions and motivations, but they lack a framework that reveals it with clarity. This is where the CVI™ becomes a powerful tool. The CVI™ is not just another human assessment, it is a map of human nature. It identifies the unchanging core values that drive your decisions, shape your contributions, and determine how you naturally move through the world.

Unlike personality tests that measure behavior, something that shifts with age, environment, and circumstance, the CVI™ measures drive. The deeper internal drivers that remain constant throughout your life. Behavior can be influenced by stress, culture, expectations, or training, but motivation is rooted in your core nature. It is the part of you that does not change. This is why the CVI™ is so different from other assessments. It doesn't tell you who you are trying to be or who you've learned to be. It reveals who you are and why you are able to rise or struggle in certain situations. It uncovers the values that sit beneath your thoughts, your instincts, your preferences, and your natural way of contributing. And because these values align perfectly with the natural flow of vision, strategy, structure, and action, the CVI™ becomes a lens through which you can understand when to step up or step back and let others shine.

Everyone has all four values, but in different proportions. Your dominant value reveals the way you most naturally create impact. Your secondary value supports and shapes your primary one. Understanding your core values and where they fall in the natural flow is like discovering the operating system running quietly beneath your life. Suddenly, patterns that once felt random begin to make sense. You understand why certain tasks feel effortless while others feel heavy. You see why you thrive in some environments and feel out of place in others. You recognize why certain conflicts repeat themselves and why certain relationships feel naturally aligned. You begin to understand not only what you do, but why you do it. And perhaps most importantly, you begin to see how your wiring points toward your purpose. Your core values are not accidental, they are clues. They reveal the kind of contributions you are uniquely equipped to make and when you should make them.

The CVI™ also helps you understand others with greater clarity and compassion. When you recognize that people are motivated by different core values, you stop expecting everyone to think, feel, or participate the way you do. You begin to appreciate the contributions others bring to the table and understand the blind spots that come with each value. You see why some people seem to always step up and lead with vision while others lead with action, why some crave clarity while others crave possibility, why some seek stability while others seek innovation. This understanding transforms relationships, teams, and communication. It allows you to collaborate more effectively, resolve conflict more gracefully, and build environments where everyone can contribute from their core values at the right moment.

The CVI™ is more than an assessment, it is a mirror. It reflects the truth of your design and invites you to live in alignment with it. It reveals the natural flow and shows you how to honor it. And as you move into the next sections, you will explore each core value in depth, discovering how the *Merchant, Innovator, Banker,* and *Builder* energies shape your life, your work, and your purpose. But before you go further, remember this: your core values are not limitations, they are your blueprint. They are the foundation of your contribution and the key to unlocking a life of clarity, alignment, fulfillment, and perfect timing.

This chapter is an invitation to recognize that the natural flow is the blueprint for the timing of your contribution, and the foundation for everything that follows. In the sections ahead, we will explore each core value in depth, discovering how the flow expresses itself through your actions, your motivations, and your natural way of moving through the world. But before you go further, hold onto this truth: the order is not just natural, it is purposeful. And when you honor that purpose, you optimize everything you do.

Vision

The *Merchant* comes first because vision always precedes everything else. The *Merchant* energy is relational, intuitive, and deeply connected to meaning and possibility. It asks, What matters? What do we value? What future are we moving toward? Without this initial spark of vision, nothing has direction or purpose. When the *Merchant* is skipped or minimized, people jump into problem-solving or planning without understanding why they are doing it. For example, imagine a team launching a new initiative without first aligning on the purpose behind it. They may work hard, but their efforts scatter because no shared vision anchors them. Or imagine a person taking action in their personal life. Changing jobs, moving cities, starting a project without first clarifying what they truly want. The result is often regret or misalignment. The *Merchant* typically leads because vision is the compass, without it, every step afterward lacks meaning and coherence.

Every meaningful endeavor begins with a spark, an idea, a possibility, a sense of what could be. This spark is the domain of the *Merchant*, the first core value in the *natural flow* of human action. Because the *Merchant* represents vision, connection, intuition, and meaning. It is the part of you that sense's purpose before you can articulate it. The part that feels possibility before you can prove it, and that sees potential in people long before anything tangible exists. Vision is the starting point because nothing in life can move forward without first being imagined. Vision is the seed from which strategy, structure, and action grow. Without it, the rest of the flow is disjointed.

Merchant energy:

- Seeks connection, harmony, and shared understanding
- Want to know that their efforts contribute to something worthwhile

- Inspires individuals and teams
- Sense emotional and relational dynamics
- People are not just roles but whole beings with potential

This ability to connect vision with humanity is what makes the *Merchant* indispensable. When vision is missing, everything else becomes misaligned. Strategy becomes clever but directionless. Structure becomes rigid and unnecessary. Action becomes frantic and unfocused. You've likely experienced this in your own life. Times when you worked hard but felt disconnected from the purpose behind your efforts, or when you pursued goals that looked good on paper but didn't resonate with your heart. Without vision, even success feels hollow. The *Merchant* prevents this by grounding every endeavor in meaning and purpose.

To understand why vision must lead, consider what happens when the order is reversed. Imagine a team that jumps straight into planning without first clarifying the vision. They may create a detailed strategy, but it will be built on assumptions rather than shared purpose. The result is misalignment, people working hard but not together. Or imagine someone who begins gathering resources before deciding what they actually want to accomplish. They may accumulate information, tools, or commitments that ultimately have nothing to do with their true goals. Or consider the person who leaps into action without any vision at all. Taking steps, making decisions, and expending energy without a clear sense of direction. These breakdowns are not failures of effort. They are failures of order.

When vision leads, everything else becomes easier. Vision clarifies priorities. It inspires commitment. It creates alignment. It gives strategy something to serve, structure something to support, and action something to accomplish. Vision is not a luxury. It is the foundation. And the *Merchant* is the keeper of that foundation. This is why vision sits at the beginning of the CVI™ process flow and at the beginning of the natural flow of human action. It is the starting point of purpose, the birthplace of meaning, and the spark that ignites every significant contribution.

As you move forward in this chapter, you will see how each core value builds on the one before it. But remember this: without vision, nothing begins. Vision is the first movement of creation. It is the whisper that says, "There is something more." When you honor the *Merchant* within you, whether it is your dominant value or a quieter part of your design, you honor the truth that every great endeavor begins with a vision.

Strategy

Once vision has taken shape, once the *Merchant* has named what matters and illuminated what could be, the next essential movement in the natural flow is strategy. This is the domain of the *Innovator*. If the *Merchant* asks, "What future are we moving toward," the *Innovator* asks, "How do we get there?" The *Innovator* is the architect of possibility, the designer of pathways, the solver of problems. It is the part of you that thrives on complexity, that sees patterns others miss, that enjoys the challenge of turning vision into something workable, elegant, and intelligent. Strategy is not merely planning. It is the art of aligning creativity with purpose. And without it, even the most inspiring vision remains suspended in imagination.

The *Innovator* follows naturally because once vision is established, strategy must take shape. Strategy cannot exist without vision, because strategy is always in service to something. When *Innovator* energy jumps ahead of the *Merchant*, strategy becomes clever but aimless. Brilliant solutions to the wrong problems. For example, a company might design an impressive product that no one actually wants, or a person might create a detailed plan for a goal that doesn't align with their values. Conversely, when strategy is skipped entirely, people move from vision straight into action, resulting in wasted effort, avoidable mistakes, and unnecessary stress. The *Innovator's* placement in the sequence ensures that the path forward is thoughtful, creative, and aligned with the original vision.

Innovator energy is:

- Analytical, inventive, and solution-oriented

- Has the ability to diagnose, design, and refine
- Asks, "How do we get there?", "What options exist?", "What's the smartest path forward?"
- Motivated by understanding, improvement, and solutions
- Drawn to questions, puzzles, and inefficiencies
- Looks for better ways to do things
- Not satisfied with surface answers
- Want to understand the underlying mechanics of a situation

When strategy is skipped entirely, when people move directly from vision to action, the consequences are equally predictable. Action without strategy leads to inefficiency, frustration, and unnecessary struggle. You may know what you want, but without a clear path, you end up taking detours, repeating mistakes, or burning energy on steps that don't move you forward. This is the person who starts a business without a plan, who jumps into a relationship without understanding their needs, or who begins a project without considering the challenges ahead. Their enthusiasm is real, but their progress is fragile. Strategy is what transforms inspiration into momentum.

To understand why the *Innovator* must come second, imagine what happens when the order is reversed. If the *Banker* (structure) comes before the *Innovator*, people gather resources without knowing what they're preparing for. They over-research, over-organize, or over-plan, only to discover that much of their effort was unnecessary. If the *Builder* (action) comes before the *Innovator*, people rush into doing without thinking, creating chaos, rework, and burnout. And if the *Merchant* tries to handle strategy alone, vision becomes idealistic rather than actionable. Each value has its place, and the *Innovator's* place is to bridge the gap between imagination and execution.

When the *Innovator* is honored, strategy becomes a source of clarity and confidence. It sharpens the vision. It identifies the smartest path. It anticipates obstacles before they appear. It ensures that the steps ahead are not only possible but purposeful. *Innovator* energy brings intelligence to inspiration, structure to creativity, and direction to desire. It is the quiet force that turns dreams into plans and plans into progress.

As you move into the next section, you will see how the *Banker* builds on the *Innovator's* work. Gathering the resources, information, and structure needed to support the strategy. But remember this: without the *Innovator*, the flow cannot move forward. Strategy is the hinge between vision and action. It is the moment when possibility evolves into practicality. And when you honor the *Innovator* within you, whether it is your dominant value or a supporting core value, you honor the truth that every meaningful endeavor requires not just imagination, but intelligent design.

Structure

Once vision has been cast by the *Merchant* and strategy has been shaped by the *Innovator*, the natural flow of human action moves into its third essential stage: structure. This is the domain of the *Banker*, the core value responsible for gathering, organizing, and stewarding the resources required to bring a strategy to life. If the *Merchant* asks, "What matters?" and the *Innovator* asks, "How do we get there?" the *Banker* asks, "What do we need," "What must be in place," and "What risks must be considered?" The *Banker* is the guardian of stability, the keeper of details, and the steward of resources. Without the *Banker*, even the most brilliant vision and strategy remain fragile, ungrounded, and unsustainable.

The *Banker* comes third because once strategy is formed, resources must be gathered, organized, and prepared. *Banker* energy is methodical, detail-oriented, and grounded in stewardship. Structure cannot precede strategy because you cannot gather the right resources until you know the plan. When *Banker* energy jumps ahead, people over-prepare, over-organize, or hoard information without knowing what is actually necessary. For example, someone might spend months researching a project they never intend to pursue, or a team might create elaborate systems before deciding on a direction. On the other hand, when *Banker* energy is skipped, action becomes chaotic and under-resourced. People run out of time, money, or clarity because they didn't prepare. The *Banker's* role ensures that the vision and strategy are supported with the right structure, making success sustainable rather than accidental.

Banker energy:

- Methodical, thoughtful, and deeply committed to accuracy
- Thrives on clarity, information, and preparedness
- Motivated by the desire to protect, preserve, and ensure that nothing essential is overlooked
- Gathers data, analyze risks, creates systems, and builds frameworks that support long-term success
- Ask questions, "Do we have enough time," "Enough money," "Enough information," "What are the potential pitfalls," and "What must be documented?"
- Brings order to complexity and stability to uncertainty

Structure must follow strategy because you cannot gather the right resources until you know what you are preparing for. When structure precedes strategy, effort is wasted and momentum stalls.

To understand why the *Banker* must come third, imagine what happens when the order is reversed. If the *Builder* (action) comes before the *Banker*, people rush into doing without the tools, information, or support they need. Mistakes multiply. Stress rises. Progress slows. If the *Merchant* tries to handle structure, vision becomes bogged down in details and loses its inspiration. If the *Innovator* tries to handle structure, strategy becomes overly complex or theoretical. Each value has its place, and the *Banker's* place is to ensure that the vision and strategy are grounded in reality and supported by the right resources.

When the *Banker* is honored, structure becomes a source of confidence rather than constraint. It creates clarity. It reduces risk. It ensures that the steps ahead are not only possible but sustainable. *Banker* energy brings order to creativity, stability to innovation, and reliability to action. It is the quiet force that ensures nothing essential is forgotten and that every endeavor has the foundation it needs to succeed.

As you move into the next section, you will see how the *Builder* completes the natural flow, turning vision, strategy, and structure into decisive action. But remember this: without the *Banker*, the flow cannot hold. Structure is not only the bridge between planning and doing, it is the moment when ideas become grounded, when risks are mitigated, and when the path ahead becomes clear and supported. And when you honor the *Banker* within you, whether it is your dominant value or a supporting core value, you honor the truth that every meaningful endeavor requires not just imagination and intelligence, but preparation and stewardship.

Action

After vision has been cast by the *Merchant*, strategy shaped by the *Innovator*, and structure secured by the *Banker*, the natural flow of human action reaches its final and essential stage: action. This is the domain of the *Builder*. If the *Merchant* asks, "What matters?", the *Innovator* asks, "How do we get there?"When the *Banker* asks, "What do we need," the *Builder* asks the questions that brings everything to life, "What must be done right now," "What is the next step," and "How do we bring this to life?" *Builder* energy is decisive, courageous, and grounded in movement. It is the force that transforms ideas into reality, plans into progress, and intentions into outcomes. Without the *Builder* energy, nothing happens. Vision remains imagination, strategy remains theory, and structure remains potential. Action is the moment when everything becomes real.

The *Builder* comes last because action is the culmination of everything that came before it. Action without vision is reckless. Action without strategy is inefficient. Action without structure is exhausting. But when action comes after the *Merchant*, *Innovator*, and *Banker* have done their work, it becomes powerful, focused, and effective. When *Builder* energy jumps ahead in the sequence, people "just start doing things" without clarity or preparation, leading to burnout, conflict, or failure. For example, a person might impulsively start a business without a plan or resources, or a team might rush into implementation before aligning on goals. The *Builder* belongs at the end because action is most impactful when it is the final expression of a well-formed vision, a smart strategy, and a solid foundation.

Builder energy is:

- Direct, practical, and intensely focused on results
- Motivated by accomplishment, momentum, and progress
- Thrive in environments where clarity meets urgency
- Don't want to talk about doing, they want to do
- Ability to cut through hesitation, eliminate unnecessary complexity, and push forward with determination
- Bring energy to stagnation, clarity to indecision, and momentum to stalled efforts
- They are the closers, the finishers, the ones who turn potential into results

When the *Builder* jumps ahead of the flow, when doing replaces thinking, the consequences are predictable. People rush into tasks without clarity, make decisions without context, or pursue goals without preparation. This is the person who makes a major life decision without considering the implications. Their drive is admirable, but their outcomes are unstable. *Builder* energy is powerful, but when it is unleashed too early, it creates chaos rather than progress.

Likewise, when the *Builder* is skipped entirely, when people stay in vision, strategy, or structure without ever taking action, the result is stagnation. Ideas pile up. Plans multiply. Resources gather dust. Nothing moves. This is the team that holds endless meetings but never executes, the individual who dreams endlessly but never begins, or the organization that prepares meticulously but never launches. Without *Builder* energy, potential remains unrealized. The flow collapses under its own weight. Action is not just the final step. It is the step that gives meaning to all the others.

To understand why the *Builder* must come last, imagine what happens when the order is reversed. If the *Banker* tries to act, structure becomes rigid and slow. If the *Innovator* tries to act, strategy becomes theoretical rather than practical. If the *Merchant* tries to act, vision becomes idealistic rather than grounded. Each value has its place, and the *Builder's* place is to complete the sequence. To take everything that has been imagined, designed, and prepared, and bring it into the world with positive contribution and clarity.

When the *Builder* is honored, action becomes powerful and purposeful. It is not frantic. It is focused. It is not reactive. It is intentional. It is not exhausting. It is energizing. *Builder* energy brings life to vision, action to strategy, and momentum to structure. It is the force that turns potential into progress and progress into impact. It is the moment when the invisible becomes visible.

Remember this: the *Builder* is not simply the end of the flow. It is the fulfillment of it. Action is the expression of everything that came before. And when you honor the *Builder* within you, you honor the truth that every meaningful endeavor must ultimately be lived, not just imagined.

When Values Are Out of Order

By now, you've seen how the natural flow of human action: vision, strategy, structure, and action, creates clarity, momentum, and alignment. You've also seen how each core value in the CVI™ mirrors this flow: *Merchant, Innovator, Banker, Builder*. When these values work in sequence, the result is a well-designed, well-resourced, and well-executed. But life doesn't always unfold in perfect order. Stress, urgency, habit, and misunderstanding can cause the flow to break down. When values are out of order, even the strongest core values can become liabilities. The purpose of this next section is to help you recognize these breakdowns, understand why they happen, and see how they affect your decisions, relationships, and results.

Builders

The most common breakdown occurs when people act before they think. When *Builder* energy jumps ahead of the flow. You've likely seen this in teams that rush into implementation before clarifying goals, or in individuals who make major decisions without considering the consequences. They may be busy, but they are not effective. Their energy scatters, their stress rises, and their outcomes sometime suffer. *Builder* energy is very powerful, but when it leads before its time, it can create chaos.

Builders face a unique and often misunderstood challenge. Their intuition is so strong, and their instinct for action so accurate, that they can produce impressive results even when the earlier steps of vision, strategy, and structure have not been fully worked through. In the *Builder's* mind, the world is a foggy road, and while others hesitate at the edge of uncertainty, the *Builder* simply steps forward, trusting that movement itself will reveal the next stretch of the path. And often, they're right. Their gut points them in the correct direction, their decisiveness cuts through confusion, and their willingness to act creates momentum that others admire. This ability to see further by moving rather than by waiting gives *Builders* a natural aura of leadership. People trust them because they get results, because their intuition proves itself again and again, and because their confidence fills the gaps where others feel doubt. But this positive contribution creates a subtle trap. *Builders* can begin to believe that the earlier steps in the natural flow: vision, strategy, and structure, are optional. After all, if they can succeed without them, why slow down? Yet this is precisely where the *Builder's* greatest growth lies. Their challenge is not learning how to act, they already excel at that. Their challenge is learning how to pause long enough to ensure that the action they take is aligned with a shared vision, supported by a thoughtful strategy, and resourced with the structure needed to sustain success. When *Builders* embrace this discipline, their impressive results become transformative results. Outcomes that not only achieve the goal but also unify the people involved. They can still anticipate challenges before they arise, and create a foundation strong enough to support long-term impact.

Bankers

Another breakdown occurs when people prepare before they plan. When *Banker* energy comes too early. This often looks like over-researching, over-organizing, or gathering information without knowing what it's for. Without strategy, structure becomes rigid and unnecessary. People create systems that don't serve the vision, collect data that doesn't matter, or build frameworks that ultimately have to be dismantled. This is the student who spends weeks color-coding notes without understanding the material, or the team that builds elaborate spreadsheets before deciding what problem they're solving. Their intentions are good, but their efforts are misaligned. *Banker* energy is essential, but when it precedes strategy, it becomes a barrier instead of a support.

Bankers face a very real and often frustrating challenge. Their gift for gathering, storing, and referencing knowledge can unintentionally become the very thing that shuts down creativity in its earliest stages. Because *Bankers* rely on what is proven, documented, or historically reliable, they often enter brainstorming or vision-scripting sessions feeling unanchored. These conversations can seem too abstract, too speculative, too ungrounded in facts to feel safe or productive. As a result, their natural instinct is to stabilize the moment by introducing data, risks, or historical patterns that are difficult for others to ignore. What they intend as helpful context can land like a wet blanket, smothering ideas before they have a chance to breathe. Their "no" is rarely rooted in negativity. It is rooted in stewardship. But in the early stages of ideation, that stewardship can feel like resistance. The challenge for *Bankers* is learning to hold back their evaluative instincts long enough for vision and strategy to take shape. Their time will come once the dreaming is done and the pathways are outlined. When the *Banker's* ability to assess feasibility, identify gaps, and ensure resources are in place becomes invaluable. When *Bankers* wait for the right moment to step in, they transform from idea-squashers into idea-sustainers, providing the structure, clarity, and stability that turn imaginative concepts into sustainable realities.

Innovator

A third breakdown happens when people strategize without vision. When *Innovator* energy tries to lead. This often looks like clever solutions to the wrong problems. Without vision, strategy becomes aimless. People design plans that don't matter, optimize processes that don't serve a purpose, or solve problems that no one actually needs solved. This is the organization that invests in innovation without understanding customer needs, or the individual who creates a detailed life plan without knowing what they truly want. Their thinking is sharp, but their direction is unclear. *Innovator* energy is brilliant, but when it precedes vision, it becomes disconnected and ineffective.

Innovators face a distinctive challenge that stems directly from their greatest contribution: their minds can run multiple pathways at once, exploring possibilities, alternatives, and improvements simultaneously. This ability is extraordinary, but it can also be disruptive at every stage of the natural flow if not managed well. *Innovators* think best when they have space (mental, emotional, and physical) to roam freely, which is why giving them a clear vision or objective and then stepping out of their way produces their best work. When too many voices crowd their thinking, or when they are forced to process ideas in real time with others, their rapid-fire thoughts can overwhelm the room and even irritate fellow *Innovators*, who are also juggling their own internal webs of ideas. Their brilliance often emerges in the quiet moments while showering, driving, decompressing after a meeting, or waking up the next morning because that is when their minds synthesize scattered insights into elegant, refined solutions. Yet this same drive to continually improve can make it difficult for them to release an idea and let the process move forward. They see what could be, and the temptation to keep refining can stall momentum. The challenge for *Innovators* is learning when to let go. When a solution is "good enough" to move into structure and action. One effective way to support them is to invite them into future iterations or follow-on versions of a product or project. Knowing they will have another opportunity to refine and elevate the work helps them release their grip on the current version, allowing the process to continue while still honoring their gift for improvement.

. . .

Merchant

Finally, a subtle but equally damaging breakdown occurs when people dream without grounding. When *Merchant* energy tries to do the work of the other values. This often looks like endless ideation, emotional enthusiasm, or a desire for harmony that avoids hard decisions. Without strategy, vision becomes idealistic. Without structure, it becomes unrealistic. Without action, it becomes unfulfilled. This is the leader who inspires but never executes. The friend who dreams big but never begins. The team that aligns beautifully but never moves forward. *Merchant* energy is inspiring, but when it tries to carry the entire flow, it becomes weightless and unanchored.

Merchants face a challenge that often emerges after the process has begun, not at the start. Because they naturally lead with vision, the early stages feel energizing and intuitive to them. They can see the future clearly, articulate meaning, and inspire others toward a shared direction. But once the process moves beyond vision and into strategy, structure, and action, the *Merchant's* relational wiring becomes both their positive contribution and their struggle. *Merchants* are deeply attuned to how decisions affect people, and when disagreement arises or when someone feels overlooked, they feel a strong internal pull to pause the process and restore harmony. Their instinct is to gather everyone back into the room, talk it through, and ensure that every voice is heard and every concern is soothed before moving forward. While unity and buy-in are important, this desire for universal agreement can unintentionally stall progress. Especially for *Innovators, Bankers,* and *Builders* who are ready to advance to the next stage. Endless meetings, repeated conversations, and attempts to secure emotional alignment can frustrate the team and slow momentum. The *Merchant's* noble intention: to protect relationships and ensure people feel valued, can become a barrier when it overrides the natural flow and interrupts the moments when other core values need to lead. Their challenge is learning to trust the process enough to let others take their turn, recognizing that disagreement does not always signal danger, and that progress can continue even when people don't perfectly align with one another. When *Merchants* embrace this position, they transform from well-meaning stallers into powerful unifiers who support the flow rather than stopping it.

Squarish CVI™ Profiles

If you remember from Chapter 3, *Squarish* CVI™ profiles face a unique challenge that doesn't show up in the same way for people with dominant core values. Their ability to bounce fluidly from one core value to another is a genuine positive contribution because it means they can participate meaningfully at every stage of the natural flow. They can help cast vision with the *Merchants*, shape strategy with the *Innovators*, build structure with the *Bankers*, and drive action with the *Builders*. But this versatility becomes a liability when they don't read the moment correctly and end up using the wrong core value for what the situation actually requires. Instead of offering clarity, they can unintentionally create confusion by shifting gears too quickly or stepping into a core value that isn't needed. In team environments, they can feel as if their contribution isn't as strong or as "pure" as those with pronounced or profound capacities. They can feel like they're always jumping in halfway rather than owning a full lane. This is where the practice of *deploy and enjoy* becomes essential. For squarish profiles, the goal isn't to out-perform others in any single value, but to deploy the right value at the right time, enjoy the part they can play, and then let the next person take over when their own capacity naturally tapers off. **A leader's capacity doesn't need to exceed the capacity of the people they lead.** True leadership is the ability to read the moment and create space for others to shine when the moment calls for their core value. When squarish profiles embrace this, their versatility becomes a stabilizing force rather than a disruptive one, and their leadership becomes a model of timing, humility, and flow.

. . .

Three Questions

I have found that there are three simple questions that can be asked by every CVI™ type to ensure they are reading the moment correctly. As work progresses through Vision, Strategy, Structure, and Action, natural transition points will occur. At these points, individuals must intentionally assess whether their contribution is still needed or whether it is time to step back so others can step up.

These three questions are:

- Where are we in the process?
- Is it my moment to step up?
- Is it someone else's moment?

Depending on the individual's wiring, their involvement should transition as work moves from one phase to the next, or when that person's capacity has reached its limit. By consistently asking these three questions, individuals stay oriented to the needs of the moment.

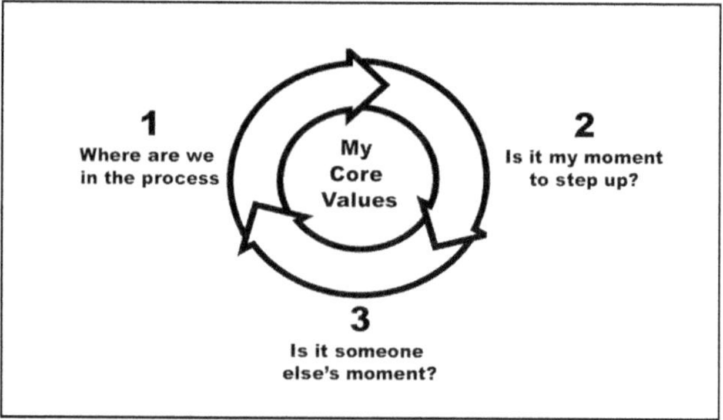

Figure 5. Three simple questions for every CVI™ type.

Practiced continuously, these questions keep teams balanced, reduces overextension and under-participation, and ensures that responsibility and leadership shift to the people best equipped to carry the work forward at each stage.

Closing Thoughts on the Natural Flow

The CVI™ reflects the true or natural order with remarkable precision. The *Merchant* leads with vision, seeing possibilities, sensing meaning, and connecting with purpose. The *Innovator* follows with strategy, solving problems, designing pathways, and determining the smartest way forward. The *Banker* comes next with structure, organizing resources, gathering information, and ensuring stability. And the *Builder* brings everything to life through action, moving decisively, courageously, and efficiently. These values are not random behavioral traits. They are expressions of the natural flow of human activity. They reveal how each person, regardless of their wiring, can contribute to the world and at what stage of the flow they best contribute.

When values are out of order, the consequences are predictable. Frustration, inefficiency, conflict, and stagnation begin to appear. But these breakdowns are not signs of failure. They reveal where the flow has been disrupted and where alignment needs to be restored. The key is not to eliminate these moments but to recognize them quickly and return to the natural sequence. When you understand the order, you can diagnose breakdowns with clarity. You can see when you're acting too soon, preparing too early, strategizing without purpose, or dreaming without grounding. And once you see it, you can correct it.

Action without vision becomes reckless. Structure without strategy becomes rigid and unnecessary. Strategy without vision becomes clever but aimless. And vision without follow-through becomes nothing more than wishful thinking. You've likely experienced these breakdowns in your own life. Times when you rushed into action without clarity, or planned endlessly without ever moving forward, or gathered information without knowing what it was for. These moments feel frustrating not because you failed, but because you were working against the natural order of how things are meant to unfold. The flow is not a suggestion. It is a blueprint.

Understanding this flow is an important step toward living and leading with greater alignment. When you honor the sequence, when you allow vision to lead, strategy to guide, structure to support, and action to complete. You begin to experience a sense of clarity and momentum that feels almost effortless. You stop fighting yourself. You stop forcing outcomes. You stop wasting energy on misaligned efforts. Instead, you begin to move in harmony with your own design. It is the doorway into a deeper understanding of how you are wired, why you think the way you do, and how you can bring your full, authentic contribution into the world.

As you move into the next chapters, you'll explore how each core value can be aggravated, become overused, how blind spots emerge, and how to bring your positive contributions back into balance. But before you go further, remember this: the flow is not fragile. It is resilient. It is always available. And every time you return to the natural order: *vision, strategy, structure, action;* you return to clarity, alignment, and the truth of the order in which you are supposed to move through the world.

CHAPTER 6
AGGRAVATING FACTORS

As we move forward, it's helpful to take a closer look at the specific conditions that can interfere with someone's ability to operate at their natural CVI™ capacity. Taylor's work makes it clear that while capacity itself is fixed, I have found that a person's access to that capacity can be disrupted by a range of internal and external pressures. Patterns like *going dark*, personal immaturity, being placed in a role that doesn't match one's core value energies, or functioning in a toxic or unstable environment can all suppress the expression of a person's innate core value capacity. These influences don't alter the CVI™ scores, they simply mask or distort them. Recognizing whether any of these factors are present in your own situation, or in the behavior of someone you're evaluating or engaging, is essential for interpreting CVI™ results accurately and compassionately. By examining each factor in detail, you'll be better equipped to distinguish between a person's true nature and the obstacles that may be limiting its expression.

In Chapter 3, capacity was described using the analogy of a high-performance car. Much like the horsepower of a high-performance engine; it is built into the machine, fixed at the factory, and doesn't change over time. No matter how the car is driven or what conditions it faces, the engine's true horsepower remains the same. What does change is how much of that horsepower can be accessed at any given moment. If the fuel line is blocked, the oil is contaminated, the driver is inexperienced, or the vehicle is placed on the wrong terrain, the engine cannot deliver its full output. Even though the power is still there. CVI™ capacity works the same way. It represents the unchanging amount of core value energy a person is capable of bringing to the world, while the conditions around them can affect how much of that energy can actually be expressed. Let's dive deeper into each aggravating factor continuing along the analogy of a high-performance car.

Going Dark

When someone "goes dark" in the CVI™ framework, it means they are operating from the *dark side* of their innate capacity. The same aspects that define their highest contribution become distorted under fear, stress, depletion, or threat. Because CVI™ capacity reflects the degree to which a person is wired to create, connect, innovate, or stabilize, their dark side emerges in direct proportion to that same capacity. A Profound-*Builder* who normally channels decisive action into progress may, when pushed past healthy limits, slip into forcefulness, impatience, or domination. A Pronounced-*Merchant*, whose natural gift is connection and encouragement, may go dark by becoming manipulative, overly emotional, or approval-seeking. *Innovators* with deep capacity for problem-solving may retreat into over-analysis, detachment, or criticism when overwhelmed. *Bankers*, who typically bring order and clarity, may become rigid, withholding, or paralyzed by fear of being wrong. Importantly, a person with meaningful capacity in all four quadrants also has the potential to go dark in all four in rapid succession because the dark side is simply the overextension or distortion of their core values. The more capacity someone has in a quadrant, the more powerful both their positive and dark expressions can be. Going dark is a signal that someone is operating out of fear of being the opposite of who they truly are, and that their innate core values are being used in ways that no longer serve them or others. Understanding this helps people recognize that their dark side is not random. It is the predictable, capacity-based inversion of their greatest contribution, and it can be navigated with awareness, boundaries, and recalibration.

Just as an engine without fuel sputters, misfires, or stalls, a person who has gone dark cannot draw on the horsepower of their innate CVI™ capacity. Their decisions become distorted, their communication becomes strained, and their performance no longer reflects who they truly are.

This doesn't mean their capacity has changed, only that it is blocked. The horsepower is still under the hood, but the fuel line is clogged. Understanding when someone has gone dark is essential because it prevents misinterpretation of their CVI™ results. Instead of assuming a lack of ability, it becomes clear that the person is temporarily unable to access their natural core value capacity. Recognizing this state allows leaders, coaches, and individuals themselves to address the underlying stressors and restore access to their true capacity.

Personal Immaturity

Personal immaturity doesn't change a person's innate CVI™ capacity, but it can dramatically limit how clearly that capacity shows up in everyday life. When someone hasn't yet developed emotional maturity, self-awareness, self-regulation, or is just a bad person with no integrity, their core values may surface in clumsy, inconsistent, exaggerated or uncharacteristic ways. In practice, this might look like over-reacting to minor setbacks, taking neutral feedback as a personal attack, interrupting without noticing, or leaping into decisions without thinking through the consequences. It's like giving a high-performance vehicle to a brand-new driver. The horsepower is real, but the driver may overcorrect, stall, or hit the gas at the wrong moment simply because they haven't learned how to handle the machine.

This is why immaturity is such a critical factor when someone's behavior doesn't seem to align with their CVI™ profile. A naturally decisive *Builder* may look impulsive instead of confident. A deeply relational *Merchant* may come across as clingy rather than collaborative. A strategic *Innovator* might seem argumentative or contrarian instead of insightful, pushing ideas without the emotional steadiness to communicate them well. A detail-driven *Banker* may appear rigid or anxious rather than dependable, clinging to information they know or rules because they haven't yet learned how to apply their knowledge with flexibility to something new.

None of these patterns indicate low capacity, they simply reveal a driver who hasn't mastered the controls yet. As individuals grow in maturity, they learn to channel their core value energy with intention rather than reactivity. They begin to recognize when to advance, when to pause, and how to navigate challenges without losing their center. The engine itself never changes. What evolves is the driver's ability to use its full power with skill, steadiness, and wisdom.

Wrong Role or Wrong Placement

When a person is placed in a role that doesn't match their core value energies, even their strongest natural abilities can feel muted or inaccessible. The misalignment creates a kind of internal friction. Tasks feel heavier than they should, motivation drops, and the person may struggle to stay engaged. In real-world situations, this can look like a naturally relational, people-focused individual being placed in a highly analytical, isolated role where they spend most of their day behind a spreadsheet. Or it might be a decisive, action-oriented person being forced into a slow, process-heavy environment where every decision requires multiple layers of approval. Their innate core values don't disappear, but the role doesn't give them the conditions to use those core values effectively. It's the same as installing a racing engine in a tractor or a tractor engine in a sports car. Both engines are powerful in their intended context, but neither can perform well when placed in the wrong machine.

This kind of mismatch often leads others to misjudge the person's true capacities. From the outside, they may appear unmotivated, inconsistent, or even incompetent, when the real issue is that the role is demanding contributions that don't align with their natural wiring. A *Builder* may look impatient or disruptive in a role that requires constant consensus-building. A *Merchant* may seem unfocused in a job that isolates them from people. An *Innovator* may appear slow or hesitant in a position that requires rapid, repetitive decision-making. A *Banker* may appear anti-social if placed in a sales position whose business requires building and maintaining rapport to get a sale versus sharing the facts and benefits of the product. None of these behaviors reflect a lack of capacity. They reflect a lack of alignment. When individuals are placed in roles that match their core values, their performance often improves dramatically and almost immediately. Tasks feel more natural, energy flows more freely, and their core values become visible without effort. In the right placement, the engine finally gets to run in the machine it was designed for, and its true horsepower becomes unmistakable.

Toxic or Unsupportive Environment

A toxic work environment, whether it's a chronically negative team, a manager who leads through intimidation or independence, or a workplace where chaos and crisis are the norm acts like grit in the gears of a high-performance engine. It creates constant friction, wears down the internal parts, and forces the engine to work far harder than it should just to keep running. Out in the world, this might look like a team where coworkers gossip or undermine each other, a supervisor who publicly shames employees, or a culture where people are expected to sacrifice personal well-being to meet unrealistic demands. Even someone with tremendous natural capacity will struggle to perform in these conditions. Their core values don't disappear, but they become harder to access because the environment is actively interfering with their ability to operate smoothly.

Over time, this corrosive atmosphere can cause a person to withdraw, shut down, or function at a fraction of their true potential. The engine still has all its horsepower, but the surrounding conditions make it unsafe (or impossible) to run at full output. In practice, this might show up as an employee who once contributed creative ideas and life to the group now staying silent in meetings, or a previously confident performer becoming hesitant and overly cautious because they fear criticism or retaliation. Recognizing the impact of environmental toxicity is essential when interpreting CVI™ results, because it helps separate a person's innate nature from the external pressures that are suppressing it. When the environment improves, or when the individual moves to a healthier workplace, their natural capacity often returns quickly and powerfully, just like an engine that roars back to life once the grit is cleared from its gears.

Chronic Stress or Overload

Chronic stress doesn't change a person's CVI™ capacity, but it can severely limit their ability to access it in day-to-day life. When someone is emotionally, mentally, or physically overloaded, they may still push themselves to perform, but the strain begins to show in subtle and not-so-subtle ways. In the real world, this can look like an employee who once handled tasks with ease now making small mistakes, forgetting details, or reacting more sharply than usual. It might show up as someone who used to enjoy problem-solving now feeling overwhelmed by even simple decisions, or a normally relational person withdrawing from conversations because they simply don't have the bandwidth. Just like an engine pushed beyond its limits, chronic stress causes a person to lose efficiency, reliability, and responsiveness. Their natural core values become harder to express, and their behavior may appear inconsistent, scattered, or uncharacteristically emotional. Not because their capacity has changed, but because the system is overheating.

If the overload continues long enough, the person may reach full burnout, where even basic functioning feels difficult. This can look like calling in sick more often, staring blankly at a computer screen unable to start a task, or feeling exhausted no matter how much, they rest. None of this reflects a loss of innate capacity. It simply means the internal system is too hot to operate safely. Once the stress is reduced; whether through rest, support, workload adjustments, or a healthier environment; the engine begins to cool, and the person can once again access their full horsepower. Recognizing the impact of chronic stress helps prevent misjudgment and encourages more compassionate expectations, allowing individuals to recover and return to expressing their true CVI™ capacity.

Misalignment Between Values and Expectations

When the expectations placed on a person don't align with their core value energies, their natural core values end up sitting idle with nowhere meaningful to go. It's like forcing a high-performance engine to idle in a parking lot. Fully capable of speed and power, yet unable to use any of it. Out in the world, this misalignment might look like a highly relational, *Merchant*-driven employee being told to "just stick to the script" and avoid personal conversations with clients, or a decisive *Builder* being required to get approval for every minor decision. An *Innovator* might be expected to follow rigid procedures with no room for problem-solving or improvement. A *Banker* might be placed in a fast-paced, constantly changing environment where procedures shift daily and expectations are ambiguous. In each case, the person may appear passive, unmotivated, or even disengaged, not because their capacity has diminished, but because the expectations around them don't allow their natural energy to be expressed.

Over time, this mismatch can drain enthusiasm and erode confidence. A person who once brought energy and creativity to their work may begin to hold back, second-guess themselves, or simply go through the motions. This isn't a reflection of their ability. It's a sign that they're being asked to operate in ways that contradict their innate wiring. When expectations shift to better match their core values, the change is often immediate and dramatic. The *Builder* who was bogged down by red tape becomes a powerhouse when given autonomy. The *Merchant* who felt stifled in a transactional role thrives when allowed to build relationships. The *Innovator* who struggled with rigid routines excels when invited to solve complex problems. The *Banker* who struggled with an ever-changing environment can bring precision once a structure is put in place. In the right alignment, the engine finally gets to run the way it was designed to run, and the person's true capacity becomes unmistakably visible.

Misreading the Moment

Not knowing *what the moment calls for* can seriously skew an individual's CVI™ capacity because it forces them to operate without clarity about which part of their innate energy should take the lead. It's a bit like driving a car without knowing whether you're supposed to be accelerating onto a highway, navigating a tight neighborhood street, or backing into a parking space. Every car can technically do all three, but each situation demands a different gear, a different level of precision, and a different kind of attention. When the driver doesn't know what's needed, they may slam the gas when finesse is required, or creep cautiously when the moment demands decisive speed. For a *Builder*, this might look like pushing forward with force and urgency when the situation actually calls for patience or collaboration, leaving others feeling bulldozed. A *Merchant* might overextend emotionally. Trying to connect, persuade, or uplift, when the moment really requires boundaries or analytical detachment, causing them to feel drained or ineffective. An *Innovator* may keep generating possibilities and rethinking the approach when what's needed is commitment to a single path, making them appear indecisive or overly abstract. And a *Banker* might default to gathering more information, double-checking details, or slowing things down when the moment calls for action, making them seem resistant or overly cautious. When people don't know which "gear" the situation requires, their natural core values can become mismatched to the moment, amplifying frustration and reducing performance. But when expectations are clear, each core value can operate in its ideal lane, allowing individuals to use their capacity with precision rather than friction.

. . .

Squarish Capacities

Having a squarish capacity profile can become a real aggravating factor when individuals fail to read the moment and instead try to do everything themselves simply because they can (at least up to a point). Their natural advantage is that they relate to all four core values and can shift from *Builder* to *Merchant* to *Innovator* to *Banker* with more ease than most people. But that flexibility can backfire when insecurity creeps in. It's like driving a car that's capable of handling city streets, highways, and rough terrain. It can do all of them reasonably well, but it's not a sports car, not an off-road machine, and not a precision-parking compact. When the driver panics and tries to push the car to perform like all three vehicles; they quickly hit the limits of what the vehicle was designed to do. The same thing happens with a squarish CVI™ profile. The *Builder* in them may try to take charge, execute, and push forward then shifting and attempting to manage relationships, refine ideas, and check details, resulting in scattered effort and half-finished action. The *Merchant* in them might try to inspire, connect, strategize, and organize in immediate succession, stretching their emotional energy thin and losing their natural warmth. The *Innovator* in them may attempt to solve, refine, act, and support in a chaotic manner, causing their clarity to blur and their solutions to become less elegant. The *Banker* in them might try to gather information, make decisions, build relationships, and take action, overwhelming themselves with data and slowing everything down. When these individuals don't read the moment, they default to "I'll just do it myself," but the outcome is capped by their capacity scores; which sit mostly in the "possible" range and only brush the lower edge of "pronounced." Their versatility is a gift, but only when paired with discernment about which core value the moment actually requires and knowing when to step back and have another step up.

Emotions

Emotions can be a powerful aggravating factor in an individual's

CVI™ capacity because they can distort how much of their natural energy is actually available in the moment. Even someone with high capacity in a core value can find that emotional overload: dislike, stress, fear, frustration, insecurity; acts like sand in the gears. It's similar to driving a car with a full tank of gas but suddenly hitting bad weather. The vehicle can perform, but visibility drops, traction weakens, and the driver becomes tense, making every maneuver less efficient. When emotions cloud the moment, people often misread what's needed and either overuse or underuse their natural core values. For a *Builder*, heightened emotion might show up as impatience, forcefulness, or pushing too hard, like flooring the accelerator on a slick road and losing control. A *Merchant* may become overly sensitive, overly accommodating, or emotionally reactive, like a driver who keeps tapping the brakes because they're nervous, slowing progress for everyone. An *Innovator* might get stuck in overthinking, second-guessing, or withdrawing, similar to a driver who keeps circling the block because they can't decide where to park. A *Banker* may retreat into rigid caution, excessive data gathering, or emotional shutdown, like a driver who refuses to merge because the traffic feels overwhelming. In each case, the emotion doesn't change the person's capacity or the car's capacity. It just blocks access to it, making their natural core values harder to use and their natural limitations more pronounced.

Closing Thoughts on Aggravating Factors

When interpreting CVI™ capacity scores, it helps to remember that a person's innate capacity is like the fixed horsepower of a high-performance engine: powerful, consistent, and unchanging; while the aggravating factors that surround them, act like conditions that determine how much of that horsepower can actually reach the road. Going dark, personal immaturity, role misalignment, toxic environments, chronic stress, emotions, and misreading moments all function like clogged fuel lines, worn-out tires, bad transmission parts, or corrosive driving conditions that interfere with the engine's ability to perform. These factors can make a high-capacity person appear inconsistent, disengaged, or underpowered, not because their engine is weak, but because something in their internal or external environment is blocking the flow of their natural energy. In real life, this might look like someone "stalling out" under stress, "idling" in a role that doesn't fit, "misfiring" when they lack the right skills, or "overheating" in a toxic workplace. Understanding these influences prevents us from misreading CVI™ results and encourages a more accurate, compassionate view of human behavior. When we separate the person's true capacity from the conditions affecting their performance, we gain a clearer picture of who a person really is and what they're capable of doing

Now that we've built a solid foundation understanding the CVI™: the four core values that shape human motivation, the concept of CVI™ capacity, and the aggravating factors that can distort or diminish how those values show up in daily life; we're ready to build upon the foundational framework of the CVI™. The next chapter will focus on how to apply CVI™ insights with intention by understanding how overusing our core values can be detrimental to performance.

CHAPTER 7
OVERUSING YOUR DOMINANT CORE VALUE

When a core value is overused, it stops functioning as a gift and begins functioning as a distortion. You see this out in the world all the time. A *Merchant* leader who keeps calling "just one more meeting" because two team members still disagree, unintentionally stalling a project that's ready to move. An *Innovator* who keeps redesigning a product long after the team is ready to build, causing deadlines to slip while they chase a more elegant solution. A *Banker* who insists on gathering more data before approving a decision, even when the team already has enough information to move forward. Or a *Builder* who charges ahead on a new initiative without waiting for a plan, leaving everyone else scrambling to catch up. Overuse happens when a person leans too heavily on their dominant value, especially under stress, uncertainty, or pressure. Instead of collaborating with the other values in the natural flow, the overused value tries to take over the entire process. The result is predictable: imbalance, frustration, and breakdown. This chapter explores how each core value becomes dysfunctional when pushed beyond its healthy boundaries, and how recognizing these patterns can restore alignment.

. . .

Merchants

Merchants, when overused, become overly relational and overly protective of harmony. Their natural gift for vision and connection becomes clouded by a fear of disappointing others or moving forward without unanimous agreement. Instead of inspiring progress, they stall it. Calling repeated meetings, seeking endless buy-in, or softening decisions to avoid conflict. Their desire to ensure everyone feels valued becomes a barrier to momentum. When the *Merchant* overextends, vision becomes emotional rather than directional, and the process becomes stuck in a loop of reassurance rather than advancement. The challenge for the *Merchant* is learning that unity does not require unanimous agreement, and that progress can continue even when every disagreement is not resolved.

Before a *Merchant* overuses their core value, there is a subtle but predictable internal shift that begins long before anyone else notices something is off. *Merchants* start by feeling a rising tension whenever they sense even mild disagreement, emotional discomfort, or relational misalignment within the group.

When overused *Merchants*:

- Anxious need to restore harmony at all costs
- Hyper-attuned to tone, body language, and unspoken reactions, reading meaning into every sigh and pause
- Replay conversations in their mind, wondering if someone misunderstood them or felt unheard
- Hesitate to move forward, feeling torn between the momentum and the emotions of people involved
- Schedule extra conversations, clarifying intentions, or seeking reassurance that everyone is still "okay," even when the team is ready to advance

In this early phase, the *Merchant* isn't trying to stall progress. They're trying to preserve connection. But if they don't recognize the shift, their relational sensitivity can quietly transform into relational overprotection, pulling the entire process off course.

When *Merchants* realize they are overusing their core value, the most powerful thing they can do is intentionally shift their focus from people's feelings back to the purpose and sequence of the process. This begins with a simple internal pause, recognizing that their discomfort with tension is not a signal to stop the process, but a cue to evaluate what is needed in the moment. *Merchants* can remind themselves that disagreement is not danger, and that progress does not require perfect emotional alignment. Practically, this means setting boundaries around how many conversations are truly needed, trusting the team to carry their part of the flow, and allowing moments of discomfort without rushing to smooth them over. It also helps for *Merchants* to articulate their concerns openly, "I'm feeling the urge to make sure everyone is okay, but I know it's time to move forward, can someone else take the lead from here?" This simple transparency invites support rather than resistance.

Others can play a crucial role as well:

- *Innovators* can reassure *Merchants* by clarifying the logic behind the next steps
- *Bankers* can provide grounding by showing that the structure is solid enough to proceed
- *Builders* can gently but firmly keep momentum by saying, "We hear the concerns, and we'll address them as we go, but it's time to take the next step"

When the team understands the *Merchant's* relational wiring, they can help create an environment where the *Merchant* feels safe enough to release control. In this shared effort, the *Merchant* learns that harmony is not lost by moving forward. It is strengthened when each value plays its rightful part in the flow.

Innovators

Innovators, when overused, become trapped in perpetual refinement. Their natural gift for strategy and problem-solving becomes a restless pursuit of the "perfect" solution. You see this in the product designer who keeps adding new features long after the team is ready to launch, or the software architect who rewrites the same module three times because they've thought of a more elegant way to structure it. They generate idea after idea, improvement after improvement, often overwhelming others with possibilities; much like the committee member who derails a simple decision by offering five alternative approaches no one asked for. Instead of clarifying the path, they complicate it. Their desire to optimize becomes a barrier to movement. When the *Innovator* overextends, strategy becomes theoretical rather than practical, and the process stalls in analysis rather than advancing toward structure or action. The challenge for the *Innovator* is learning that a solution does not need to be perfect to be effective, and that progress often requires releasing an idea before it feels complete.

Before an *Innovator* begins overusing their core value, there is a familiar internal pattern that starts to unfold. Subtle at first, then increasingly consuming. A new idea, a fresh angle, or a clever improvement that suddenly appears in their mind. But instead of settling into a single direction, their thoughts begin branching rapidly, multiplying into parallel paths that all seem equally compelling.

When overused *Innovators*:

- Must explore every option before choosing one
- Replay conversations, mentally redesigning solutions, or waking up with new insights
- Meetings feel too slow or too linear
- Struggle to stay present in meetings as mind races ahead
- Feel restless, impatient with constraints, and increasingly protective of their ideas
- Compelled to keep improving, adjusting, rethinking
- Spiral into analysis paralysis

When *Innovators* recognize that they are overusing their core value, the most effective step they can take is to intentionally create boundaries around their ideation and refinement process. This begins with acknowledging that their mind will always generate more possibilities and that this is a positive contribution, not a flaw but also recognizing that not every possibility needs to be explored right now. *Innovators* can set personal checkpoints such as, "I'll choose one direction by the end of the meeting," or "I'll refine this idea for 30 minutes, then hand it off." These self-imposed limits help them shift from endless improvement to purposeful progress. It also helps for *Innovators* to externalize their thinking; writing down additional ideas in a "version 2.0 and beyond" list so they don't feel lost or wasted. Knowing they can revisit these ideas later makes it easier to release the current version.

Others play a crucial role as well:

- *Merchants* can help *Innovators* reconnect to the original vision, reminding them of the purpose behind the work
- *Bankers* can provide grounding by clarifying what resources or constraints matter most, helping narrow the field of possibilities
- *Builders* can gently but firmly keep momentum by saying, "This is good enough to move forward. We can improve it in the next iteration."

When the team understands the *Innovator's* wiring, they can create an environment where the *Innovator* feels both supported and contained, allowing their brilliance to shine without derailing the flow. In this shared effort, the *Innovator* learns that progress is not the enemy of excellence and that sometimes the most innovative act is knowing when to let go.

Bankers

Bankers, when overused, become rigid, risk-averse, and overly cautious. Their natural gift for structure and stewardship becomes a fixation on what could go wrong. You see this in the project manager who insists on collecting "just a little more data" even after the team already has enough to make a decision, or the compliance-minded manager who creates a 20-step approval process for something that used to take two. They gather more information than necessary, create more systems than required, and raise more concerns than the moment demands. Much like the committee member who halts a promising initiative because they want to review three years of historical reports before allowing it to move forward. Instead of supporting the process, they slow it down. Sometimes to a halt. Their desire to protect becomes a barrier to possibility. When the *Banker* overextends, structure becomes suffocating rather than stabilizing, and the process becomes bogged down in preparation rather than moving toward action. The challenge for the *Banker* is learning that not all risks can be eliminated, and that progress often requires stepping forward before every detail is known.

Before a *Banker* begins overusing their core value, there is a noticeable internal shift that starts quietly and grows stronger as uncertainty increases. It often begins with a subtle sense that something important might be missing. An overlooked detail, an unexamined risk, or an assumption that hasn't been validated.

When overused *Bankers*:

- Gather more information, double-check facts, or revisit previous decisions "just to be sure"
- Worry that the foundation isn't solid enough yet
- Reread documents, expand spreadsheets, or ask numerous clarifying questions
- Feel that the pace of meetings is too fast, ideas too untested, or enthusiasm too detached from reality
- Feel responsible for preventing mistakes and protecting the team from risk
- Increasingly aware of pitfalls/imagine worst-case scenarios
- Mind becomes crowded with "what ifs"
- Uneasy when decisions made without exhaustive evidence

When *Bankers* recognize that they are overusing their core value, the most effective step they can take is to intentionally shift from protecting the process to supporting it. This begins with acknowledging that their instinct to gather more information or build more structure is coming from a place of care (not fear) but also recognizing that too much caution can quietly become obstruction. *Bankers* can practice setting limits on their research or preparation, such as deciding in advance how much data is truly necessary or identifying a clear point at which they will hand the process off to the next stage for action. It also helps for them to articulate their concerns openly and concisely saying, "Here are the top two risks I see," rather than listing every possible scenario. This not only clarifies their thinking but also prevents others from feeling overwhelmed.

Others can play a vital role as well:

- *Merchants* can reassure *Bankers* by reconnecting them to the vision and reminding them why the work matters
- *Innovators* can help narrow the field by identifying risks are worth addressing and which are unlikely to materialize
- *Builders* can gently but firmly keep momentum by saying, "We have enough to move forward, let's take the next step and adjust as we go"

Leaders and supervisors can tell the *Banker* to not engage during brainstorming sessions, but instead, write down every pitfall or error they are seeing and provide their inputs to them post session. When the team understands the *Banker's* wiring, they can create an environment where the *Banker* feels safe enough to release control, trusting that the process will not collapse without exhaustive preparation. In this shared effort, the *Banker* learns that their contribution is not diminished by letting go and that progress often requires stepping forward even when the foundation isn't perfect.

Builders

Builders, when overused, become forceful, impatient, and dismissive of the earlier stages of the flow. Their natural gift for action becomes a compulsion to move now, fast, and with little tolerance for discussion. You see this in the manager who launches a new initiative before the team even understands the goal, or the contractor who starts construction without waiting for finalized plans because "we'll figure it out as we go." They push forward without waiting for vision to be clarified, strategy to be shaped, or structure to be secured. Much like the sales leader who announces a new process on Monday morning without consulting operations, leaving everyone scrambling to catch up. Instead of driving progress, they create chaos. Their desire to accomplish becomes a barrier to alignment. When the *Builder* overextends, action becomes reckless rather than effective, and the process becomes reactive rather than intentional. The challenge for the *Builder* is learning that speed is not the same as progress, and that the strongest outcomes come from honoring the steps that precede action.

Before a *Builder* begins overusing their core value, there is a familiar internal shift that starts long before their behavior becomes outwardly forceful or impatient. It often begins with a rising sense of urgency. An almost physical pressure that something needs to happen now. *Builders* start to feel restless when conversations drag on, when decisions aren't made quickly, or when others seem hesitant to act. What feels like "stalling" to them triggers an internal frustration, as if the entire process is being weighed down by unnecessary steps.

When overused *Builders*:

- Fidget in meetings, mentally jumping ahead to execution
- Thoughts become increasingly focused on momentum, progress, and tangible results
- Irritated by perceived overthinking or excessive caution
- Believe if they don't take charge, nothing will move forward
- Feel responsible for pushing the process ahead, even if it means bypassing conversations or ignoring questions
- Compulsion to act prematurely

When *Builders* recognize that they are overusing their core value, the most effective thing they can do is intentionally slow their internal pace long enough to reconnect with the larger flow of the process. This doesn't mean suppressing their drive. It means channeling it. *Builders* can start by pausing before taking action and asking themselves one grounding question, "Has the steps before mine been completed?" This simple check helps them resist the urge to jump ahead. They can also practice delegating or inviting others to lead portions of the discussion, which creates space for vision, strategy, and structure to take shape before action begins. It often helps for *Builders* to verbalize their impatience in a constructive way. Saying something like, "I'm feeling ready to move, but I know we need clarity first," which signals to the team that they're trying to stay aligned rather than take over.

Others play a crucial role as well:

- *Merchants* can help *Builders* reconnect to the purpose behind the work, reminding them why the early stages matter
- *Innovators* can offer clear strategic reasoning that satisfies the *Builder's* need for direction
- *Bankers* can provide the structure and checkpoints that reassure *Builders* action will be taken

When the team understands the *Builder's* wiring, they can support momentum without letting it become chaos. In this shared effort, the *Builder* learns that action is most powerful when it is timed well and that honoring the steps before theirs doesn't slow them down, it sets them up to succeed.

Squarish Profiles

Squarish CVI™ profiles bring a unique kind of complexity to the natural flow because they don't stay anchored in one value for long. Instead, they bounce rapidly between core values, shifting gears in ways that can feel unpredictable or even jarring to the people around them. Unlike someone who overuses a single core value, squarish profiles overuse the switching itself. They can only operate from one core value at a time, so when pressure rises, they may jump from *Merchant*-style enthusiasm to *Banker*-level caution within the same meeting, or from *Innovator*-level ideation to *Builder*-level urgency in the span of a single conversation. This constant pivoting can leave teams feeling jerked around. Never quite sure which version of the person they're going to get. In the real world, this looks like the leader who starts a meeting with a big, inspiring vision (*Merchant*), then suddenly slams on the brakes because they want more data (*Banker*), only to shift again into rapid-fire problem-solving (*Innovator*) before ending the meeting by pushing everyone to act immediately (*Builder*). Or the project manager who tells the team to "dream big" on Monday, demands strict adherence to process on Tuesday, and insists on launching early by Wednesday. When squarish profiles overuse the wrong value at the wrong moment: like bringing *Builder* urgency into the vision stage or *Banker* caution into the action stage. They disrupt the entire flow, confuse roles, and create emotional whiplash for everyone involved. Their contribution is versatility, but without aware-ness and timing, that versatility becomes volatility, making the process harder for everyone to navigate.

Before a squarish CVI™ profile begins overusing their core values, they often experience an internal tug-of-war that feels both energizing and destabilizing. Because they have multiple core values of nearly equal capacity, their mind starts rapidly shifting between them the moment pressure, uncertainty, or urgency enters the picture. At first, this feels like versatility. They can see multiple angles, anticipate different needs, and adapt quickly. But as the internal tension builds, the switching becomes less intentional and more reactive.

When overused Squarish CVI™ profiles:

- Feel deeply aligned with one value only to feel an equally strong pull from another core value moments later
- Feel restless, unfocused, or oddly impatient, sensing that something is "off"
- Thoughts speed up, their emotional tone shifts, and they begin second-guessing decisions
- Champion bold action, then suddenly worry about missing details, then inspire the team, then become overly cautious in a short span of time
- Try to reconcile powerful internal drivers that all feel right
- Experience disruptive value-switching

When squarish CVI™ profiles recognize that they are overusing their core values by bouncing unpredictably between them, the most powerful step they can take is to slow down long enough to identify which value the moment actually requires. Because their internal switching feels natural and even helpful, they often don't realize how disruptive it becomes until the team looks confused or momentum starts to wobble. A practical strategy is for them to pause and ask themselves, "Which *hat* am I wearing right now and is it the right core value for this stage of the process?" Naming the core value, they are operating from helps them stay anchored instead of ricocheting between impulses. It can also help to set intentional boundaries, such as committing to stay in one core value for the duration of a meeting or deferring the other impulses to a "later list" so they don't hijack the flow. Transparency is another powerful tool. Saying something like, "I feel all of my values pulling, help me stay aligned with the stage we're in," invites collaboration rather than confusion.

Others play an essential role as well:

- *Merchants* can gently remind them of the vision when they drift into premature action or excessive caution
- *Innovators* can help them sort through competing impulses by clarifying which value best serves the strategy
- *Bankers* can ground them with structure, helping them stay consistent rather than reactive
- *Builders* can keep momentum steady by reinforcing which step the team is currently in

When the team understands the squarish profile's internal tug-of-war, they can help create an environment where versatility becomes an asset rather than a source of chaos. With awareness and support, squarish profiles learn to channel their multiple contributions intentionally, bringing flexibility without volatility and leadership without whiplash.

· · ·

Closing Thoughts on Overusing Your Dominate Core Value

Overuse is not a flaw. It is a signal. It reveals where a person is leaning too heavily on their dominant value and neglecting the contributions of the others or the part of the process they are in. It shows up where the natural flow has been disrupted and where balance needs to be restored. The key is not to suppress your dominant core value but to introduce it at the appropriate moment. When each value operates in its proper place: vision first, strategy second, structure third, action last, the contributions of each become amplified rather than distorted. Recognizing overuse is the first step toward reclaiming that balance.

As you move into the next chapter, you will explore the deeper blind spots that accompany each core value. Patterns that are harder to see, harder to admit, and harder to change. But before you go further, remember this: your core values are not the problem. Overuse is. And when you learn to honor your core values and the part of the process you are in, you unlock the full power of your capacity and those you are with.

CHAPTER 8
BLIND SPOTS

Blind spots are the unseen forces that shape outcomes, decisions, and interpretations without our conscious awareness. They form when we rely so heavily on our values, habits, or assumptions that we stop noticing the limitations that come with them. A blind spot isn't necessarily a flaw, it's simply a part of ourselves we don't see clearly, much like the area a driver can't view through mirrors alone. Yet these unseen tendencies can quietly hinder outcomes. They can cause us to misread situations, overlook important information, or assume others see the world the way we do. For example, someone who prides themselves on being decisive may rush into choices without gathering enough context. Someone who values harmony may avoid necessary conflict, allowing problems to fester. Blind spots narrow our field of vision, and when we don't recognize them, they can lead to misunderstandings, stalled progress, and repeated patterns that feel frustratingly familiar. The moment we become aware of them, we regain the ability to choose rather than react, opening the door to more intentional and effective outcomes.

Within the CVI™ framework, each core value: *Merchant, Innovator, Banker,* and *Builder* has its own predictable blind spots that arise from its greatest contribution. *Builders,* who thrive on action and results, may overlook the emotional or relational nuances that others consider essential. *Merchants*, who excel at connection and inspiration, may miss practical constraints or avoid difficult conversations. *Innovators*, gifted at problem-solving and conceptual thinking, may get stuck analyzing possibilities instead of committing to a direction. *Bankers*, who bring stability and deep knowledge, may resist change or become overly cautious when speed is required. These blind spots aren't personal shortcomings. They are simply the natural shadows cast by each value's positive contribution. When individuals understand how their core value shapes their blind spots, they can catch themselves before slipping into automatic patterns. This awareness allows them to balance their core values with the perspectives of others, creating more effective communication, smoother collaboration, and wiser decision making.

Merchants

Merchants, with their natural gift for connection, enthusiasm, and relational intelligence, often carry blind spots that arise from the very contributions that make them so influential. One common blind spot is over-idealizing people, assuming others have the same positive intentions they do. For example, a *Merchant* leader might continue trusting a team member who repeatedly misses deadlines because they believe "they're really trying," even when the pattern shows otherwise. Another blind spot is avoiding necessary conflict. A *Merchant* may sidestep a difficult conversation with a colleague to preserve harmony, only to watch the unresolved issue grow into a larger problem. A third blind spot is overcommitting in an effort to support everyone. A *Merchant* might enthusiastically say "yes" to multiple projects, later realizing they've stretched themselves too thin and can't deliver on all their promises. A fourth blind spot is taking things personally. Interpreting neutral feedback as a relational threat, hearing "this proposal needs more detail" and feeling unappreciated rather than recognizing it as constructive input. These blind spots don't diminish the *Merchant's* abilities. They simply show how the desire to uplift, inspire, and connect can unintentionally cloud judgment. When *Merchants* become aware of these tendencies, they gain the ability to set clearer boundaries, engage in healthy conflict, and balance empathy with discernment, allowing their natural relational gifts to shine without creating unintended strain.

Merchants can overcome their blind spots by learning to balance their natural relational contributions with intentional structure, boundaries, and self-awareness. The first step is recognizing that empathy and optimism, while powerful, can sometimes cloud judgment so *Merchants* benefit from pausing to verify facts rather than relying solely on their instinct to believe the best in others. When they notice themselves over-idealizing someone, they can ask grounding questions like, "What evidence supports this belief?" or "What patterns am I seeing?" To counter their tendency to avoid conflict, *Merchants* can reframe difficult conversations as acts of care rather than threats to connection. By preparing talking points, setting a clear intention, and reminding themselves that honesty strengthens relationships, they can step into conflict with confidence instead of fear. To address overcommitment, *Merchants* can practice saying to themselves, "Let me check my schedule first" before agreeing to new tasks, giving themselves space to evaluate whether they can realistically follow through. And to soften the habit of taking things personally, they can learn to separate feedback from identity. Viewing input as information rather than criticism. When *Merchants* adopt these practices, they don't lose their warmth or enthusiasm. Instead, they gain clarity, resilience, and discernment. Their relationships become healthier, their commitments more sustainable, and their leadership more grounded. In this way, awareness transforms blind spots into opportunities for growth, allowing *Merchants* to express their core value with greater wisdom and impact.

Innovators

Innovators, known for their ability to see patterns, solve complex problems, and envision elegant solutions, often develop blind spots that stem directly from their intellectual capacity. One common blind spot is overanalyzing situations, which can lead to paralysis. For example, an *Innovator* might spend weeks refining a product concept because they keep discovering "a better way," causing the team to miss critical deadlines. Another blind spot is detaching emotionally when conversations become inefficient or overly emotional. An *Innovator* may unintentionally appear aloof or dismissive when a colleague expresses frustration, simply because they're focused on solving the problem rather than acknowledging the feeling. A third blind spot is assuming others understand their logic, leading to communication gaps. An *Innovator* might present a solution that makes perfect sense to them but leaves the rest of the team confused because of their ability to understand complex issues. A fourth blind spot is becoming defensive when their ideas are challenged. Because *Innovators* invest deeply in the elegance of their solutions and their wisdom, they may interpret questions as criticism rather than collaboration, shutting down dialogue. These blind spots don't diminish the *Innovator's* brilliance, they simply reveal how a mind wired for insight can sometimes overlook the human, practical, or time-sensitive elements of a situation. When *Innovators* recognize these tendencies, they gain the ability to pair their intellectual gifts with greater clarity, empathy, and adaptability, making their contributions even more impactful.

Innovators can overcome their blind spots by intentionally grounding their brilliance in structure, empathy, and shared understanding. To counter the tendency to overanalyze, *Innovators* benefit from setting clear decision thresholds such as defining what "good enough" looks like before beginning a project, so they know when to stop refining and start executing. They can also use time-boxing techniques to limit how long they explore possibilities before choosing a direction. To address emotional detachment, *Innovators* can practice pausing before offering solutions and acknowledging the feelings in the room with simple statements like, "I hear your frustration" or "Let's take a moment to understand what's important here." This small shift helps others feel seen rather than bypassed. To overcome the assumption that everyone follows their logic, *Innovators* can slow down and narrate their thinking step-by-step, checking in with questions like, "Does this make sense so far?" or "Should I walk through the reasoning behind this?" This ensures their insights land clearly instead of creating confusion. And to soften defensiveness when their ideas are challenged, *Innovators* can reframe feedback as collaboration rather than critique, reminding themselves that questions often strengthen solutions rather than diminish them. When *Innovators* adopt these practices, they retain their gift for elegant problem-solving while becoming more accessible, more collaborative, and more effective. Their ideas gain traction, their relationships deepen, and their ability to influence grows because their brilliance is now paired with clarity, humility, and connection.

Bankers

Bankers, whose contributions lie in knowledge, accuracy, and thoughtful analysis, often develop blind spots that emerge from their deep commitment to getting things right. One common blind spot is over-prioritizing information, where a *Banker* becomes so focused on gathering data that they delay action. For example, a *Banker* might postpone approving a new software tool because they want to review every possible security scenario, causing the team to miss an opportunity for an on-time delivery. Another blind spot is resisting change, especially when existing systems feel safe and proven such as a *Banker* pushing back on a new workflow simply because "the old way works," unintentionally slowing innovation. A third blind spot is communicating with too much detail, overwhelming others with lengthy explanations or exhaustive documentation. A *Banker* might send a 20-page report when the team only needed a one-page summary, leaving colleagues confused or disengaged. A fourth blind spot is being perceived as rigid or inflexible, especially when they insist on following rules or procedures even in situations that call for adaptability. For instance, insisting on a formal process for a quick, time-sensitive decision. These blind spots don't diminish the *Banker's* value. They simply show how their positive contribution for precision and stability can unintentionally create bottlenecks or disconnects.

When *Bankers* become aware of these tendencies, they can balance their careful nature with greater openness, flexibility, and responsiveness, allowing their deep knowledge to support progress rather than slow it.

Bankers can overcome their blind spots by learning to balance their natural caution and depth of knowledge with intentional flexibility, prioritization, and clearer communication. To counter the tendency to over-prioritize information, *Bankers* can set predefined limits on research such as identifying the "minimum viable data" needed before moving forward so they don't get stuck waiting for perfect certainty. They can also practice checking in with others early in the process to confirm what level of detail is actually required, which prevents unnecessary deep dives. To soften resistance to change, *Bankers* can experiment with small, low-risk trials rather than committing to full-scale shifts. This allows them to test new ideas while still honoring their need for stability. When it comes to communication, *Bankers* can focus on leading with the headline, summarizing the key point first, then offering additional detail only if requested so their expertise becomes more accessible and less overwhelming. And to avoid appearing rigid, they can practice asking clarifying questions like, "What outcome are we aiming for?" or "Where is flexibility most important here?" This helps them understand when rules truly matter and when adaptability serves the greater goal. By integrating these habits, *Bankers* preserve their positive contributions: accuracy, reliability, and thoughtful analysis while becoming more agile and collaborative. Their knowledge becomes a catalyst for progress rather than a brake and their presence becomes both grounding and empowering for the teams they support.

Builders

Builders, known for their drive, decisiveness, and ability to take action quickly, often develop blind spots that stem from their intense focus on results and forward momentum. One common blind spot is moving too fast, assuming that speed equals effectiveness. For example, a *Builder* might launch into a project without gathering input, only to discover later that key details were missed. Another blind spot is communicating too bluntly. A *Builder* may give short, direct instructions like, "Just do it this way," unintentionally coming across as harsh or dismissive to colleagues who need more context. A third blind spot is taking over instead of collaborating. When a *Builder* sees a task stalling, they may jump in and do it themselves, inadvertently disempowering the team and creating dependency. A fourth blind spot is overconfidence in their instincts, leading them to make quick decisions without fully considering risks or alternative perspectives, for instance, approving a major purchase or strategic shift based solely on gut feeling. These blind spots don't diminish the *Builder's* contributions, they simply reveal how a natural bias toward action and control can sometimes overshadow patience, listening, and shared ownership. When *Builders* become aware of these tendencies, they can channel their powerful energy more effectively and create environments where both progress and people thrive.

Builders can overcome their blind spots by intentionally slowing down just enough to create space for clarity, collaboration, and thoughtful decision making, without losing the momentum that defines them. One of the most powerful shifts a *Builder* can make is learning to pause before acting, even briefly, to gather essential input from others. This doesn't mean sacrificing speed. It simply means asking quick grounding questions like, "What am I missing?" or "Who else needs to weigh in to avoid costly rework later?" To soften blunt communication, *Builders* can practice adding one or two sentences of context before giving direction, which helps others feel informed rather than commanded. When they feel the urge to take over a task, *Builders* can instead delegate with clear expectations and resist the temptation to jump in unless truly necessary. This builds trust and strengthens the team's capability. And to counter overconfidence in instinct, *Builders* can adopt a habit of checking key assumptions with someone they trust, especially for high-impact decisions. These small adjustments don't dilute the *Builder's* power, they refine it. By pairing their natural drive with a bit more patience, curiosity, and openness, *Builders* become not only effective doers but also inspiring leaders who create environments where people feel empowered, respected, and action-oriented.

Squarish CVI™ Profiles

A "squarish" CVI™ profile comes with its own unique set of blind spots that differ from those of individuals with a dominant value. Because squarish profiles can see merit in multiple perspectives, one common blind spot is difficulty prioritizing, as they may weigh all options equally and struggle to choose a clear direction. For example, they might spend too long debating between two viable strategies because each aligns with a different internal value. Another blind spot is shifting gears too frequently, trying to honor all parts of themselves. One moment they are acting decisively like a *Builder*, the next diving into details like a *Banker*, leaving others unsure of what to expect. A third blind spot is over-accommodating, because they naturally understand and empathize with all value types. A squarish leader might adjust their approach so often to meet others' needs that they lose sight of their own preferences or boundaries. A fourth blind spot is appearing inconsistent, especially when their internal balance causes them to change their stance depending on which value feels most activated in the moment. For instance, supporting a bold idea during a brainstorming session but later slowing things down to analyze its risks. These blind spots don't reflect a lack of capability, rather they highlight the challenge of having many internal core values competing for outward expression. When squarish individuals become aware of these tendencies, they can learn to anchor themselves in clarity and intentionality, using their versatility as a positive contribution rather than a source of confusion.

A squarish CVI™ profile can overcome their blind spots by learning to anchor their natural versatility with intentional clarity, consistent decision-making habits, and a stronger sense of internal priority. Because squarish individuals can genuinely see value in all four core energies, one of the most effective strategies is to choose a primary lens for each situation. For example, squarish leaders can determine where in the natural flow they are and then decide whether the moment calls for *Builder* action, *Merchant* connection, *Innovator* analysis, or *Banker* precision. This prevents the internal tug-of-war that leads to indecision or inconsistency. To counter difficulty prioritizing, squarish profiles can adopt simple frameworks like, "What matters most right now?" or "Which value best serves the moment?" which helps them commit rather than endlessly weighing options. To avoid shifting gears too frequently, they can communicate their process openly, saying things like, "I'm switching into *Innovator* mode for a moment" or "Let's stay in *Innovator* energy until we finalize the plan" which helps others follow their transitions instead of feeling confused. To address over-accommodating tendencies, squarish individuals benefit from setting personal boundaries and checking in with themselves before adapting to others, ensuring they don't lose their own values in the process. And to reduce the appearance of inconsistency, they can document decisions, articulate the reasoning behind shifts, and revisit their intentions regularly. When squarish profiles practice these habits, their balanced nature becomes a powerful asset. They can integrate perspectives, bridge differences, and adapt fluidly, without getting lost in the very contributions that make them so uniquely capable.

Closing Thoughts on Blind Spots

Blind spots are an inevitable part of being human, and the CVI™ offers a powerful lens for understanding how they show up differently in each of us. Whether someone leads with the relational warmth of the *Merchant*, the analytical depth of the *Banker*, the inventive clarity of the *Innovator*, the decisive drive of the *Builder*, or the balanced versatility of a squarish profile, every core value casts a shadow when used unconsciously. *Merchants* may overextend themselves or avoid conflict, *Innovators* may overanalyze or detach, *Bankers* may resist change or drown others in detail, *Builders* may move too fast or take over, and squarish individuals may struggle to prioritize or appear inconsistent. Yet the beauty of recognizing these blind spots is that awareness transforms them from hidden obstacles into opportunities for growth. When each individual learns to pause, reflect, and intentionally balance their natural tendencies; communication becomes clearer, collaboration becomes smoother, processes run effectively, and decision making becomes more grounded. Blind spots stop being sources of friction and instead become catalysts for maturity, alignment, and deeper connection. Ultimately, understanding blind spots (our own and others') restores the natural flow of human interaction, allowing each core value to contribute its best without unintentionally creating breakdowns along the way.

CHAPTER 9
STEREOTYPES AND LABELS

abels are powerful. They help us make sense of complexity, communicate quickly, and understand ourselves and others with greater clarity. But labels also have a way of shrinking people. When we start treating them as fixed identities rather than necessary insights, they stop being helpful and start becoming harmful. Even in assessments like the CVI™ that were never meant to negatively label people. This misuse creates a quiet tragedy. Instead of using the CVI™ to understand how someone naturally contributes, people use it to predict, limit, or excuse behavior. They see a colleague's highest core value and assume they already know how that person will think or act. Even more damaging, individuals sometimes look at their own "painful" or low-energy values and use them as a reason to disengage. "I'm not good at that" becomes a shield. "That's not my core value" becomes a permission slip to give minimal effort. In these moments, the CVI™ stops being a tool for growth and becomes a justification for avoidance.

But the CVI™ was never designed to restrict anyone. I believe its purpose is to illuminate where we naturally thrive and where we may need to be more intentional. It's a map of capacity, not a map of capability. Every core value has something meaningful to offer, and every person has the ability to stretch beyond their comfort zone when the moment calls for it. The real skill is in reading the situation and knowing which part of yourself to bring forward. Sometimes your strongest value should take the lead. Other times, the wisest move is to step back and let someone else's core value take center stage. And occasionally, growth requires leaning into a value that feels uncomfortable, not as a permanent identity shift, but as a conscious act of contribution.

Healthy teams understand this balance. They don't expect everyone to excel in every area. Instead, they create space for each person's natural contributions while encouraging thoughtful stretch when needed. They recognize that a *Builder* can collaborate, a *Merchant* can analyze, a *Banker* can innovate, and an *Innovator* can execute. The question isn't "Is this my top value?" but "What does this moment require, and how can I contribute within my capacity?" When people approach their core values this way, the CVI™ becomes a living framework rather than a static label.

The Possible and Painful Merchant

People with a "possible" (10-18) or "painful" (9 and below) *Merchant* value often fall into a predictable pattern of self-limiting stories, behaviors, and excuses that quietly undermine their ability to contribute. Because the *Merchant* value is tied to connection, persuasion, and relational energy, individuals who score low in this area may convince themselves that they "just aren't people-persons," using that label as a shield rather than a starting point. They may say things like, "I'm not good with people," "I don't do small talk," "I'm not the relationship type," or "I'll just let someone else handle the people stuff." These statements sound harmless, but they become a box, one that keeps them from engaging, collaborating, or stretching themselves. In meetings, they might stay silent because they assume their voice won't resonate. When conflict arises, they may withdraw entirely, telling themselves, "I don't want to deal with emotions," or "I'm not wired for that kind of conversation." They may avoid networking opportunities, skip team-building activities, or resist roles that require influence or interpersonal nuance. Even simple relational gestures: checking in on a colleague, offering encouragement, or asking clarifying questions can feel like heavy lifting, so they rationalize their absence by saying, "That's just not what I am good at." The irony is that these behaviors often reinforce the very discomfort they're trying to avoid. By opting out, they never build the relational muscles that would make these moments easier. Instead, they stay in the safe but limiting identity of "not a *Merchant*," missing opportunities to connect, collaborate, and contribute in ways that would stretch them.

A possible/painful *Merchant* can overcome both external stereotypes and their own self-imposed limitations by approaching relational moments with intention rather than avoidance, gradually proving (to themselves and others) that low energy in a value does not equal low capability. The first step is reframing the narrative. Instead of saying "I'm not good with people," they can shift to "Relationship-heavy moments take more energy for me, but I can still show up with purpose." This mindset opens the door to small, manageable actions that build confidence. They can start by practicing simple relational behaviors that don't require dramatic personality shifts, asking one clarifying question in a meeting, offering a brief word of appreciation to a teammate, or initiating a short check-in with someone they work closely with. These micro-interactions accumulate, signaling to others that they are engaged and willing to connect, even if it doesn't come naturally. They can also prepare for relational situations the way others prepare for technical tasks: by planning talking points, setting clear intentions, or identifying one person they want to connect with rather than trying to "work the room." When conflict arises, instead of withdrawing, they can focus on listening first, which reduces pressure to perform and still demonstrates presence. Over time, these intentional choices challenge the stereotype that they are aloof, uninterested, or disconnected. Just as importantly, they challenge the internal stereotype that they are incapable of relational contribution. By showing up in small but consistent ways, a painful or possible *Merchant* proves that while connection may not be their primary energy source, it is still a skill they can develop and a meaningful part of how they contribute.

· · ·

The Possible and Painful Innovator

People with a "possible" or "painful" *Innovator* value often fall into a pattern of self-protection that looks like avoidance, rigidity, or over-simplification, all rooted in the belief that they "just aren't creative" or "aren't idea people." Because the *Innovator* value is tied to problem-solving, strategy, and creative solutions, individuals who score low in this area may convince themselves that they should stay out of conversations that require brainstorming or conceptual thinking. They might say things like, "I'm not the creative type," "I don't do strategy," "Just tell me what to do," or "I'm not good at coming up with ideas." These statements become a box they willingly climb into. A box that keeps them from contributing insights they do have, even if those insights take more effort to articulate. In meetings, they may stay quiet during ideation sessions, telling themselves, "I don't want to slow the group down," or "Someone else will come up with something better." When faced with ambiguity or open-ended problems, they may shut down or push for overly simple solutions, saying, "Let's not overthink this," or "Can we just pick something and move on." They might avoid roles or tasks that require innovation, such as designing processes, improving systems, or troubleshooting complex issues, rationalizing it with, "That's not what I am good at," or "I'm not wired for that kind of thinking." Even when they do have a good idea, they may hesitate to share it out of fear it won't measure up, telling themselves, "It's probably obvious," or "It's not worth mentioning." Over time, these behaviors reinforce the stereotype (both in their own mind and in the minds of others) that they lack creativity or strategic insight, even though the truth is simply that these tasks require more energy and intention for them. By opting out, they never build the confidence that would make these moments easier, and the possible or painful *Innovator* identity becomes a self-fulfilling limitation.

A possible or painful *Innovator* can overcome both internal and external stereotypes by approaching problem-solving with preparation, intention, and a willingness to engage even when the path forward feels unclear. Instead of defaulting to "I'm not creative" or "I don't do strategy," they can reframe their mindset to something more accurate and empowering, such as "Innovative thinking takes more energy for me, but I can still contribute thoughtfully." This shift opens the door to practical steps that build confidence over time. They can start by preparing in advance for brainstorming sessions. Reviewing the topic, jotting down a few observations, or identifying one question they want to ask. Questions are a powerful tool for possible or painful *Innovators* because they reduce the pressure to generate ideas on the spot while still moving the conversation forward. They can also break complex problems into smaller, concrete pieces, allowing them to engage without feeling overwhelmed by ambiguity. When someone else proposes an idea, they can contribute by clarifying assumptions, identifying risks, or offering practical refinements. Forms of innovation that don't require being the "big idea" person. Over time, these consistent, intentional contributions challenge the stereotype that they lack creativity or strategic insight. Just as importantly, they challenge the internal belief that they have nothing to offer in conceptual discussions. By showing up with preparation, curiosity, and a willingness to stretch, a possible or painful *Innovator* proves that innovation isn't a personality trait, it's a practice, and one they are fully capable of contributing to.

The Possible and Painful *Banker*

People with a "possible" or "painful" *Banker* value often fall into a predictable pattern of avoidance, self-doubt, and over-simplification because they believe they're "just not detail-oriented" or "not the organized type." Since the *Banker* value is tied to knowledge, accuracy, structure, and information management, individuals who score low in this area may convince themselves that anything involving data, documentation, or precision is beyond their capability. They might say things like, "I'm terrible with details," "I don't do paperwork," "I'm not a numbers person," or "Someone else should handle the logistics." These statements become a box they willingly climb into, a box that keeps them from learning, improving, or contributing in areas that require careful thought. In practice, this can look like avoiding tasks that require tracking information, procrastinating on documentation, or rushing through details with the excuse, "I'm more of a big-picture person." They may resist processes or systems, saying, "This is too rigid," or "I don't need all these steps," even when those steps would make their work easier. When asked to analyze data or verify information, they might deflect with, "I'll let someone who's good at that take it," or "I don't want to mess it up." In meetings, they may tune out when conversations shift toward facts, metrics, or procedures, telling themselves, "This isn't my lane." Even simple organizational tasks like keeping notes, following a checklist, or maintaining a calendar, can feel overwhelming, so they rationalize their inconsistency by saying, "I work better when things are loose." Over time, these behaviors reinforce the stereotype that they're unreliable with details or uninterested in accuracy, even though the truth is simply that these tasks require more energy and intention for them. By opting out, they never build the confidence or establish the workarounds that would make these moments easier, and for the possible or painful *Banker*, the identity becomes a self-fulfilling limitation.

A possible or painful *Banker* can overcome both internal and external stereotypes by approaching detail-oriented work with structure, preparation, and small, repeatable habits that build confidence over time. Instead of defaulting to "I'm terrible with details" or "I'm not a numbers person," they can adopt a more accurate mindset such as, "Precision takes more energy for me, but I can still handle it with the right approach." This shift opens the door to practical strategies that make *Banker*-type tasks far more manageable. They can start by using simple tools: checklists, templates, reminders, or step-by-step workflows that reduce cognitive load and create consistency. Breaking tasks into smaller pieces helps prevent them from becoming overwhelmed, and reviewing information in short, focused bursts can make accuracy feel less draining. When documentation or data work is required, they can prepare by gathering what they need ahead of time, setting a clear intention, and giving themselves a defined window to focus. They can also contribute meaningfully by asking clarifying questions, verifying assumptions, or summarizing key points, forms of precision that don't require deep technical expertise but still demonstrate reliability. Over time, these intentional behaviors challenge the stereotype that they're disorganized or inattentive. Just as importantly, they challenge the internal belief that they "can't" handle detail-heavy tasks. By showing up with structure, curiosity, and a willingness to stretch, a possible or painful *Banker* proves that accuracy isn't an impossible goal, it's part of a core value that can be done and a valuable part of their contribution.

The Possible and Painful Builder

People with a "possible" or "painful" *Builder* value often fall into a pattern of hesitation, overthinking, and self-protection because they believe they're "not decisive," "not action-oriented," or "not the take-charge type." Since the *Builder* value is tied to initiative, courage, and forward motion, individuals who score low in this area may convince themselves that anything requiring quick decisions, assertiveness, or hands-on execution is outside their capability. They might say things like, "I don't want to make the wrong call," "I'm not comfortable taking the lead," "Someone else should decide," or "I need more information before I can act." These statements become a box they willingly step into, a box that keeps them from building confidence through action. In practice, this can look like delaying decisions until the last possible moment, waiting for others to take the first step, or avoiding tasks that require boldness or confrontation. They may over-analyze simple choices, saying, "Let's think about this a little longer," or "I'm not sure we're ready yet," even when the situation clearly calls for movement. When asked to take charge of a project or make a call, they might deflect with, "I'm better in a support role," or "I don't want to step on anyone's toes." In group settings, they may hold back their opinions, telling themselves, "It's not my place," or "Someone else will speak up." Even small acts of initiative, like starting a meeting, making a phone call, or giving direct feedback can feel intimidating, so they rationalize their avoidance by saying, "I don't want to come off too strong," or "I'm just trying to be respectful." Over time, these behaviors reinforce the stereotype that they lack drive or confidence, even though the truth is simply that decisive action requires more energy and intention for them. By opting out, they never build the muscle that would make these moments easier, and the possible or painful *Builder* identity becomes a self-fulfilling limitation.

A possible or painful *Builder* can grow past these limitations by embracing small, intentional acts of initiative that build confidence without requiring a dramatic personality shift. Instead of defaulting to "I'm not decisive" or "I'm not the take-charge type," they can adopt a more accurate mindset such as, "Taking action takes more energy for me, but I can still move things forward in meaningful ways." This reframing opens the door to practical strategies that make *Builder*-type behaviors far more accessible. They can start by committing to one clear, simple action whenever they feel stuck sending the email, making the call, outlining the first step because momentum often matters more than perfection. Preparing ahead of time for situations that require assertiveness can also help. Writing down key points before a meeting, rehearsing a difficult conversation, or identifying the one decision they want to influence. When leadership moments arise, they don't need to dominate. They can contribute by offering direction in small doses, such as clarifying next steps or volunteering to handle a specific piece of the work. Over time, these consistent, manageable actions challenge the stereotype that they lack drive or courage. Just as importantly, they challenge the internal belief that they "aren't built for action." By showing up with preparation, intention, and a willingness to stretch, a possible or painful *Builder* proves that taking initiative is something they are fully capable of doing.

The Squarish Stereotype

People with a squarish CVI™ profile often fall into a unique kind of self-limiting box. The belief that because they aren't "dominant" in any one area, they don't have a clear identity, specialty, or standout core value. Instead of seeing their balanced profile as a tremendous asset, they may say things like, "I'm not really the expert at anything," "I don't have a strong value like other people," or "I'm just kind of average across the board." These statements become a quiet excuse to stay in the background, avoid taking ownership, or defer to others who appear more specialized. In group settings, they might hesitate to speak up because they assume someone else is more qualified. When asked to lead, they may respond internally with, "Someone with a stronger profile should take this," or say to the group "I'm not the best fit for this role." They may downplay their versatility by saying, "I can help a little, but I'm not the go-to person," or "I'll just support whoever has the strongest value here." Even when they perform well, they might attribute it to luck or circumstance. In decision-making moments, they may overthink their options because no single value feels like a natural anchor, leading them to say, "I'm torn, I don't really lean one way or another," or "I'm indifferent." Over time, these behaviors reinforce the stereotype (internally and externally) that they lack a clear lane, even though their balanced profile actually gives them adaptability, perspective, and the ability to bridge gaps between others. Instead of recognizing that they can flex into whatever the moment requires, they sometimes shrink into the identity of "not being strong enough" in any one area, turning their greatest advantage into a self-imposed limitation.

A squarish CVI™ profile can step into contribution with far more confidence by embracing the truth that versatility is not a lack of identity, it's a superpower. Instead of thinking, "I'm not the strongest in any one area," they can reframe their mindset to, "I can flex into whatever the moment requires, and that makes me uniquely valuable." This shift allows them to see their balanced profile as a stabilizing force rather than a diluted one. They can start by noticing the situations where their adaptability naturally shines: mediating between strong personalities, bridging gaps between departments, translating ideas across different work styles, or stepping into roles that require someone who can wear multiple hats. Because they understand all four values well, they can often spot blind spots others miss, anticipate friction before it happens, and bring harmony to teams that might otherwise struggle with imbalance. To build confidence, they can intentionally claim small leadership moments, clarifying next steps, offering a balanced perspective, or volunteering for tasks that require coordination rather than specialization. Over time, these actions help others see them not as "generalists without a lane" but as integrators, connectors, and stabilizers who make teams more effective. Just as importantly, these actions help the squarish individual rewrite their internal narrative: they are not undefined, they are multidimensional, and their ability to flex is precisely what makes them indispensable.

Closing Thoughts on Labels & Stereotypes

Stereotypes, whether about possible/painful values, dominant values, or even balanced CVI™ profiles, become dangerous the moment people start treating them as fixed truths rather than starting points for understanding. A possible or painful *Merchant* may hide behind the belief that they "aren't good with people," a possible or painful *Innovator* may shrink from creative problem-solving, a possible or painful *Banker* may avoid details, and a possible or painful *Builder* may hesitate to act. Even those with a squarish CVI™ profile can fall into the trap of thinking they lack a clear identity or standout core value. In every case, the stereotype becomes a box. A convenient explanation for disengagement, a shield against discomfort, and a quiet limiter on growth. But the reality is that these labels only hold power when people accept them as permanent. Each core value, whether high, low, or evenly distributed, comes with both opportunities and challenges, and none of them define a person's capability. When individuals recognize that their "painful" areas simply require more intention, not avoidance, they begin to stretch in meaningful ways. When they see their core values as tools rather than identities, they become more adaptable. And when they stop using labels as excuses, they reclaim the freedom to contribute, grow, and collaborate without being confined by stereotypes. Ultimately, the CVI™ becomes most powerful not when it explains who people are, but when it helps them see how they can contribute.

The tragedy isn't that people have different levels core value capacities.   It's that they sometimes use those core value capacities as excuses. The real opportunity is learning to balance self-awareness with adaptability. When individuals stop hiding behind labels and start showing up with intention, collaboration becomes richer, communication becomes more honest, and contribution becomes more meaningful. The CVI™ becomes what it was always meant to be: a guide, not a cage.

CHAPTER 10
LEADERSHIP STYLE

Leadership comes in many styles and approaches, and no single style holds a monopoly on effectiveness. Some leaders are visionary, inspiring others with big-picture thinking and a clear sense of direction. Think of someone who rallies a team around a bold future. Others are servant leaders, focusing on lifting others up, removing obstacles, and creating an environment where people thrive. There are transformational leaders who challenge the status quo and motivate people to grow, and transactional leaders who excel at structure, clarity, and accountability. Some lead through collaboration, pulling people together and building consensus, while others lead through decisive action, stepping in quickly when the moment calls for it. These styles show up everywhere, in workplaces, families, volunteer groups, and even childhood playground dynamics. Leadership isn't a single behavior. It's a spectrum of approaches shaped by how a person naturally sees the world and chooses to influence it.

When you look at leadership through the lens of the CVI™, these styles become even more understandable. Because the CVI™ reflects a person's innate hardwiring, their natural way of contributing, deciding, and interacting, leadership tendencies often emerge early in life and remain consistent across roles and environments. A *Builder* may lead through action and decisiveness, an *Innovator* through problem-solving and strategy, a *Merchant* through connection and inspiration, and a *Banker* through structure and precision. None of these styles is "better" than another. Each one brings contributions that are essential in different moments. The most successful leaders aren't the ones who try to mimic someone else's style, they're the ones who lead through their core values while also reading the moment and allowing other values to step forward when needed. A *Merchant* can lean into *Banker* precision when the situation demands accuracy. A *Builder* can pause and draw on *Innovator* analysis before acting. A *Banker* can stretch into *Merchant* connection to strengthen relationships. This ability to stay rooted in one's innate wiring while flexing intentionally based on their capacity and the capacity of others is what creates balanced and resilient leadership. Leadership that works not because it fits a mold, but because it honors the individual, others, and the moment.

Merchant Leader

A *Merchant* leads through connection, inspiration, and the ability to make people feel seen, valued, and part of something meaningful. Their leadership style is rooted in emotional intelligence and relational awareness. They naturally tune into the energy of a room, sense what people need, and build trust through authenticity. *Merchant* leaders excel at creating environments where people feel safe to contribute and motivated to give their best. A *Merchant* leader might start a meeting by checking in with the team on a personal level, making sure everyone feels grounded before diving into tasks. They often use storytelling to communicate vision, helping others understand not just what needs to be done but why it matters. When conflict arises, they lean into empathy, facilitating conversations that restore harmony rather than allowing tension to linger. They're the leaders who remember birthdays, notice when someone seems off, and take the time to ask, "How are you really doing." They build loyalty by being approachable and consistent, and they influence not through authority but through relationship. A *Merchant* leader might rally a team around a new initiative by highlighting shared values, celebrating small wins, and recognizing individual contributions publicly. They're often the glue in a group, bridging gaps between personalities, smoothing rough edges, and ensuring everyone feels included. Even in high-pressure situations, they lead with encouragement, offering reassurance and reminding people of their positive contributions. Their leadership is less about directing and more about connecting, less about commanding and more about inspiring. And because they lead from the heart, people don't just follow them, they believe in them.

When a *Merchant* leader goes "dark," the very contributions that normally make them inspiring and connective begin to twist into their shadow forms, creating confusion, emotional volatility, and relational pressure for the people around them. Instead of using empathy to understand others, they may use it to manipulate outcomes. Subtly guilt-tripping, withdrawing affection, or leveraging emotional influence to get their way. A dark *Merchant* might say things like, "I just thought we were closer than this," or "I guess I'm the only one who cares," turning connection into a weapon rather than a bridge. Their natural desire for harmony can morph into avoidance, where they refuse to address conflict directly but still expect others to "just know" what's wrong. They may triangulate, venting to one person about another instead of having the hard conversation themselves. Their gift for reading people can become hypersensitivity, interpreting neutral comments as personal attacks or assuming negative intent where none exists. In leadership settings, a dark *Merchant* might over-promise to keep everyone happy, then quietly resent the pressure they created for themselves. They may become inconsistent, warm and affirming one moment, cold and withdrawn the next leaving their team unsure how to approach them. They might avoid making decisions because they fear disappointing someone, or they may make decisions based solely on who they want to please rather than what the situation requires. When stressed, they can slip into martyrdom, saying things like, "I'm doing everything I can and no one appreciates it," or "I guess I'll just handle it myself," using self-sacrifice to gain sympathy or control. At their darkest, *Merchant* leaders stop leading through genuine connection and start leading through emotional pressure, approval-seeking, or subtle manipulation, behaviors that erode trust and leave others feeling drained rather than inspired.

A *Merchant* can prevent themselves from going dark by staying grounded in self-awareness, emotional regulation, and clear communication, three practices that help them lead from genuine connection rather than reactive emotion. Because *Merchants* feel deeply and read people intuitively, they must learn to pause before interpreting or responding, especially when they sense tension or disappointment. Simple habits like checking their assumptions, "What else could be true," naming their feelings without acting on them, and setting boundaries around their emotional energy can keep them from slipping into guilt, manipulation, or avoidance. *Merchants* thrive when they feel connected, so proactively nurturing healthy relationships, rather than waiting until they feel insecure, helps them stay balanced. They can also prevent dark patterns by being honest about their needs, asking for clarity instead of guessing, and reminding themselves that conflict is not a threat to connection. On the other side, people around a *Merchant* can play a huge role in keeping them from going dark. Offering direct but kind communication, expressing appreciation for their relational contributions, and addressing issues early (before the *Merchant* starts filling in the emotional blanks) helps them feel secure. Giving them space to talk through feelings without judgment, being consistent in tone and behavior, and avoiding abrupt or unexplained changes in relationship dynamics also keeps them steady. When others are clear about expectations, avoid triangulation, and approach disagreements with warmth rather than sharpness, *Merchants* remain at their best: open, encouraging, and deeply connective.

Innovator Leader

An *Innovator* leads through insight, clarity, and the ability to see patterns and possibilities that others often miss. Their leadership style is rooted in problem-solving and strategic thinking. They naturally gravitate toward understanding how things work, why something is happening, and what the smartest path forward might be. *Innovator* leaders excel at diagnosing issues quickly and offering elegant, efficient solutions. An *Innovator* leader might pause a chaotic discussion and say, "Let's step back and look at what's really going on," instantly bringing order to confusion. They often ask sharp, clarifying questions that cut through noise and reveal the core issue. When a team is stuck, they're the one who sketches a model on the whiteboard, reframes the problem, or proposes a new approach no one else considered. They lead by offering thoughtful analysis rather than emotional persuasion, and people trust them because their ideas consistently make things better. *Innovator* leaders are also skilled at anticipating obstacles before they appear, flagging risks, identifying dependencies, and designing systems that prevent future problems. They might streamline a workflow, redesign a process, or create a tool that saves the team hours of frustration. In meetings, they listen carefully, synthesize information quickly, and then offer a solution that feels both simple and brilliant. They're calm under pressure because they rely on logic and clarity, and they help others feel grounded by explaining the "why" behind decisions. Their leadership is less about charisma and more about competence. Less about rallying emotion and more about illuminating the smartest path. When *Innovators* lead well, teams feel smarter, more focused, and more capable because the *Innovator* has given them a clear, well-designed way forward.

When an *Innovator* leader goes "dark," their natural positive contribution of clarity, analysis, and problem-solving begin to harden into patterns that feel cold, dismissive, or intellectually overpowering to the people around them. Instead of using insight to illuminate the path forward, they may use it to dismantle others' ideas with cutting precision, interrupting with comments like, "That won't work," "You're missing the point," or "We've already solved this," shutting down contributions before they're fully expressed. Their ability to see patterns can morph into relentless fault-finding, where every suggestion is met with, "Here's the problem," or "That's inefficient," leaving the team feeling deflated and hesitant to speak. A dark *Innovator* might retreat into analysis paralysis, endlessly researching, refining, or modeling scenarios while avoiding decisions because nothing feels perfect enough. They can become so focused on logic that they dismiss emotional cues entirely, responding to someone's frustration with, "That's irrelevant," or "Let's stay objective," which makes others feel unseen. Their calm demeanor can turn icy, creating distance rather than stability. In meetings, they may dominate the conversation with long, complex explanations that leave others confused or intimidated, or they may withdraw completely, offering only cryptic critiques from the sidelines. When stressed, they might become rigid, insisting that their solution is the only rational one and refusing to consider alternatives. They may also become impatient with slower thinkers, saying things like, "Why is this taking so long," or "I shouldn't have to explain this again," unintentionally belittling the team. At their darkest, *Innovator* leaders stop using their wisdom to elevate others and instead use it as a shield, a weapon, or a barrier, leaving people feeling dismissed, overruled, or intellectually steamrolled rather than guided.

An *Innovator* can prevent themselves from going dark by staying grounded in humility, emotional awareness, and intentional collaboration, three practices that help them use their insight as a gift rather than a weapon. Because *Innovators* naturally see patterns, flaws, and solutions faster than most, they must learn to slow down long enough to bring others with them. This means pausing before critiquing, asking clarifying questions instead of jumping to conclusions, and remembering that not every problem needs to be solved immediately or perfectly. They can also check their tone, since what feels like "just being direct" to them can land as dismissive or cold to others. Practicing empathy, reminding themselves that people process information differently, helps them stay patient and open. *Innovators* thrive when they feel intellectually respected, so seeking feedback, inviting alternative viewpoints, and acknowledging others' contributions keeps them balanced and connected. They can also prevent dark patterns by setting boundaries around overthinking. Choosing a decision deadline, limiting research time, or sharing early drafts instead of waiting for perfection. On the other side, people around an *Innovator* can play a huge role in keeping them from going dark. Offering clear, concise communication helps them stay focused rather than frustrated. Asking for their insight directly, "What patterns do you see here" signals respect for their natural core value. Giving them space to think without interruption, while also gently nudging them toward decisions when they get stuck, keeps them productive without overwhelming them. Others can also prevent dark behavior by not taking their analytical tone personally, by asking for clarification when something feels sharp, and by expressing appreciation for the clarity and solutions they bring. When both sides work together, *Innovators* regulating their intensity and others engaging them with clarity and respect; *Innovators* remain at their best: insightful, steady, and brilliantly effective.

Banker Leader

A *Banker* leads through clarity, consistency, and a deep commitment to accuracy, offering a stabilizing presence that keeps teams grounded, informed, and protected from unnecessary risk. Their leadership style is rooted in structure and reliability. They make sure information is correct, processes are followed, and decisions are based on solid facts rather than impulse. *Banker*-aligned leadership excels at creating order out of chaos and ensuring that nothing important slips through the cracks. A *Banker* leader might begin a project by outlining expectations, documenting responsibilities, and establishing a clear timeline so everyone knows exactly what success looks like. They're the ones who maintain organized records, track progress meticulously, and ensure that decisions are supported by data rather than assumptions. When a team is brainstorming, they listen carefully and then ask grounding questions like, "What evidence do we have," "What are the risks," or "How will we measure this," helping others think more clearly. They lead by providing stability. Double-checking details, verifying information, and making sure the team is prepared before moving forward. In meetings, they often summarize key points, clarify misunderstandings, and ensure that action items are captured accurately. When conflict arises, they bring calm logic, focusing on facts rather than emotion. They might say, "Let's look at what actually happened," or "Here's what the data shows," helping people separate feelings from reality. *Banker* leaders also shine in compliance, budgeting, documentation, and quality control, areas where precision matters. Their leadership is less about charisma and more about dependability. Less about bold moves and more about protecting the team from avoidable mistakes. When *Bankers* lead well, people feel safe, informed, and confident that nothing important will be overlooked.

When a *Banker* leader goes "dark," their natural contributions of accuracy, structure, and risk-awareness can twist into rigidity, control, and an almost suffocating focus on what might go wrong. Instead of using details to support the team, they may weaponize them, correcting people harshly, pointing out every small mistake, or shutting down ideas with comments like, "That's not documented," "We don't have enough data," or "We can't move forward until everything is known." Their desire for order can morph into micromanagement, where they comb over tasks, demand constant updates, or refuse to delegate because "no one else will do it correctly." A dark *Banker* might slow projects to a crawl by insisting on more research, more verification, or more approvals, creating bottlenecks that frustrate everyone. They can become overly cautious, rejecting new ideas with, "There are too many unknowns," or "This isn't how we've done it before," even when innovation is needed. Their calm logic can turn cold and dismissive, making them seem unapproachable when people bring emotional concerns. In meetings, they may dominate with long lists of risks, compliance issues, or procedural requirements, leaving others feeling overwhelmed or shut down. They might cling to outdated processes, resist change simply because it introduces uncertainty, or correct people publicly in ways that feel shaming. When stressed, they can become territorial about information. Hoarding data, refusing to share updates until they're "fully verified," or using their knowledge as leverage. At their darkest, *Banker* leaders stop using structure to protect the team and instead use it to control, restrict, or slow everyone down, leaving people feeling scrutinized, constrained, and unable to move forward with confidence.

A *Banker* can prevent themselves from going dark by intentionally balancing their need for accuracy and structure with openness, flexibility, and trust in others. Because *Bankers* naturally see risks, details, and potential errors, they benefit from pausing before reacting, asking themselves, "Is this a real threat or just my wiring wanting more certainty." This simple moment of reflection helps them avoid slipping into rigidity or micromanagement. They can also set healthy boundaries around perfectionism by defining what "good enough" looks like before starting a task, rather than chasing flawless outcomes that drain their energy and frustrate others. Practicing delegation, starting with small, low-risk tasks, helps them build confidence in the team and reduces the urge to control every detail. *Bankers* thrive when they feel informed, so proactively asking for clarity rather than assuming something is missing keeps them grounded. They can also prevent dark patterns by communicating their needs openly, "I need a bit more detail to feel comfortable," or "Can we walk through the steps together." On the other side, people around a *Banker* can play a huge role in keeping them from going dark. Providing clear expectations, organized information, and timely updates helps them feel secure rather than anxious. When presenting ideas, offering a bit of data or rationale goes a long way. Others can also prevent dark behavior by avoiding last-minute surprises, being consistent in follow-through, and acknowledging the *Banker's* contributions to accuracy and stability. Giving them space to review details without pressure, while also gently nudging them forward when they get stuck in analysis, keeps them balanced. When both sides work together, *Bankers* regulating their need for control and others offering clarity and reliability, *Bankers* remain at their best: steady, thoughtful, and deeply dependable.

Builder Leader

A *Builder* leads with action, momentum, and a powerful sense of direction, driving progress through decisiveness, confidence, and an instinctive ability to cut through hesitation. *Builder*-aligned leadership thrives when there is something to do, something to fix, or something to move forward. They are the leaders who walk into a stalled meeting and say, "Alright, here's what we're doing," instantly shifting the energy from discussion to execution. *Builders* lead by example, often being the first to roll up their sleeves, jump into the work, or take responsibility when others are still weighing options. They value efficiency and clarity, so they tend to communicate in direct, straightforward language, "Let's get this done," "Here's the next step," or "We're overthinking this." When a team is stuck in analysis paralysis, a *Builder* will break the logjam by making a call and mobilizing people around it. They excel in crisis because they don't freeze. They assess quickly, act decisively, and keep others calm by projecting certainty. A *Builder* leader might reorganize a chaotic workflow on the spot, redirect a team that's drifting off course, or push through obstacles that would discourage others. They're also highly protective of their people, stepping in when someone is being treated unfairly, confronting issues head-on, or advocating fiercely for resources the team needs. Their leadership is grounded in momentum, courage, and a bias toward action. When *Builders* lead well, teams feel energized, focused, and confident that progress will happen, not someday, but today.

When a *Builder* leader goes "dark," their natural contributions of decisiveness, action, and forward momentum can twist into forcefulness, impatience, and a tendency to bulldoze others in the pursuit of getting things done. Instead of using their confidence to energize the team, they may use it to dominate, cutting people off with comments like, "We don't have time for this," "Just do what I said," or "Why is this taking so long," shutting down collaboration in favor of speed. Their bias for action can morph into recklessness, where they make snap decisions without consulting anyone, override important details, or push ahead even when clear risks are present. A dark *Builder* might take over tasks they previously delegated, not because others failed but because "it's faster if I do it myself," leaving the team feeling disempowered and mistrusted. They can become visibly frustrated when others hesitate or ask questions, interpreting thoughtful analysis as resistance or incompetence. In meetings, they may dominate the conversation, dismiss alternative viewpoints, or pressure the group into decisions before they're ready. Under stress, they might become confrontational, raising their voice, issuing ultimatums, or using intimidation to force compliance. They may also become overly controlling, insisting that things be done their way even when other approaches are equally valid. When deadlines loom, they can push people past healthy limits, saying things like, "We just need to power through," or "Everyone needs to step up," without acknowledging burnout or capacity. At their darkest, *Builder* leaders stop using their drive to move the team forward and instead use it to push, pressure, and overpower, leaving people feeling rushed, unheard, and steamrolled rather than motivated.

A *Builder* can prevent themselves from going dark by intentionally slowing down just enough to stay self-aware, grounded, and connected to the people they're leading. Because *Builders* are wired for action, they often move so quickly that they don't notice rising frustration, impatience, or the subtle shift from "driving progress" to "driving over people." One of the most powerful things a *Builder* can do is build in micro-pauses, moments to ask themselves, "Is this urgency real or just my wiring," or "Have I given people enough clarity to act." These small check-ins help them avoid snapping, bulldozing, or taking over tasks prematurely. They can also prevent dark patterns by delegating intentionally and resisting the urge to reclaim work the moment someone hesitates. Practicing curiosity asking, "What do you need to move forward," instead of assuming resistance, keeps them collaborative rather than combative. *Builders* thrive when they feel momentum, so setting clear priorities and celebrating progress (even small wins) helps them stay energized without slipping into pressure mode. On the other side, people around a *Builder* can play a huge role in keeping them from going dark. Offering concise communication, clear expectations, and quick updates helps *Builders* feel confident that things are moving. When someone needs more time or clarity, stating it directly, "I can get this done, but I need X first," prevents the *Builder* from assuming inaction. Others can also help by not taking their directness personally, by matching their straightforward tone, and by addressing issues early before frustration builds. Giving *Builders* room to act, while also gently reminding them when the team needs a moment to think or regroup, keeps them balanced. When both sides work together, *Builders* regulating their intensity and others engaging them with clarity and momentum, *Builders* remain at their best: decisive, energizing, and powerfully effective.

. . .

Squarish Leaders

A squarish CVI™ profile leads with a uniquely balanced, integrative style that draws from all four core values, making them one of the most adaptable and situationally aware types of leaders. Instead of relying on a single dominant core value, they naturally shift gears depending on what the moment requires, leaders who can "read the room," bridge gaps, and bring harmony to diverse teams. In one moment, they may lead like a *Builder*, stepping in decisively when a project is stuck and saying, "Let's move this forward." In another, they may lean into their *Merchant* side, sensing tension on the team and pausing to check in with people before pushing ahead. When clarity is needed, their *Innovator* wiring surfaces, they ask thoughtful questions, reframe the problem, or help the group see a smarter path. And when accuracy or structure becomes essential, their *Banker* instincts take over, they document next steps, clarify expectations, or ensure the team has the information needed to avoid mistakes. Squarish leaders often act as translators between strong personalities, helping a high-*Builder* colleague understand a high-*Banker's* concerns, or helping a *Merchant* and *Innovator* find common ground. They're the ones who can sit in a meeting full of competing priorities and say, "Here's what everyone is trying to accomplish, let's find a way to integrate these goals." Their leadership is steady, flexible, and relationally intelligent. They don't overpower or dominate. Instead, they create cohesion by seeing multiple perspectives and adjusting their approach fluidly. Because they can flex into any of the four values without losing themselves, squarish leaders often become the glue that holds teams together, balancing speed with thoughtfulness, connection with clarity, and structure with innovation.

When a squarish leader goes "dark," the very versatility that normally makes them balanced, adaptive, and relationally intelligent can collapse into inconsistency, confusion, and emotional whiplash for the people around them. Because they can flex into all four core values, their dark side shows up as over-flexing, shifting so rapidly between modes that others can't predict what version of them will show up. One moment they may act like a dark *Builder*, pushing too hard, taking over tasks, or snapping, "We just need to get this done," and the next they may swing into dark *Merchant* behavior, withdrawing emotionally, seeking reassurance, or using guilt-tinged comments like, "I just thought we were all on the same page." When stressed, they might slip into dark *Innovator* tendencies, overanalyzing, poking holes in every idea, or stalling decisions because "there are too many variables." Then, without warning, they may shift into dark *Banker* mode. Micromanaging details, nitpicking mistakes, or insisting that nothing can move forward until everything is perfectly documented. This unpredictability can leave teams feeling like they're walking on eggshells, unsure whether they're about to encounter intensity, detachment, criticism, or control. A dark squarish leader may also lose their sense of identity, trying so hard to meet everyone's expectations that they become chameleons, agreeing with one person in private, then contradicting themselves in the next meeting. They may overcommit to please the *Merchants*, over-structure to satisfy the *Bankers*, over-analyze to impress the *Innovators*, and over-drive to match the *Builders*, leaving themselves exhausted and others frustrated. At their darkest, squarish leaders stop being integrators and become reactors pulled in every direction, inconsistent in tone, and unable to provide the stability and clarity their teams rely on.

A squarish CVI™ leader can prevent themselves from going dark by anchoring in clarity about who they are and how they naturally operate, rather than trying to be everything for everyone. Because they can flex into all four core values, their greatest risk is losing their center so one of the most powerful things they can do is intentionally define their "home base," their dominant core value they return to when they feel overwhelmed or pulled in too many directions. Regular self-check-ins help tremendously asking, "Which value am I operating from right now," "Is this the right one for the moment," and "Am I shifting because it's needed or because I'm trying to please someone or the moment?" This keeps their adaptability intentional rather than reactive. They can also prevent dark patterns by setting boundaries around over-committing, since squarish leaders often say "yes" to too many roles because they can flex into them. Prioritizing rest, clarity, and honest communication helps them stay grounded. They have a tendency to be the single point of failure where all work stops because they have to see and decide on everything. To prevent this from happening, they need to set aside a dedicated time to complete these task or don't accept them in the first place. When they feel themselves swinging between modes too quickly, pausing to name the stressor and using the value to lead from restores stability. They also benefit from surrounding themselves with people who appreciate their versatility but don't exploit it, and from giving themselves permission to not solve every interpersonal or operational gap on the team.

People around a squarish leader can play a huge role in keeping them from going dark by offering consistency, clarity, and direct communication. Because squarish leaders are highly attuned to the needs of others, unclear expectations or shifting emotional dynamics can send them into reactive mode. Being straightforward, "Here's what I need," "Here's what I'm concerned about," "Here's what success looks like" helps them stay centered. Others can also prevent dark behavior by not pulling them in multiple directions at once, by avoiding triangulation, and by not assuming the squarish leader will automatically fill every gap. Acknowledging their ability to flex while also encouraging them to choose a lane in moments of stress helps them feel supported rather than stretched thin. When all sides work together, squarish leaders grounding themselves in intentionality and others offering clarity and stability, these leaders remain at their best: balanced, integrative, and remarkably effective at guiding teams through complexity.

Opposing Contribution Type™ Leaders

Individuals who's top two CVI™ core values fall in opposite Contribution Types™ lead with a dynamic, multidimensional style that blends two very different ways of operating, creating leaders who are both complex and uniquely effective. A *Builder–Banker* leader, for example, combines decisive action with meticulous structure. They move fast but with precision, launching initiatives quickly while also double-checking details, setting clear procedures, and ensuring nothing important gets missed. They might say, "Let's get this rolling today, and here's the checklist we'll follow," blending urgency with order. A *Builder–Merchant* leader brings boldness wrapped in warmth, they inspire through energy and personal connection, rallying people with statements like, "We've got this, let's go together," and then charging ahead with confidence. They're the type who motivates a team through a tough deadline by both pushing hard and making everyone feel valued. A *Builder–Innovator* leader is a strategist in motion. They act decisively but only after identifying the smartest path forward. They might pause a chaotic moment to say, "Hold on, here's the real issue," and then immediately mobilize the team toward a clear solution. A *Banker–Merchant* leader blends stability with empathy, they create safe, predictable environments where people feel supported, often saying things like, "Let's make sure everyone has what they need before we move on." They're the ones who quietly ensure the team is both emotionally grounded and operationally prepared. A *Banker–Innovator* leader is a master of clarity and logic. They build systems, refine processes, and solve problems with calm precision, often stepping in with, "Let's map this out so we can make the best decision." They lead through thoughtful structure rather than force. Finally, a *Merchant–Innovator* leader blends emotional intelligence with insight, they read people deeply while also seeing patterns others miss. They might say, "I hear what everyone is feeling, and here's the direction that honors all perspectives," guiding teams through complexity with both empathy and brilliance. Across all pairings, opposite-type leaders shine because they bridge worlds, action and thought, structure and emotion, speed and depth, making them some of the most versatile and compelling leaders in any environment.

When individuals with opposite-type CVI™ pairings go "dark," the tension between their two contrasting core values becomes amplified, creating leadership patterns that feel contradictory, unpredictable, or overwhelming to the people around them. A *Builder–Banker* leader may swing between forceful urgency and rigid control, one moment barking, "Just get it done now," and the next freezing progress with, "We can't move forward until every detail is verified." They might micromanage fiercely, take tasks away from others, or shut down ideas because they're "too risky," creating a stop-start environment that exhausts their team. A *Builder–Merchant* leader can become emotionally volatile, pushing people hard with intense energy, then flipping into guilt, frustration, or emotional pressure when others don't keep up. They may say things like, "Why isn't anyone stepping up," followed minutes later by, "I just feel like no one cares as much as I do," leaving the team unsure how to respond. A *Builder–Innovator* leader may oscillate between impulsive action and paralyzing over analysis, charging ahead with half-formed plans, then abruptly halting everything because they've suddenly noticed a flaw or new angle. They might dismiss others' ideas as "not smart enough," then later criticize the team for not moving fast enough. A *Banker–Merchant* leader can become both controlling and emotionally reactive, correcting people harshly, clinging to rules, or withholding approval while simultaneously seeking reassurance or feeling personally wounded by minor feedback. They may say, "That's not the right process," followed by, "I just don't feel supported," creating confusion about whether the issue is procedural or emotional. A *Banker–Innovator* leader may retreat into cold intellectualism. Nitpicking details, poking holes in every idea, or shutting down progress with endless analysis. They might insist, "We need more data," while offering no path forward, leaving the team stuck in a loop of critique without action. Finally, a *Merchant–Innovator* leader can become manipulative or aloof, using emotional insight to influence others subtly, then withdrawing into detached analysis when things get uncomfortable. They may say, "I just thought you understood how important this is to me," followed by, "Logically, your idea doesn't make sense," blending emotional pressure with intellectual superiority. Across all pairings, dark-side behavior emerges when the two opposing values stop balancing each other and instead pull the leader in conflicting directions, creating inconsistency, tension, and a leadership style that feels unstable rather than integrated.

Leaders who's top two CVI™ values sit in opposite Contribution Types™ can prevent themselves from going dark by learning to intentionally integrate their contrasting core values rather than letting them compete for control. A *Builder–Banker* can stay balanced by pausing before acting, asking, "Do I need speed or accuracy right now," and choosing one consciously instead of swinging between urgency and rigidity. A *Builder–Merchant* can ground themselves by checking their emotional temperature before pushing forward, making sure their drive isn't turning into pressure and their empathy isn't turning into guilt. A *Builder–Innovator* can prevent dark patterns by setting a clear decision window. Giving themselves enough time to think without slipping into over analysis, but not so little time that they act impulsively. A *Banker–Merchant* can stay centered by separating facts from feelings asking, "Is this a procedural issue or an emotional one," so they don't mix control with sensitivity. A *Banker–Innovator* can prevent going dark by setting limits on analysis, defining what "enough information" looks like, and remembering that progress matters as much as precision. A *Merchant–Innovator* can stay healthy by naming their assumptions out loud, checking whether their emotional read or their intellectual interpretation is driving their reaction. Across all pairings, the key is self-awareness. Noticing which value is taking over and intentionally choosing balance rather than reacting from stress.

People around these leaders can play a major role in keeping them from going dark by offering clarity, consistency, and direct communication. Opposite-type leaders are highly sensitive to mixed signals, so giving them clear expectations and steady follow-through helps them stay grounded. When a *Builder*-blend starts pushing too hard, others can slow the pace by offering structured updates or asking for priorities. When a *Banker*-blend becomes rigid, others can gently remind them of the bigger picture or provide reassurance that progress is safe. When a *Merchant*-blend becomes emotionally reactive, others can offer calm, factual grounding. When an *Innovator*-blend gets stuck in analysis, others can ask for a recommended next step to help them move forward. Most importantly, people can prevent dark behavior by not pulling these leaders in opposite directions, avoiding triangulation, being honest about needs, and acknowledging the leader's effort to balance two very different internal drives. When all sides work together, these leaders remain at their best: integrated, steady, and uniquely capable of bridging worlds that others struggle to connect.

· · ·

Closing Thoughts on Leadership Styles

Leadership is never one-size-fits-all, and the CVI™ provides the clearest framework for understanding why. Each leader's natural style, whether driven by *Builder* action, *Merchant* connection, *Innovator* wisdom, *Banker* knowledge, or a *Squarish* blend of all four, shapes how they make decisions, motivate others, solve problems, communicate expectations, and navigate conflict. The CVI™ reveals the hardwired preferences behind every leadership behavior. *Builders* lead through momentum and decisiveness, *Merchants* through inspiration and relationships, *Innovators* through strategy and insight, *Bankers* through structure and accuracy, and *Squarish* leaders through balance and adaptability. Recognizing these patterns helps leaders lean into their core values while also understanding where blind spots may appear. It also reminds us that effective leadership isn't about copying someone else's style, it's about leading from your authentic wiring while learning to honor the wiring of the people you serve. The key takeaway is simple: the CVI™ doesn't just describe leadership styles, it gives leaders a roadmap for self-awareness, team alignment, communication, decision-making, and long-term effectiveness, allowing them to lead in a way that is both natural and deeply impactful.

CHAPTER 11

DECISION MAKING

ecision-making is shaped by a wide mix of internal and external factors that interact in subtle ways. Personal values often sit at the center, someone who prioritizes financial security, for example, may choose a stable job over a more exciting but risky startup role. Emotions also play a powerful role. A person feeling anxious might avoid making a big purchase, while someone feeling confident may take on a new investment. Social influences matter too, such as friends encouraging someone to try a new restaurant or a workplace culture nudging employees toward certain behaviors. Past experiences shape choices as well. Someone who once had a bad experience with a contractor may be far more cautious when hiring again. Finally, cognitive biases can steer decisions without people realizing it. Confirmation bias might lead a person to buy a car from a brand they already believe is "the best," even if objective comparisons suggest otherwise. These factors blend together constantly, creating a decision-making landscape that is rarely simple and always deeply personal.

An individual's CVI™ profile provides an insightful layer by highlighting the innate motivational drivers that guide how they approach decisions. Someone with a strong *Builder* energy may make choices quickly and confidently, preferring decisive action over prolonged analysis. A person with dominant *Merchant* energy might prioritize relationships and long-term vision, choosing options that strengthen connections or create future opportunities. Those with strong *Innovator* energy tend to analyze problems deeply, seeking elegant solutions and relying on logic to guide their choices. Meanwhile, individuals with high *Banker* energy often prefer thorough research and data, making decisions only after gathering enough information to feel secure. In general terms, a CVI™ profile doesn't dictate what someone will choose, but it strongly influences how they choose, whether they move fast or slow, rely on intuition or data, focus on people or processes, and ultimately what feels most natural and aligned with their core motivations.

Merchant

A *Merchant's* thought process is rich, intuitive, and deeply relational, driven by a desire to create connection, harmony, and long-term opportunity. When a *Merchant* evaluates a decision, the first and most influential factor is often the impact on people, how the choice will affect relationships, trust, collaboration, and the emotional climate around them. They naturally scan for alignment with their values, especially authenticity, vision, and mutual benefit. They consider whether the decision will inspire others, strengthen bonds, or open doors for future growth. *Merchants* also weigh the long-term narrative, "Does this choice move us toward a meaningful future," "Does it feel aligned with who we want to become?" Intuition plays a major role, as they often "feel" it before they can fully articulate it. On the other hand, factors that tend to sit lower on a *Merchant's* decision-making list include rigid data analysis, highly technical details, or purely transactional considerations. While they appreciate information, they rarely let spreadsheets or procedural rules override their sense of people and purpose. They may also deprioritize short-term efficiency if it conflicts with long-term relationships or vision. In essence, a *Merchant's* decision-making process is guided by heart and foresight, seeking outcomes that uplift people, build trust, and create a future worth moving toward.

When a *Merchant* goes dark, their decision-making process can shift dramatically. Instead of relying on their usual intuition, relational awareness, and long-term vision, they may become overly emotional, reactive, or approval-seeking. A dark *Merchant* might fixate on how others might feel rather than what is actually true, leading them to avoid decisions altogether or make choices purely to keep the peace. They can become hypersensitive to perceived rejection or conflict, reading negative intent where none exists. In this state, they may over-promise in an attempt to maintain harmony, even when they lack the capacity to follow through. Their natural gift for seeing future possibilities can turn into unfocused idealism or unrealistic expectations, causing them to chase "feel-good" options rather than grounded ones. They may also become indecisive, bouncing between choices because they fear disappointing someone or damaging a relationship. Instead of using their persuasive contributions positively, a dark *Merchant* might slip into manipulation, subtle guilt-tripping, emotional appeals, or selective sharing of information to steer outcomes in their favor. Ultimately, a *Merchant* when dark is still driven by the desire for connection and vision, but those motivations become distorted by fear, insecurity, and emotional overload, leading to decisions that lack clarity, boundaries, or long-term stability.

When interacting with a *Merchant* to help them make decisions, the most effective approach is to speak in a way that honors their relational, intuitive, and future-oriented nature. *Merchants* respond best when they feel genuinely heard, valued, and emotionally connected to the conversation, so it helps to begin by acknowledging their perspective with phrases like "I see what you're envisioning," "Your instincts here make a lot of sense," or "I appreciate how you're thinking about the people involved." They gain confidence when others affirm the long-term purpose behind a choice, so highlighting shared goals, "This aligns with the future you're trying to build," can be grounding. *Merchants* also appreciate open dialogue rather than rigid directives, so asking collaborative questions such as "How does this option feel to you?" or "What outcome would strengthen relationships the most?"

keeps them engaged and reassured. Actions matter too. Maintaining warm eye contact, giving them space to talk through their thoughts, and showing genuine enthusiasm for their ideas helps them feel supported. When addressing concerns, it's helpful to speak to emotional and relational impacts rather than drowning them in data. Offering reassurance like, "Everyone involved will be taken care of," "We've thought through how this affects the team," "We coordinated this across the team and we are in agreement," or "This choice keeps your values at the center" gives them comfort that the decision is aligned with what matters most to them. Ultimately, a *Merchant* feels confident when they sense trust, connection, and shared vision so the more you reinforce those elements, the more empowered they become in their decision-making process.

Innovator

An *Innovator's* thought process is deliberate, analytical, and rooted in a desire to understand how things work and how they could work better. When faced with a decision, an *Innovator* instinctively begins by examining the underlying problem, often breaking it down into smaller components to understand the mechanics at play. They highly value logic, efficiency, and elegant solutions, so they tend to ask questions like "What is the smartest way to approach this?" or "What solution solves the root issue rather than just the symptoms?" *Innovators* also consider long-term sustainability and system-wide impact, preferring decisions that create clarity, reduce friction, and improve processes. They are comfortable sitting with complexity and ambiguity while they analyze patterns, gather information, and test ideas mentally. On the other hand, factors that tend to rank lower in their decision-making include emotional considerations, social dynamics, or decisions based purely on tradition or "the way we've always done it." *Innovators* may also deprioritize speed if it compromises the quality of the solution, and they are less influenced by popularity or group pressure. Their focus is on accuracy, logic, and improvement, not appeasing others or rushing to closure. Ultimately, an *Innovator's* decision-making process is guided by a commitment to solving problems intelligently and designing outcomes that make systems, relationships, or environments function more effectively.

When an *Innovator* goes dark, their decision-making process can shift from thoughtful and analytical to rigid, detached, and overly critical. Instead of calmly exploring possibilities, they may fixate on flaws, risks, or inefficiencies to the point of paralysis. A dark *Innovator* can become hyper-analytical, endlessly dissecting problems without moving toward a solution, or they may swing the other way and make abrupt, overly logical decisions that ignore emotional or relational consequences. Their natural gift for seeing patterns can turn into suspicion or over-interpretation, causing them to assume hidden motives or problems that aren't actually there. They may become dismissive of others' ideas, believing only their own reasoning is sound, and their communication can grow sharp, overly blunt, or condescending. In this state, they often undervalue collaboration without refelection and may withdraw to avoid what they perceive as unnecessary emotional noise. Factors like empathy, group morale, or the human impact of a decision drop low on their priority list, replaced by a narrow focus on "fixing the problem" or proving their logic is correct. Ultimately, a dark *Innovator's* decisions tend to be driven by fear of being wrong, misunderstood, or out of control, leading them to overthink, over-criticize, or over-isolate behaviors that obscure their natural positive contributions in clarity, insight, and elegant problem-solving.

When interacting with an *Innovator* to help them make decisions, the most effective approach is to speak in a way that honors their need for clarity, logic, and thoughtful problem-solving. *Innovators* feel most at ease when they know the situation has been examined thoroughly, so offering structured information and walking through the reasoning behind options can be incredibly grounding. Phrases like "Here's the core issue as I see it," "Let's break this down step by step," or "I want to make sure the solution is efficient and well-designed" signal that you respect their analytical process. They also appreciate when others acknowledge the importance of accuracy and systems thinking, so statements such as "I checked the details to make sure nothing was overlooked" or "This approach solves the root problem, not just the symptoms" help them feel understood. Actions matter just as much. Giving them space to think without pressure, allowing pauses in conversation, and presenting information in a clear, organized way all help them feel comfortable. *Innovators* also respond well to calm, rational dialogue rather than emotional intensity, so maintaining a steady tone and focusing on facts can keep the conversation productive. When addressing their concerns, it helps to explicitly confirm that the logic holds up, "I've tested this from multiple angles," "The data supports this direction," or "This solution minimizes long-term friction." Ultimately, an *Innovator* gains confidence when they sense that the decision is grounded in sound reasoning, that the problem has been fully understood, and that the chosen path is both elegant and effective.

Banker

A *Banker's* thought process is methodical, data-driven, and grounded in a desire for accuracy, stability, and well-informed choices. When a *Banker* approaches a decision, they instinctively begin by gathering information, facts, historical data, documented patterns, and any relevant details that help them build a complete picture. They highly value reliability and clarity, so they take time to verify sources, cross-check assumptions, and ensure that nothing important has been overlooked. Their internal questions often sound like, "Do we have enough information?", "What does the data actually show?", or "What are the risks if we move forward?" *Bankers* also consider long-term security and consistency, preferring decisions that minimize uncertainty and protect against potential problems. They are naturally cautious, not because they fear change, but because they want to make sure the change is justified and well-supported. On the lower end of their decision-making priorities are emotional appeals, intuition-based arguments, or decisions made simply to satisfy group pressure or speed. They are less swayed by charisma, enthusiasm, or "gut feelings," and they tend to deprioritize options that feel rushed, ambiguous, or poorly documented. Ultimately, a *Banker's* decision-making process is guided by a commitment to thoroughness, precision, and responsible stewardship, ensuring that choices are grounded in solid evidence and structured thinking rather than impulse or uncertainty.

When a *Banker* goes dark, their decision-making process can become rigid, overly cautious, and dominated by worst-case thinking. Instead of using their natural contribution for gathering accurate information and creating stability, they may fixate on gaps, uncertainties, or potential risks to the point where no amount of data feels sufficient. A dark *Banker* can become paralyzed by the fear of making the wrong choice, leading them to delay decisions indefinitely or insist on endless research, documentation, or verification. Their communication may grow cold, overly formal, or dismissive as they retreat into analysis and distance themselves from emotional or relational input. They may also become hypercritical (of themselves and others), pointing out flaws without offering solutions, or rejecting ideas simply because they feel unproven or unfamiliar. In this state, they tend to undervalue intuition, collaboration, and forward momentum, instead clinging to what is known, safe, and historically reliable. Their desire for accuracy can morph into perfectionism, and their instinct for caution can turn into fear-based obstruction. Ultimately, a *Banker* in the dark is still trying to protect stability, but their protective instincts become distorted, causing them to over-control, over-analyze, or shut down entirely rather than move toward a balanced, well-supported decision.

When interacting with a *Banker* to support their decision-making, the most effective approach is to communicate with clarity, structure, and respect for their need for accurate, well-verified information. *Bankers* feel most confident when they know the facts are solid and the risks have been thoroughly examined, so offering organized details, documented evidence, and clear reasoning helps them feel grounded. Using phrases like "Here's the information we've confirmed," "I've double-checked the data," or "These are the documented outcomes from similar situations," signals that you understand and value their need for precision. They also appreciate when others acknowledge the importance of thoroughness and caution, so statements such as, "Take the time you need to review this" or "I want to make sure you have all the details before deciding," show respect for their process. Actions matter just as much. Providing written summaries, offering supporting documents, outlining steps in a logical sequence, and giving them space to analyze without pressure all help them feel secure. When addressing concerns, it's helpful to speak directly to accuracy and risk management, "We've accounted for the potential downsides," "Here's the historical data that supports this choice," or "This plan minimizes uncertainty over the long term." Ultimately, a *Banker* gains comfort when they sense the decision is grounded in reliable information, that nothing important has been overlooked, and that they are being given the time and structure needed to make a responsible, well-supported choice.

Builder

A *Builder's* thought process is direct, action-oriented, and grounded in a desire to create movement, achieve results, and maintain control over outcomes. When a *Builder* approaches a decision, they instinctively look for the most efficient path forward, what needs to be done, who is responsible, and how quickly progress can be made. They highly value clarity, authority, and decisiveness, so they tend to ask questions like, "What's the objective?", "What's the fastest way to get this done?", or "Who's accountable for each step?" *Builders* are motivated by tangible results and prefer solutions that produce immediate, measurable impact rather than abstract or theoretical benefits. They also consider whether a decision strengthens their ability to lead, protect, or take charge of a situation. On the lower end of their decision-making priorities are prolonged discussions, emotional processing, or decisions that require extensive analysis without clear action steps. They are less influenced by group consensus, relational-based arguments, or highly detailed data unless it directly supports forward momentum. *Builders* may also deprioritize long-term hypotheticals if they feel those conversations slow down execution. Ultimately, a *Builder's* decision-making process is guided by a drive for efficiency, clarity, and decisive action, favoring choices that create movement and produce concrete results while minimizing anything that feels like hesitation, ambiguity, or unnecessary complexity.

When a *Builder* goes dark, their decision-making process can become forceful, reactive, and overly controlling. Instead of using their natural contribution of decisiveness, courage, and forward momentum, they may shift into a mode where speed and dominance override clarity and collaboration. A dark *Builder* often feels an urgent need to regain control, which can lead them to make snap decisions without considering consequences or input from others. They may become impatient, dismissive, or blunt, pushing ahead simply to "get it done" rather than ensuring the choice is truly effective. Their natural drive for action can turn into aggression or rigidity, causing them to bulldoze obstacles (or people) rather than work with them. They may also become hyper-focused on winning, being right, or asserting authority, even when the situation doesn't require it. Emotional nuance, long-term implications, and relational impacts tend to fall to the bottom of their priority list, replaced by a narrow focus on immediate control or resolution. In this state, a *Builder's* protective instincts become distorted. Instead of creating stability through decisive leadership, they may create tension, conflict, or rushed outcomes that don't serve the bigger picture. Ultimately, a dark *Builder* is still trying to protect progress and maintain order, but fear and pressure twist those instincts into behaviors that feel harsh, inflexible, or prematurely forceful.

When interacting with a *Builder* to help them make decisions, the most effective approach is to communicate with clarity, confidence, and a focus on action. Builders feel most grounded when they know exactly what needs to happen, who is responsible, and how quickly progress can be made, so speaking in direct, concise language is essential. Phrases like, "Here's the plan," "This is the fastest path forward," or "I've already handled the key obstacles" reassure them that momentum is being maintained. They appreciate when others demonstrate competence and decisiveness, so offering concrete steps, "First we'll do this, then we'll move to that," helps them feel in control of the process. Actions matter just as much. Showing up prepared, eliminating unnecessary delays, and presenting solutions rather than problems all signal respect for their time and leadership instincts. When addressing concerns, it helps to speak to efficiency and authority, "We've removed the bottlenecks," "You'll have full control over the final call," or "This option gets us results the quickest." *Builders* also respond well when others match their pace and avoid excessive emotional processing or over-explaining. Ultimately, a *Builder* gains comfort when they sense that the situation is under control, the path forward is clear, and the people around them are capable, decisive, and ready to move.

Squarish Profiles

A "squarish" CVI™ profile tends to approach decision-making with a blended, integrative thought process that shifts from multiple core values rather than relying heavily on a single dominant style. When this person evaluates a decision, they naturally consider a wide range of factors: the practical steps required to move forward (*Builder*), the relational and long-term human impact (*Merchant*), the logic and structural soundness of the solution (*Innovator*), and the accuracy or reliability of the information involved (*Banker*). Because no single value energy overwhelmingly drives them, they often take a more holistic view, weighing efficiency, relationships, logic, and data in a way that feels balanced and thoughtful. They may ask themselves questions like, "Does this make sense?", "Is this the right thing for the people involved?", "Do we have enough information?", and "What's the most effective path forward?" This versatility can make them adaptable and fair-minded, but it can also create tension when different internal priorities conflict. Factors that tend to fall lower on their decision-making list include extreme positions, purely emotional choices without structure, purely data-driven decisions that ignore people, or impulsive action without analysis. They are also less likely to be swayed by group pressure or by any single perspective that feels too narrow. Ultimately, a squarish CVI™ thinker strives for decisions that are well-rounded, stable, and consid-erate of multiple dimensions, making them natural integrators who seek balanced, sustainable outcomes rather than quick wins or one-sided solutions.

When a squarish CVI™ profile goes "dark," their normally balanced, integrative decision-making style becomes conflicted, stalled, and internally chaotic. Because they naturally draw from all four value energies, they usually make decisions by blending action, logic, relationships, and data. But under stress, those energies stop cooperating and begin competing. Instead of harmony, they experience internal tug-of-war. The *Builder* part of them may push for quick action, while the *Banker* part demands more information. The *Merchant* side may worry about how people will feel, while the *Innovator* side insists on analyzing the problem further. This creates a loop where every internal voice cancels out the others, leading to indecision, frustration, or second-guessing. In this dark state, they may become unusually hesitant, overwhelmed by the fear of choosing "wrong" because no single value energy feels strong enough to take the lead. They might also swing unpredictably between extremes, acting impulsively one moment, then freezing the next, over-accommodating people, then abruptly withdrawing, over-analyzing details, then ignoring them entirely. Their natural contribution (seeing all sides) turns into a burden as they become hyperaware of every possible consequence, risk, or emotional ripple. Factors that normally help them stay balanced, like gathering input or weighing multiple perspectives, can backfire and amplify their confusion. Ultimately, a squarish profile in the dark looks like someone stuck between competing internal priorities, unable to find clarity because the very contributions that make them adaptable become sources of internal conflict rather than alignment.

When interacting with a squarish individual, the most effective approach is to help them create clarity by organizing the many internal voices they naturally juggle. Because they take into account action, people, logic, and data; they feel most supported when others acknowledge the full range of their concerns rather than pushing them toward a single perspective. Speaking to them in a balanced, structured way can be grounding. Phrases like "Let's look at this from all angles," "Here's the information we know so far," or "These are the practical steps we can take next," help them feel that each part of their internal process is being respected. They also appreciate when someone names the tension they may be feeling, "It makes sense that you're weighing several priorities here," because it reassures them that their complexity is normal, not a flaw. Actions that help include summarizing options clearly, outlining pros and cons without pressure, and giving them space to reflect without rushing them toward a decision. They feel comfort when they see that emotional impacts (*Merchant*), logical structure (*Innovator*), reliable information (*Banker*), and actionable steps (*Builder*) have all been addressed. Ultimately, a squarish individual gains confidence when they sense that the decision has been explored thoroughly yet efficiently, that no major dimension has been ignored, and that they have the time and clarity needed to integrate their many closely measured core values into a choice that feels balanced and authentic.

Competing Contribution Types™

When someone has a CVI™ profile made up of opposite and closely scored Contribution Types™ such as *Builder/Banker* or *Merchant/Innovator*, their decision-making process becomes a blend of contrasting motivations that must coexist, negotiate, and sometimes compete with one another. A *Builder/Banker*, for example, weighs both speed and certainty. The *Builder* side wants decisive action and clear direction, while the *Banker* side demands thorough information, risk assessment, and accuracy. This creates a thought process where they highly consider efficiency, control, and tangible results, but only when supported by solid data and well-documented reasoning. Emotional factors, group consensus, or open-ended brainstorming tend to fall lower on their list. A *Merchant/Innovator*, by contrast, blends relational intuition with analytical problem-solving. They care deeply about how decisions affect people and long-term vision (*Merchant*), while also scrutinizing logic, structure, and root-cause solutions (*Innovator*). They highly consider harmony, future potential, and elegant solutions, but may deprioritize rigid rules, excessive caution, or decisions that feel purely transactional. A *Builder/Merchant* profile mixes drive and connection. They want to move quickly and decisively, but they also care about how their choices impact relationships and morale. They prioritize momentum, trust, and shared purpose, while placing less weight on deep analysis or exhaustive data. Meanwhile, a *Banker/Innovator* profile blends precision with insight. They want decisions grounded in facts, patterns, and well-reasoned logic, valuing accuracy and elegant problem-solving above all. They tend to deprioritize emotional considerations, speed, or decisions based on intuition alone. A *Builder/Innovator* weighs speed and action against analysis and structural clarity. They want to move quickly and decisively, but only when the solution feels smart, efficient, and well-designed. They highly consider practicality, logic, and forward momentum, yet they tend to place less emphasis on emotional nuance or lengthy consensus-building. A *Merchant/Banker*, on the other hand, blends relational awareness with a strong need for accuracy and reliability. They care deeply about how decisions affect people and long-term trust, while also wanting to ensure the facts are correct and the risks are well understood. They highly consider harmony, stability, and documented information, but may deprioritize rapid action or purely theoretical problem-solving. Across pairings, the tension between their opposing energies shapes a decision-making process that is thoughtful, layered, and often more complex than it appears on the surface, with each side influencing what they prioritize and what naturally falls lower on their list.

Figure 6. Decision Making Overview

Closing Thoughts on Decision Making

Across all the CVI™ profiles and combinations we explored, a clear theme emerges. Every core value and Contribution Type™ brings a distinct lens to decision-making, and understanding those lenses is the key to communicating effectively and supporting others in moments of clarity or stress. *Builders* prioritize action, direction, and momentum. *Merchants* focus on relationships, intuition, and long-term harmony. *Innovators* seek logic, elegant solutions, and root-cause understanding. *Bankers* value accuracy, stability, and well-supported information. When these energies pair, whether in opposite combinations like *Builder/Banker* or *Merchant/Innovator*, or in balanced "squarish" profiles, the internal dialogue becomes more complex, creating tension when priorities conflict. In their natural states, each type contributes clarity, purpose, and unique contributions to decision-making. When dark, those same core values can distort into rigidity, indecision, emotional overwhelm, or over-control. What consistently helps across all profiles is communication that honors their core motivations: clarity and efficiency for *Builders*, empathy and vision for *Merchants*, logic and process for *Innovators*, and accuracy and structure for *Bankers*. Squarish individuals benefit from balanced, organized conversations that acknowledge all angles. Ultimately, the heart of effective interaction lies in recognizing what each profile values most and what they tend to overlook so decisions can be made with confidence, alignment, and respect for the diverse ways people naturally think and contribute.

CHAPTER 12
COMMUNICATION

ommunication is far more complex than simply exchanging words. It's a blend of personal preference, perception, and presentation that shapes how messages are received. People communicate in countless ways. Some rely on direct, concise language, while others prefer storytelling, emotional nuance, or visual cues to express their ideas. At the same time, listeners aren't just absorbing content. They're tuning in to tone, pacing, body language, confidence, and even the speaker's intent. Many people listen for clarity, credibility, empathy, or shared values, and these elements can dramatically influence how a message lands. A single speech can be interpreted in completely different ways depending on factors like the speaker's delivery style, the structure of the information, the emotional energy behind the words, and the listener's own expectations or experiences. When a message is presented with warmth and authenticity, it may be seen as inspiring, while the same message delivered in a rushed or monotone manner might feel unconvincing or detached. Ultimately, communication is a dynamic interaction where how something is said can matter just as much, if not more, than what is said, shaping the listener's understanding, trust, and overall impression.

The CVI™ offers a powerful lens for understanding why people communicate the way they do, because it identifies the innate, unchanging drivers: *Merchant, Innovator, Banker,* and *Builder* that shape how individuals process information, express themselves, and interpret the world. When you look at communication through this framework, it becomes clear that both the speaker and the listener are guided by their hardwiring long before they consciously choose their words. A *Builder*-driven speaker may communicate with directness and urgency, while a *Merchant*-oriented listener may be tuning in for emotional connection and shared values. An *Innovator* might craft messages rich with nuance and problem-solving logic, yet a *Banker* listener may be evaluating the precision, accuracy, and structure of the information instead. These mismatches explain why the same message can land as inspiring to one person and confusing or unconvincing to another. This dynamic is so influential that it inspired the idea of *The Human Cheat Code*™: the realization that everything we do and receive is not taken in or randomly done but deeply tied to our CVI™ profile. Once you understand the hardwired patterns driving communication on both sides of the conversation, you begin to see that effective communication isn't just about crafting the right message, it's about speaking in a way that resonates with the listener's core values and decoding how their wiring shapes what they hear, prioritize, and respond to.

Merchants

When you're communicating with a *Merchant*, the key is understanding that they listen through the lens of connection, purpose, and relationship. Their core value is rooted in people, how they feel, how they're treated, and how they're inspired, so they naturally tune in to messages that reinforce trust, collaboration, and shared meaning. Although the CVI™ framework doesn't provide a script, it consistently shows that *Merchants* want communication that feels sincere, human, and aligned with a bigger mission. They want to hear that their presence and the presence of others matter, that relationships are valued, and that the work being done has emotional or social impact. They respond best when the message acknowledges the heart behind the effort, not just the effort itself. To communicate effectively with a *Merchant*, it helps to include elements such as:

- A clear sense of shared purpose or mission
- Appreciation for who they are and how they contribute
- Stories or examples that highlight human impact or emotional meaning
- An optimistic, inspiring vision of what is possible together

Examples of *Merchant*-friendly communication include statements like, "Your influence made a real difference," "We achieved this because of our efforts together," "Here's how people were positively impacted," "We're building something meaningful together," and "Your insight and presence matter." When these elements are present, *Merchants* feel energized, valued, and motivated. When they're missing, the message can feel cold, transactional, or disconnected from what matters most to them. Understanding this hardwiring makes it clear why tailoring communication to a *Merchant's* core values isn't just helpful, it's essential for creating alignment, engagement, and genuine connection.

When meeting with a *Merchant* leader, it's essential to let them know from the very beginning all the people involved. Who contributed, how they collaborated, and the relationships that made the effort possible. *Merchants* are naturally drawn to stories of teamwork, shared purpose, collective commitment, and for tasks, people they trust who were involved in the process. Opening with acknowledgment of the group's effort immediately aligns with what they value most. If the path forward was agreed upon by all participants, highlight that unity and emphasize the sense of partnership that shaped the decision. If there wasn't full agreement, don't gloss over it. Instead, acknowledge the differing perspectives with respect and transparency. A *Merchant*-aligned way forward in moments of disagreement is to reaffirm the shared mission, emphasize the importance of maintaining trust, and propose a collaborative next step. Something like bringing the group together again if time permits, an effort to explore common ground, ensured everyone felt heard, valued, and included in shaping the solution moving forward. Having every voice heard and valued is important even if a perspective doesn't move forward in the effort. Don't fall into the common trap of telling the leader that having 100% buy-in before moving forward is necessary if the group is awaiting the next step after the leader's approval.

Innovators

When communicating with an *Innovator*, the key is recognizing that they listen for logic, clarity, problem-solving structure, and the underlying "why" behind any message. Their core value is rooted in wisdom, which means they naturally gravitate toward communication that is thoughtful, well-reasoned, and intellectually coherent. The broader CVI™ framework consistently shows that *Innovators* want to hear information that is organized, purposeful, and grounded in a clear understanding of how things work. They appreciate when a speaker demonstrates that they've considered multiple angles, anticipated challenges, and crafted a solution that makes sense both practically and conceptually. *Innovators* also listen for efficiency. Messages that avoid fluff, emotional excess, or unnecessary repetition and they respond best when communication respects their need for autonomy and their desire to improve systems, processes, or outcomes. To communicate effectively with an *Innovator*, it helps to include elements such as:

- A clear explanation of the problem or situation
- The reasoning behind decisions or recommendations
- Evidence that multiple options were considered
- A logical path forward that solves the root issue
- Opportunities for them to refine, improve, or optimize

Examples of *Innovator*-friendly communication include statements like, "Here's the core issue we're solving," "These were the options we evaluated and why this one makes the most sense," "Here's the logic behind the approach," "I'd value your insight on how to improve this," and "This solution addresses both the immediate need and the long-term impact." When these elements are present, *Innovators* feel engaged and intellectually stimulated. When they're missing, they may view the message as shallow, incomplete, or lacking strategic thought. Understanding this hardwiring makes it clear why tailoring communication to an *Innovator's* core values is essential. They want to hear the logic, the structure, and the deeper reasoning that allows them to fully grasp the situation and contribute meaningfully.

When meeting with an *Innovator*, the best way to draw them in from the beginning is to immediately establish clarity, logic, and purpose, because these are the elements that signal the conversation will align with what they value most. *Innovators* feel grounded when they understand the core problem being addressed, the reasoning behind the effort, and the structure guiding the discussion. They want to know why the work matters, how the team approached it, and what assumptions or constraints shaped the decisions. Giving them comfort means demonstrating that the effort is thoughtful, well-designed, and aimed at solving a meaningful issue rather than just checking a box. *Innovators* appreciate communication that highlights the analytical process, the options considered, and the rationale behind the chosen direction. Examples of what resonates with them include statements like, "Here's the root issue we're solving," "These were the three approaches we evaluated and why this one is strongest," "Here's the logic behind our recommendation," "We identified a pattern that helped shape our solution," "This approach reduces long-term risk and increases efficiency," and "We'd value your insight on how to refine this further." When communication starts with structure, reasoning, and a clear path forward, *Innovators* feel respected, engaged, and confident that the effort aligns with their core value of wisdom and their desire to improve systems in meaningful, sustainable ways.

Bankers

When communicating with a *Banker*, the most important thing to remember is that they listen for accuracy, clarity, and factual grounding above all else. Their core value is knowledge, which means they want information that is complete, precise, and supported by evidence. The broader CVI™ framework makes it clear that *Bankers* feel most confident when a message is structured, detailed, and free of ambiguity. They want to hear the data behind decisions, the historical context, the risks, and the safeguards. They value communication that is methodical and well-researched, and they are quick to notice gaps, inconsistencies, or missing details. To communicate effectively with a *Banker*, it helps to include elements such as:

- Clear, accurate facts and verified information
- Historical data or past performance that supports message
- Well-defined terms, timelines, and expectations
- Risks, constraints, and the rationale behind decisions
- Documentation, references, or evidence

Examples of *Banker*-friendly communication include statements like, "Here are the numbers that support this conclusion," "Based on the data from the last three quarters, here's the trend we're seeing," "These are the risks we identified and how we plan to mitigate them," "Here is the documented process we followed," and "This recommendation is based on verified information from multiple sources." When these elements are present, *Bankers* feel grounded, respected, and confident in the message. When they're missing, they may view the communication as incomplete, unreliable, or lacking credibility. Understanding this hardwiring is essential because *Bankers* don't just want information; they want accurate, complete, and well-supported information that allows them to trust the message and make sound decisions.

Builders

When communicating with a *Builder*, the most important thing to remember is that they listen for action, clarity, and forward momentum, because their core value (Power) is expressed through getting things done and driving results. *Builders* want communication that is direct, purposeful, and free of unnecessary detail. *Builders* thrive when they hear what needs to happen, why it matters, and how quickly progress can be made. They want to know the objective, the obstacles, and the specific actions required to move forward. *Builders* also value confidence and decisiveness in communication. They want to feel that the speaker understands the situation and is ready to take action rather than theorize. To communicate effectively with a *Builder*, it helps to include elements such as:

- A clear statement of the goal or desired outcome
- The immediate actions required and who is responsible
- The timeline or urgency associated with the work
- The obstacles or challenges that must be addressed
- The expected impact or result once the work is completed

Examples of *Builder*-friendly communication include statements like, "Here's the objective and what we need to do next," "These are the three steps that will move us forward," "Your leadership is needed to remove this roadblock," "This action will get us most of the way there," and "Once we complete this phase, we can begin implementation." When these elements are present, *Builders* feel energized and ready to act. When they're missing, they may view the communication as vague, inefficient, or lacking direction. Understanding this makes it clear why tailoring communication to a *Builder's* core values is essential. They want to hear what needs to be done, how to do it, and how quickly they can move toward meaningful results.

When meeting with a *Builder*, the best way to draw them in from the beginning is to immediately establish clarity, direction, and action; the elements that signal the conversation will align with what they value most. *Builders* feel grounded when they know exactly what the goal is, what needs to happen next, and how their involvement will move things forward. They want to hear the purpose of the effort stated plainly, the obstacles that stand in the way, and the concrete steps required to achieve results. Giving them comfort means demonstrating that the work is practical, relevant, and ready for execution rather than theoretical or overly conceptual. *Builders* appreciate communication that is direct, confident, and focused on outcomes rather than emotions or abstract ideas. Examples of what resonates with them include statements like, "Here's the objective and what we need to do first," "These are the immediate actions that will create momentum," "We need your leadership on this effort," "This step will get us most of the way there," "Once we complete this action, we can move directly into implementation," and "Here's the timeline we're working against and why it matters." When communication begins with purpose, action, and a clear path forward, *Builders* feel energized and confident that the effort aligns with their core value of power, turning intention into meaningful, tangible results.

Squarish CVI™ Profiles

A "squarish" CVI™ profile listens for a unique blend of elements when information is communicated to them. Squarish CVI™ profiles draw meaning, motivation, and clarity from all four value energies rather than leaning heavily on just one or two. Because of this, a squarish profile wants communication that is well-rounded, structured, relational, logical, actionable, and evidence-based. They want to hear that the work has purpose (*Merchant*), that the reasoning is sound (*Innovator*), that the facts are accurate (*Banker*), and that the path forward is clear and doable (*Builder*). They feel most comfortable when communication honors each of these dimensions rather than over-favoring one. To communicate effectively with a squarish CVI™ profile, it helps to include elements such as:

- A clear purpose or "why" behind the effort
- Logical reasoning that explains how decisions were made
- Accurate facts, data, or evidence supporting the message
- Action steps, responsibilities, and next-move clarity
- Acknowledgment of the people involved and the relationships that made progress possible

Examples of communication that resonates with a squarish profile include statements like, "Here's the purpose behind this effort and why it matters," "These were the options we evaluated and the logic behind our choice," "Here are the key data points that support this direction," "These are the next steps and who will take them," and "This progress was possible because of the collaboration across the team." When these elements are present, a squarish individual feels balanced, respected, and fully informed. When they're missing, they may feel that the message is lopsided, too emotional, too vague, too data-heavy, or too theoretical. Understanding this profile is powerful because it reminds us that some people don't just listen through one lens, they listen through all four, and communication must reflect that breadth to truly connect.

Communication Trick

The bigger the audience, the more diverse the core values are in the room, and the less likely you are to know each person's CVI™ profile. That's why tailoring communication that touches every core value is essential when speaking to a large group of people. A message that touches on all four core values ensures that everyone hears something that resonates with them:

- Emotional connection and shared purpose for *Merchants*
- Logic and conceptual clarity for *Innovators*
- Accuracy and detail for *Bankers*
- Action and direction for *Builders*

When communication is balanced in this way, it feels complete, inclusive, and grounded. It avoids the pitfalls of leaning too heavily into one value at the expense of others, and it creates a sense of alignment across a wide range of listeners. In essence, speaking to all four core values is speaking to everyone and doing so increases the likelihood that your message will be understood, appreciated, and acted upon.

As discussed in Chapter 5, every effective process naturally flows through the sequence of *Merchant → Innovator → Banker → Builder*, and a well-crafted speech should follow this same rhythm. You would begin with the *Merchant* energy by opening with a story about the vision of the effort, the people involved, the relationships that made progress possible, and the shared purpose driving the work. Then you transition into *Innovator* energy by explaining the core problem, the insights gained, and the reasoning behind the chosen direction. Next, you shift into *Banker* energy by presenting the data, the evidence, the historical context, and the risks that were evaluated. Finally, you land in *Builder* energy by outlining the next steps, the actions required, and the clear path forward. A speech following this flow might sound like this:

"We came together this year wanting to be the innovation leader in our industry and from across our organization, people came together in ways that strengthened our relationships and together, put us on a path to achieve our goal. As we looked at the challenges we faced, we explored several approaches and identified the one that would create the most sustainable impact and change the way we do business forever. The data we collected shows a positive glide slope, and our analysis confirms that this direction is both sound and achievable and will allow us to be the industry leader in the next couple of years. Now here's what we're going to do next, and how we'll execute it together."

You would of course put more details into the speech above for each core value area but the idea is that this structure ensures that every core value is honored and every listener finds a point of connection.

Some may initially view this approach as manipulation, but in reality, it is the opposite. Most issues in organizations (and in relationships) stem from miscommunication, and much of that miscommunication is filtered through the lens of an individual's CVI™ profile. People don't just hear words, they interpret them through their CVI™ wiring…their natural way of processing the world. Speaking in a way that intentionally reaches past those biases isn't about controlling people, it's about creating clarity, reducing misunderstanding, and ensuring that everyone has equal access to the message. When we communicate in ways that honor all four core values, we build bridges instead of barriers, and we create the conditions for alignment, trust, and meaningful progress. This is how relationships are strengthened, great teams function, how strong cultures are built, and how extraordinary outcomes become possible.

Figure 7. Communication Overview

Closing Thoughts on Communication

Communication is never just about the words we choose, it is an expression of our wiring, our values, and the way we naturally interpret the world. The CVI™ reveals why people speak, listen, and respond so differently, and it gives us a practical framework for understanding those differences with clarity instead of frustration. *Merchants* listen for connection and purpose, *Innovators* listen for logic and structure, *Bankers* listen for accuracy and completeness, *Builders* listen for action and direction, and *Squarish* profiles listen for a balanced blend of all four. When we tailor our communication to honor these core values, messages land more clearly, trust grows, and collaboration becomes easier. The *Human Cheat Code*™ concept reminds us that none of this is random. Every reaction, every misunderstanding, and every moment of alignment is shaped by our innate wiring. And when speaking to groups, the most effective approach is to intentionally touch all four energies, following the natural flow of *Merchant* → *Innovator* → *Banker* → *Builder* so every listener finds a point of connection. The key takeaway is simple but transformative: communication becomes powerful, inclusive, and effective when we stop speaking from our own wiring alone and start speaking to the wiring of the people we're trying to reach.

CHAPTER 13
CONFLICT MANAGEMENT

onflict management recognizes, addresses, and resolves disagreements in ways that strengthen rather than damage relationships. People tend to approach conflict in a variety of ways, some take an avoidant route, stepping back to keep the peace even if important issues go unaddressed. Others adopt a competitive stance, pushing hard for their own viewpoint. Some prefer accommodation, prioritizing harmony by yielding to others. Many try compromise, where each side gives up something to reach middle ground. Typically, the most constructive approach is collaboration, where people work together to find a solution that meets the needs of all involved. Understanding these styles matters because the way you handle conflict directly shapes the tone and effectiveness of your relationships. When you deal with conflict in healthy, intentional ways: listening actively, expressing your needs clearly, and seeking solutions rather than victories, you create an environment of trust and psychological safety. This doesn't just improve one-on-one interactions, it strengthens team dynamics by reducing tension, encouraging open communication, and helping groups move through challenges with resilience and respect.

The CVI™ describes how people's deepest motivational drivers shape how they respond to conflict, and each core value brings its own contributions and blind spots to tense situations. *Builders*, driven by power and action, tend to confront conflict head-on. They prefer clear decisions, quick resolutions, and direct communication, sometimes pushing for control when stress rises. *Innovators*, motivated by wisdom and problem-solving, approach conflict analytically. They step back, gather information, and look for logical, well-designed solutions, though they may appear detached or slow to engage emotionally. *Bankers*, grounded in knowledge and stability, handle conflict by seeking clarity, structure, and predictability. They want all the facts before responding and may withdraw until they feel secure enough to re-enter the conversation. *Merchants*, fueled by love and connection, focus on preserving relationships. They try to understand everyone's feelings, build harmony, and find win-win outcomes, but may avoid necessary confrontation to keep the peace. Together, these approaches show that conflict isn't just about the issue at hand, it's about how people's core motivations shape their reactions. Understanding these patterns helps relationships and teams appreciate each other's instincts and navigate disagreements with more empathy and effectiveness.

Merchant

Merchants tend to handle conflict with a strong emphasis on connection, empathy, and preserving relationships, which often makes them the emotional glue in teams. When tension arises, they instinctively try to understand everyone's feelings and motivations, looking for solutions that allow all parties to feel heard and valued. This relational approach can diffuse hostility quickly. Think of a team meeting where two colleagues are arguing over project priorities, and the *Merchant* steps in to acknowledge each person's concerns, reframe the disagreement in a positive light, and guide the group toward a collaborative compromise. In customer-facing roles, this contribution is especially powerful. For example, a *Merchant* salesperson might calm an upset client by validating their frustration, expressing genuine care, and working together to find a mutually satisfying path forward. Their natural ability to build trust and restore harmony makes them invaluable during emotionally charged moments.

However, the *Merchant's* desire to maintain harmony can also create challenges. Because they dislike confrontation and fear damaging relationships, they may avoid addressing issues directly or delay difficult conversations. This can lead to unresolved problems simmering beneath the surface such as a *Merchant* manager who notices a team member repeatedly missing deadlines but hesitates to address it, hoping the issue will resolve itself. In group settings, their tendency to prioritize feelings over facts can slow decision-making, especially when tough trade-offs are required. For example, during a budget-cutting discussion, a *Merchant* might struggle to support necessary reductions if they worry someone will feel undervalued or excluded. Their conflict-avoidant tendencies can unintentionally create confusion or frustration for others who prefer direct, timely resolution.

When conflict arises, a *Merchant's* internal dialogue often sounds like, "Why is this happening? Did I do something wrong? How can I bring everyone back together?" or "If I can just get them to see how this affects the relationship (or team), we can fix it." They instinctively look for common ground, try to soothe tension, and want everyone involved to feel heard and valued. But when a *Merchant* goes "dark," their conflict style can shift dramatically. Instead of leaning into empathy, they may become overly emotional, passive-aggressive, or manipulative in subtle ways. For example, a dark *Merchant* might withdraw affection or communication to signal displeasure, hoping others will notice and repair the relationship for them. They might say things like, "I guess it doesn't matter how I feel," using guilt as a tool rather than direct communication. They may triangulate (bringing in a third party to validate their feelings instead of addressing the issue directly). They might catastrophize the situation, thinking, "This relationship is falling apart," even if the conflict is minor. In darker moments, they can become overly idealistic and disappointed when others don't meet their emotional expectations, leading them to lash out with moral judgment or emotional intensity. They may over-personalize neutral comments, assume negative intent, or try to "fix" the other person rather than address the actual issue. A dark *Merchant* might also avoid conflict entirely, smiling on the surface while internally stewing, then later exploding in an emotional outburst that feels disproportionate to the original problem. In short, when healthy, *Merchants* bring warmth, connection, and understanding to conflict. When dark, they can become reactive, guilt-driven, indirect, and emotionally volatile, still trying to protect the relationship, but doing so in ways that often make the conflict worse.

To avoid unnecessary conflict with a *Merchant,* individuals should approach them with openness, warmth, and respect for their relational focus. *Merchants* respond best when others communicate with sincerity and avoid abrupt or overly blunt language. Providing context, expressing appreciation, and showing that you value the relationship helps prevent misunderstandings, for instance, starting a conversation with "I really appreciate how much you care about the team, and I want to work through something together" sets the right tone. If conflict does occur, the quickest way to get back on task is to reestablish an emotional connection. Acknowledge their feelings, reaffirm shared goals, and invite collaboration. For example, if a disagreement derails a planning session, you might say, "I know we both want this project to succeed. Let's figure out a solution that works for both of us." Once the *Merchant* feels the relationship is intact, they can reengage productively and help guide the group toward a cooperative resolution.

Innovator

Innovators tend to handle conflict with a calm, analytical mindset that brings clarity and structure to emotionally charged situations. Their instinct is to step back, gather information, and understand the problem from every angle before reacting. This makes them excellent at de-escalating conflict by removing emotional heat and focusing on logic and long-term solutions. For example, if a team is arguing about the best approach to a new product launch, an *Innovator* might pause the discussion, outline the key variables on a whiteboard, and guide the group toward a logic-driven decision that satisfies the core objectives. In a family setting, an *Innovator* might respond to a disagreement about finances by reviewing the budget, identifying patterns, and proposing a practical plan that reduces stress for everyone. Their ability to stay composed and think strategically often leads to solutions that others might overlook in the moment.

The downside of the *Innovator's* conflict style is that their analytical detachment can sometimes be misinterpreted as aloofness, indecision, or emotional distance. Because they prefer to process internally and avoid rushed decisions, they may withdraw from conflict or delay addressing it until they feel fully prepared. This can frustrate people who want immediate engagement or emotional validation. For instance, in a workplace disagreement about workload distribution, an *Innovator* might ask for time to "think it through," leaving colleagues feeling unheard or dismissed. In personal relationships, a partner might express hurt feelings, only to receive a series of questions from the *Innovator* aimed at understanding the situation rather than offering immediate empathy. Their focus on logic over emotion can unintentionally escalate tension when others interpret their calmness as a lack of concern.

Innovators approach conflict with a calm, analytical mindset, often stepping back to observe the situation before engaging. Their internal monologue might sound like, "What's the real problem here? What's the most elegant solution? How can I fix this without unnecessary emotion?" They tend to value clarity, logic, and efficiency, so they prefer to de-escalate tension by breaking issues down into solvable components. *Innovators* often try to remove emotional noise from the conversation, focusing instead on root causes and long-term solutions. But when an *Innovator* goes "dark," their conflict style can shift into something far more detached, cold, or even condescending. In this state, they may think, "This is irrational. Why can't they just be logical? I'm wasting my time," or "If they can't follow my reasoning, that's their problem." A dark *Innovator* might withdraw completely, shutting down communication and retreating into silence as a way to avoid emotional intensity. They may become hyper-critical, nitpicking details to assert control or superiority. They might weaponize logic, using it to invalidate others' feelings or to "win" the argument rather than resolve it. They can become dismissive, saying things like, "This isn't worth discussing," or "You're overreacting," which can escalate conflict rather than calm it. In darker moments, they may appear aloof or uncaring, prioritizing efficiency over empathy and leaving others feeling unheard. They might also procrastinate on addressing the conflict, hoping it will resolve itself, or they may mentally check out while pretending to engage. Some dark *Innovators* become subtly passive-aggressive, responding with clipped answers, sarcasm, or intellectual superiority. Others may double down on perfectionism, insisting that their solution is the only "correct" one. Ultimately, while healthy *Innovators* bring clarity, insight, and problem-solving to conflict, their dark side can manifest as emotional detachment, intellectual arrogance, avoidance, and a rigid insistence on logic at the expense of human connection.

To avoid unnecessary conflict with an *Innovator*, it helps to approach them with clarity, structure, and respect for their need to think before responding. They appreciate when others present issues logically, avoid emotional exaggeration, and give them space to analyze without pressure. For example, instead of confronting an *Innovator* with "You never listen to me," a more effective approach would be, "I'd like to talk through something that's been affecting our workflow. Can we walk through it together?" If conflict does arise, the best way to get back on task is to reestablish a shared problem-solving mindset. Acknowledge their need for thoughtful analysis and invite them to help design a solution, "I know you think deeply about these issues. Can we map out the key points so we can move forward?" Once the *Innovator* feels the conversation has returned to logic, clarity, and purpose, they reengage quickly and can help steer the relationship or group toward a well-reasoned, sustainable resolution.

Banker

Bankers handle conflict with a steady, methodical approach that brings structure and clarity to situations that might otherwise feel chaotic. Their instinct is to gather all relevant information, verify facts, and ensure that decisions are grounded in accuracy rather than emotion or impulse. This makes them incredibly valuable during disagreements that require precision such as a workplace dispute over budget discrepancies, where a *Banker* might calmly pull financial records, highlight inconsistencies, and guide the team toward a data-supported resolution. In family settings, if siblings argue about how to divide household responsibilities, a *Banker* might create a clear schedule or checklist to ensure fairness and prevent future misunderstandings. Their commitment to thoroughness and stability often prevents conflicts from escalating and helps groups make well-informed decisions.

The downside of the *Banker's* conflict style is that their need for certainty and complete information can slow down resolution or create frustration for others who want quicker engagement. Because they prefer to retreat and analyze before responding, they may withdraw from conflict or appear unresponsive when emotions are high. For example, if a team member confronts a *Banker* about a missed deadline, the *Banker* might immediately start reviewing emails and documents rather than addressing the emotional tension in the moment, which can make the other person feel dismissed. In personal relationships, a partner expressing hurt feelings may feel unheard when the *Banker* responds with factual corrections instead of empathy. Their focus on accuracy can unintentionally come across as nitpicking or rigidity, especially when others are looking for reassurance or emotional connection rather than detailed explanations.

Bankers tend to handle conflict through structure, facts, and a desire for stability, because their core drive is to preserve order and ensure that decisions are grounded in reliable information. When conflict arises, a *Banker's* internal thoughts often sound like, "What are the facts? What actually happened? Let's slow down and make sure we're not missing anything," or "If everyone would just follow the process, we wouldn't be in this situation." They prefer calm, methodical conversations and often try to de-escalate tension by clarifying details, reviewing past patterns, or establishing clear expectations. They want to understand the root cause before taking action, and they dislike emotional volatility or impulsive reactions. But when a *Banker* goes "dark," their conflict style can shift into rigidity, judgment, and withdrawal. In this state, their thoughts may turn into, "This is chaotic. I can't trust these people," or "If they won't follow the rules, then I'm done trying." A dark *Banker* might shut down communication entirely, retreating into silence as a way to regain control. They may become hyper-critical, pointing out every flaw or inconsistency in the other person's argument. They might weaponize rules or policies, insisting on strict adherence even when flexibility would help. They can become stubborn, refusing to compromise because they believe their way is the only "correct" or "safe" option. Some dark *Bankers* become passive-aggressive, dragging their feet, withholding information, or quietly sabotaging progress or a person to prove a point. Others may retreat into data and documentation, burying themselves in details to avoid emotional engagement. They might say things like, "That's not my responsibility," or "Show me proof," even when the issue is relational rather than factual. In their darkest moments, *Bankers* can become pessimistic, assuming the worst about others' intentions, or they may cling to past grievances as evidence that the current conflict is part of a larger pattern of unreliability. When healthy, *Bankers* bring stability, clarity, and thoughtful analysis to conflict. When dark, they can become rigid, distant, overly cautious, and emotionally unavailable, trying to protect themselves through control, but often making the conflict feel colder and harder to resolve.

To avoid unnecessary conflict with a *Banker*, individuals should approach them with clarity, preparation, and respect for their need for accurate information. *Bankers* respond best when others present issues calmly, avoid emotional exaggeration, and provide concrete details. For example, instead of saying, "You never communicate," a more effective approach would be, "I noticed we missed two key updates last week. Can we review how we're sharing information?" If conflict does occur, the quickest way to get back on task is to reestablish a sense of structure and predictability. Acknowledge their need for facts and invite them to help organize the path forward, "Let's outline the steps we need to take so we can move ahead." In a real-world scenario, say a project meeting derails due to miscommunication, resetting with a shared checklist or timeline can help the *Banker* reengage and contribute. Once they feel the situation is grounded in clarity and order, they return to being a stabilizing force who helps the team move forward with confidence.

Builder

Builders approach conflict with directness, decisiveness, and a strong drive to take action, which often brings clarity and momentum to situations that might otherwise stall. When tension arises, they prefer to address it immediately rather than let issues linger, and their straightforward communication style can cut through confusion quickly. For example, if a project team is stuck debating priorities, a *Builder* might step in, outline the top objective, assign responsibilities, and get everyone moving again. In a family setting, if siblings argue about weekend plans, the *Builder* might quickly propose a plan, set a timeline, and ensure everyone knows what needs to happen next. Their confidence and willingness to take charge can stabilize a group and prevent conflicts from spiraling into unproductive territory.

The downside of the *Builder's* conflict style is that their intensity and directness can sometimes feel overwhelming to others, especially those who prefer a more collaborative or reflective approach. *Builders* may push for quick decisions before others feel ready, or they may unintentionally dominate conversations, leaving quieter voices unheard. For instance, in a workplace disagreement about resource allocation, a *Builder* might insist on their preferred solution without fully considering alternative viewpoints, causing teammates to feel dismissed or pressured. In personal relationships, a partner might express a concern gently, only to receive a blunt, solution-focused response that feels abrupt or insensitive. Their desire for efficiency and control can escalate conflict if others interpret their assertiveness as aggression or impatience.

Builders tend to handle conflict with directness, decisiveness, and a strong bias toward action, because their core drive is to get things done and remove obstacles that slow progress. When conflict arises, a *Builder's* internal thoughts often sound like, "What's the quickest way to fix this?" or "Why are we still talking about this instead of doing something?" They prefer straightforward communication, clear expectations, and practical solutions. *Builders* don't enjoy long emotional discussions or theoretical debates, they want clarity, commitment, and movement. They often step into a leadership role during conflict, taking charge and pushing for resolution so the team can get back to work. But when a *Builder* goes "dark," their conflict style can shift into forcefulness, impatience, and control. In this state, their thoughts may turn into, "This is a waste of time," or "If they won't step up, I'll just take over," or even "I'm done dealing with incompetence." A dark *Builder* might bulldoze the conversation, interrupt others or shutting them down to push their own solution through. They may become blunt to the point of harshness, using statements like, "Just do it," or "This isn't complicated," without considering how their tone lands. They can become domineering, insisting that their way is the only efficient path forward. Some dark *Builders* become visibly irritated, crossed arms, clipped responses, or a sharp edge in their voice. Others may escalate the conflict by issuing ultimatums, withdrawing cooperation, or taking unilateral action without consulting anyone. They might dismiss others' feelings as irrelevant, saying things like, "We don't have time for this," or "Stop being so sensitive." In darker moments, they may micromanage, criticize effort, or label others as weak or unreliable. They can also become reactive, making snap decisions just to end the discomfort of the conflict, even if those decisions aren't well-considered. When healthy, *Builders* bring clarity, momentum, and courage to conflict. When dark, they can become intimidating, impatient, and overly forceful, trying to regain control through sheer willpower, often leaving others feeling steamrolled rather than supported.

To avoid unnecessary conflict with a *Builder*, individuals should communicate clearly, concisely, and with a sense of purpose. *Builders* appreciate when others get to the point, avoid excessive emotional buildup, and demonstrate confidence in their own perspective. For example, instead of saying, "I'm not sure how I feel about this project direction," a more effective approach would be, "Here's the specific concern I have, and here's what I propose." If conflict does occur, the best way to get back on task is to acknowledge the *Builder's* need for action and offer a concrete path forward. You might say, "I hear that you want to move quickly. Let's agree on the next two steps so we can keep things moving." In a real-world scenario, say a heated debate during a team meeting. Resetting with a clear agenda or decision point can help the *Builder* reengage productively. Once they see a structured plan and a path toward progress, they shift out of conflict mode and back into their natural contribution: driving results.

Squarish CVI™ Profiles

A "squarish" CVI™ profile tends to handle conflict with a blend of emotion, decisiveness, structure, and practicality, which can be incredibly effective in high-pressure situations. They bring the *Builder's* directness and action orientation together with the *Banker's* need for accuracy and stability, allowing them to cut through confusion while keeping decisions grounded in facts. In a workplace disagreement about project deadlines, for example, a squarish individual might quickly gather the relevant data, identify the bottleneck, and assign clear next steps to keep the team moving. In a family setting, if there's conflict about household responsibilities, they might create a simple, efficient system, like a rotating chore chart, to eliminate ambiguity and prevent future disputes. Their ability to combine speed with structure often leads to swift, well-reasoned resolutions.

The downside of a squarish conflict style is that their intensity and focus on correctness can sometimes overshadow emotional nuance. Because they value efficiency and factual clarity, they may come across as rigid, blunt, or dismissive of feelings, especially when others need empathy or time to process. For instance, during a team conflict about workload fairness, a squarish person might respond with, "Here's what the numbers say, so this is what we're doing," unintentionally shutting down colleagues who feel overwhelmed or unheard. In personal relationships, a partner expressing frustration might receive a solution-oriented response rather than emotional validation, which can escalate tension. Their tendency to push for quick, fact-based decisions can make others feel pressured or steamrolled, particularly those with *Merchant* or *Innovator* energies who prefer collaboration or reflection.

Squarish CVI™ profiles tend to handle conflict in a uniquely complex way because no single instinct dominates their response. Instead, they often cycle through multiple internal reactions bouncing from one to the other, "I want to fix this quickly" (*Builder*), "I want everyone to feel understood" (*Merchant*), "I need to analyze what's really going on" (*Innovator*), and "I should check the facts before I act" (*Banker*). This internal push-and-pull can make them appear adaptable and diplomatic, but it can also create hesitation or internal tension as they try to satisfy all four drives throughout the process. In healthy moments, squarish profiles can be remarkably balanced in conflict. They can listen empathetically, think logically, act decisively, and stay grounded in facts. But when they go "dark," the very balance that makes them versatile can become a source of confusion, inconsistency, or emotional overload. A dark squarish person might think, "I have to fix this now," followed seconds later by, "I don't want to upset anyone," then, "This doesn't even make sense," and finally, "I need more information before I say anything." This internal conflict can lead to paralysis, abrupt mood shifts, or unpredictable reactions. They might withdraw completely because they can't decide which instinct to trust. They may become overly controlling, trying to impose structure (*Banker*) while simultaneously demanding emotional reassurance (*Merchant*). They might over-explain or intellectualize the issue (*Innovator*), then suddenly snap with impatience (*Builder*). Some dark squarish profiles become chameleons, shifting their stance depending on who they're talking to, which can come across as inconsistent or even manipulative. Others may catastrophize emotionally (*Merchant*), nitpick details (*Banker*), or retreat into cold logic (*Innovator*) in rapid succession. They might try to "fix" the conflict from every angle, offering solutions, soothing feelings, analyzing motives, and reviewing facts, only to overwhelm themselves and others. In their darkest moments, they can feel internally fragmented, frustrated that no single approach feels right, and may lash out, shut down, or oscillate between extremes. When healthy, squarish profiles are balanced, wise, and flexible. When dark, they can become scattered, contradictory, and emotionally overloaded, struggling to reconcile the competing voices inside them.

To avoid unnecessary conflict with a squarish CVI™ profile, individuals should communicate clearly, concisely, and with well-prepared information. These individuals appreciate directness, respect for their time, and a logical structure to the conversation. For example, instead of saying, "I feel like this project is a mess," a more effective approach would be, "Here are the three specific issues I'm seeing, and here's what I propose we adjust." If conflict does occur, the best way to get back on task is to acknowledge their need for clarity and action while also grounding the conversation in shared goals. You might say, "I know you want us to move forward efficiently. Let's outline the key steps we agree on so we can reset and keep progressing." In a real-world scenario, say a heated debate during a planning meeting, reestablishing structure with a short agenda or decision matrix can help the squarish individual reengage productively. Once they see a clear path forward, they shift quickly from conflict to execution, helping the team regain momentum.

All Out Conflict

When conflict erupts, each of the four core values has a predictable way of "taking over," and when these instincts collide without awareness, the interaction can spiral so quickly that resolution becomes nearly impossible. The *Merchant* may jump in first with emotional Vision, saying things like, "We're losing trust here," or "I just need to know we're okay," pulling the conversation toward feelings and connection. The *Innovator* then shifts the focus to Strategy, responding with something like, "Let's slow down and figure out what the real issue is," which can feel dismissive to the *Merchant*, who interprets the calm analysis as emotional distance. The *Banker* steps in next with Structure, saying, "We need the facts before we go any further," which can frustrate the *Innovator*, who sees the *Banker* as getting stuck in details, and overwhelm the *Merchant*, who feels the emotional core is being ignored. Finally, the *Builder* pushes for action, often with blunt statements like, "Enough talking, here's what we're going to do," which can feel controlling to the *Merchant*, reckless to the *Banker*, and premature to the *Innovator*. Each person's instinctive reaction triggers the next. The *Merchant's* emotional intensity activates the *Innovator's* detachment, the *Innovator's* detachment activates the *Banker's* rigidity, the *Banker's* rigidity activates the *Builder's* forcefulness, and the *Builder's* forcefulness reactivates the *Merchant's* emotional escalation. This loop continues and ping pongs through each core value until everyone feels misunderstood, unheard, or invalidated. The CVI™ reminds us that efforts must follow the natural flow of Vision → Strategy → Structure → Action, and when individuals skip steps or impose their preferred step on others at the wrong time and in the wrong way, the process breaks down. To navigate conflict effectively, people must recognize where they are in the flow, understand their internal biases based on their CVI™ wiring, consider the wiring of the individuals they're engaging, read the moment accurately, and then use CVI™ insights to act intentionally rather than react instinctively. When people honor the sequence and respect each other's core values, conflict can become a coordinated process rather than a chaotic collision of instincts.

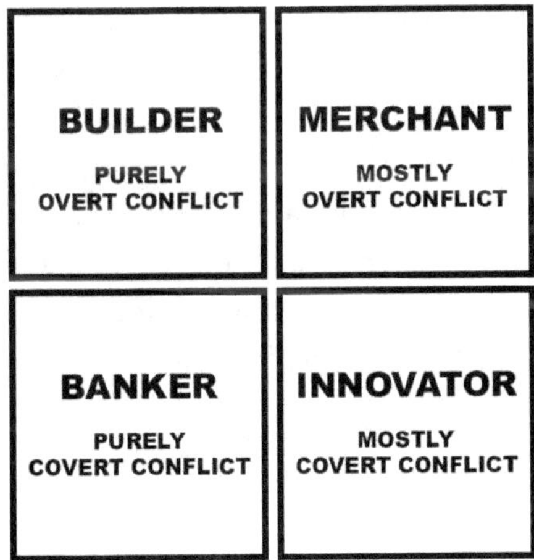

Figure 8. Conflict Management Overview

. . .

Closing Thoughts on Conflict Management

When you look at conflict through the lens of the CVI™, patterns that once felt confusing suddenly make sense, almost like discovering a *cheat code* for human interaction. Each core value brings its own predictable contributions and blind spots into moments of tension. *Merchants* soothe conflict with empathy and connection, *Innovators* bring calm analysis and thoughtful problem-solving, *Bankers* stabilize situations with facts and structure, *Builders* cut through chaos with decisive action, and squarish profiles blend firmness, precision, thought, and connection to drive efficient resolution. When you understand these instinctive responses, you stop taking behavior personally and start seeing it as a reflection of someone's core motivational wiring. A *Merchant* isn't avoiding the issue; they're protecting the relationship. An *Innovator* isn't disengaging, they're processing. A *Banker* isn't nitpicking, they're ensuring accuracy. A *Builder* isn't being harsh; they're trying to move things forward. And a squarish profile isn't being rigid; they're anchoring the situation finding a balanced approach. This perspective transforms conflict from a source of frustration into a roadmap for communication. Instead of reacting emotionally, you can anticipate how someone will respond, adjust your approach, and guide the interaction toward resolution with far less friction. In teams, this creates psychological safety, reduces misunderstandings, and accelerates collaboration. In personal relationships, it deepens empathy and prevents unnecessary escalation. When you understand the CVI™, you're not just managing conflict, you're navigating human behavior with insight, intention, and a level of interpersonal fluency that feels almost unfair in how effective it is.

CHAPTER 14
ENERGY MANAGEMENT

When you think about energy management, it's really about treating your time and attention as limited resources that deserve intention rather than autopilot. If we want to get the most out of our day, you have to deliberately invest your energy in activities that leave you feeling fulfilled, capable, and aligned with who you want to be and minimize the time you spend on things that drain you or pull you away from your contributions. In the real world, energizing activities might look like:

- Collaborating on a creative project where ideas flow
- Exercising or moving your body in a way that feels good and leaves you mentally sharper
- Having a meaningful conversation with someone who inspires you or challenges you in a healthy way

On the flip side, draining activities often show up as:

- Sitting in meetings with no clear purpose or role for you
- Completing tasks that don't align with your core values

- Spending time with people who consistently complain, criticize, or create emotional friction

The more aware you become of what fills your tank versus what empties it, the more you can design your day around energy, not just time.

From a CVI™ perspective, this becomes even more precise. Your CVI™ profile reveals the innate energies that drive you, whether you're naturally wired as a *Merchant, Innovator, Banker,* or *Builder,* and it gives you a blueprint for how much time you need to spend each day in activities that match those core values to feel balanced and effective. For example, a high *Merchant* thrives on connection and vision, so they need daily time spent influencing, inspiring, or building relationships. A high *Banker* needs space for analysis, structure, and thoughtful decision-making. A high *Builder* needs action, momentum, and tangible progress. A high *Innovator* needs problem-solving, creativity, and freedom to explore new ideas. When you align your daily efforts with your CVI™ most valued core values, even if it's just 20–40% of your day, you operate with more clarity, confidence, and energy. When you don't, you feel friction, fatigue, and frustration. Your CVI™ doesn't just describe who you are, it tells you exactly where your energy comes from and how to manage your day so you're working with your natural wiring instead of against it.

Energy Management Formula

There is a simple formula I learned from Justin Erickson from Hardwired Coaching LLC that allows you to calculate how many minutes per day you should spend in activities aligned with each of your CVI™ energies. The accuracy of this formula is often surprising to people the first time they use it. My formula was modified slightly from 9.6 to 9.9 to make it easier to remember and still get similar results. Once you jot down your assigned time for each core value: *Merchant, Innovator, Banker,* or *Builder,* you'll notice something fascinating. When you're operating inside your natural *energy zone*, motivation, clarity, and fulfillment flow almost effortlessly, but the moment you exceed that time, there's a sharp drop off in enthusiasm and effectiveness. It's not subtle. It's immediate and noticeable, as if your internal wiring simply refuses to keep pushing in a direction that doesn't match your innate capacities. The beauty of this formula is that it resets every single day, giving you a fresh opportunity to structure your schedule intentionally so you're spending the right amount of time in the right kinds of activities. When you plan your day around these energy windows, rather than forcing yourself into tasks that drain you; you get more done, feel more aligned, and show up better in every engagement. This chapter breaks down the formula itself and explores the types of activities that correspond to each core value, helping you design your days in a way that honors your natural wiring and maximizes your energy. To determine your specific energy preference, turn to your *Weighted Energy Preference Chart* in your CVI™ Individual Report. In Figure 9, a portion of the Weighted Energy Preference Chart is provided below:

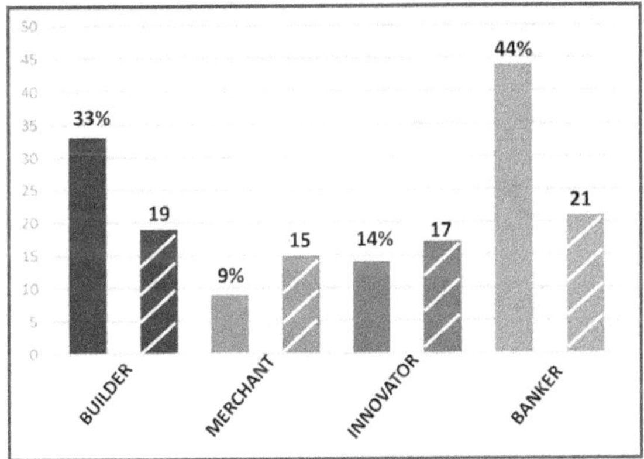

Figure 9. Sample of Weighted Energy Preference Chart

In the example on the previous page, you would take the percentages (solid bars in graph) and multiply each of them by 9.9 to get the number of minutes you should be spending each day in that particular core value (This 9.9 formula will get you within 99% of your drop off point). Note: The *striped bars* represent your CVI™ scores from your individual report. If you want to determine the number of hours a day, divide that multiplied number by 60.

Core Value% x 9.9 = minutes in a day (Divide by 60 to get hours)

This formula accounts for a 16.5-hour day since I'm assuming you spend the remaining hours sleeping (~6.0 – 7.0 hours) or efforts not requiring much capacity like getting ready to work, etc. (~0.5 - 1.0 hours).

In Figure 10 below, here is the math for Figure 9:

Core Value	Core Value Percentage (%)	x 9.9 (Minutes Per Day)	Divided by 60 (Hours Per Day)
BUILDER	33%	326.7 minutes	5.445 hours
MERCHANT	9%	89.1 minutes	1.485 hours
INNOVATOR	14%	138.6 minutes	2.31 hours
BANKER	44%	435.6 minutes	7.26 hours

Figure 10. Weighted Energy Time Breakdown for Figure 9.

As you can see in Figure 10, this particular individual would be more fulfilled if they spent more time doing *Banker*-type activities, followed by *Builder*-type activities. The two combined is almost 13-hours a day for *Banker/Builder-type* activities. Now imagine if this individual was a psychiatrist or counselor/coach where the majority of their day would be spent talking with individuals and trying to walk them through their emotional or personal issues? I have personally found that when I talk to people who are frustrated with their jobs, there is almost always a misalignment to their CVI™ wiring. Sure, they can do the job some of the time but even when they do their job well, they find themselves worn out with nothing to give when they get home. They usually find themselves trying to decompress the moment they walk into their home from a job that is misaligned to their core values.

Side note: I have personally found that if you do activities that are draining at the end of your day, go to bed, and then get back up to that same draining activity, the energy level still feels depleted. With this in mind, I consider this formula more of a 24-hour day formula that doesn't fit nicely in our actual day-to-day. So keep this in mind since we can't pause life and restart it when it is convenient for us. For planning purposes, this formula is great for scheduling your day and understanding when you will experience the drop off in energy in a 24-hour period.

The energy management formula is an amazing revelation for a lot of people I talk to. I often find that individuals approach to work changes after they understand how their CVI™ wiring was impacting their fulfillment in the job. While they are still required to go back to that job, they understand why they weren't finding fulfillment and that alone helped them deal with going to work everyday. In some cases, I received reports that individuals have left their current job and would only apply and interview for jobs that were aligned to the wiring. Just recently, I had an individual change jobs based on our CVI™ discussion and she is now more fulfilled and engaged in her current job.

With this in mind, here are a few activities that can bring fulfillment, and a few that create energetic drag, for each of the four core values. As you read through them, you'll likely feel an immediate sense of recognition for the ones that match your own CVI™ profile. *Builders* will resonate with action-oriented tasks that create momentum, while feeling drained by slow, repetitive processes. *Merchants* will light up around connection and vision, yet lose energy in isolation or environments lacking emotional engagement. *Innovators* thrive when solving problems or creating new approaches, but feel depleted when forced into rigid routines or tasks with no room for thought. *Bankers* feel fulfilled when organizing, analyzing, and bringing clarity to complexity, but drained by chaotic, unstructured, or overly emotional situations.

As you plan your day, keep these patterns in mind. Your CVI™ profile isn't just a description of who you are, it's a guide to how your energy flows. When you intentionally align your schedule with the activities that fuel your core values and minimize the ones that drain them, you'll move through your day with more clarity, motivation, and ease.

Merchants

Merchants draw their energy from connection, vision, and meaningful interaction. They thrive when they're building relationships, inspiring others, or communicating ideas that matter.

Activities that energize *Merchants* include:

- Having meaningful one-on-one conversations
- Brainstorming future possibilities with others
- Collaborating on projects requiring inspiration
- Encouraging someone who needs support
- Meeting new people with interesting stories
- Sharing ideas in a group setting where energy flows
- Discussions aligning people around a shared purpose
- Expressing appreciation or recognition to others
- Engaging in creative planning sessions
- Mentoring or coaching someone toward growth
- Participating in team-building activities
- Talking through challenges with someone to find a positive path forward

- Building or strengthening relationships
- Exploring new opportunities, partnerships, or collaborations

Activities that drain *Merchants* include:

- Working alone for long stretches with no interaction
- Repetitive or highly detailed administrative tasks
- Being in environments with conflict, criticism, or negativity
- Sitting through meetings with no engagement or purpose
- Doing work that requires strict routines or rigid structure
- Tasks that involve heavy data analysis or technical detail
- Forced to follow processes with no creativity or connection
- Engaging in transactional conversations with no depth
- Working under leaders who lack vision
- Isolated from team dynamics or collaborative opportunities
- Managing tasks that require long-term focus without variety
- Navigating environments where people are disengaged
- Completing tasks that feel disconnected from meaning
- Required to make decisions without considering people or relationships
- Individuals who drain emotional energy
- Environments that lack optimism and connection

Merchants feel most fulfilled when they're influencing, encouraging, or guiding people toward a shared purpose. When their day includes space for emotional connection and big-picture thinking, their natural enthusiasm and charisma come alive.

Innovators

Innovators are fueled by problem-solving, creativity, and the freedom to explore new ideas. They gain energy from activities that challenge their mind, allow them to design solutions, or give them room to think independently. *Innovators* thrive when they're analyzing complex issues, experimenting with new approaches, or refining systems to make them better.

Activities that energize *Innovators* include:

- Solving complex problems that require fresh thinking
- Exploring new ideas, systems, or approaches
- Designing/improving processes making them more efficient
- Exploring multiple solutions to a single challenge
- Working independently with freedom to think and create
- Analyzing patterns, inconsistencies, or inefficiencies
- Experimenting with new tools, methods, or technologies
- Strategizing long-term plans or innovative pathways
- Refining concepts until they're elegant and effective
- Asking deep questions that reveal root causes
- Collaborating with others to troubleshoot or innovate
- Creating frameworks, models, or conceptual maps
- Taking things apart and imagining how they could be better
- Tackling open-ended problems with no predefined answer
- Engaging in thoughtful discussions that challenge assumptions

Activities that drain *Innovators* include:

- Following rigid routines with no room for adaptation
- Completing repetitive or highly structured tasks
- Being micromanaged or given overly detailed instructions
- Working in environments where creativity isn't valued
- Tasks that require strict adherence to rules without flexibility
- Meetings with no problem-solving or strategic purpose
- Work with excessive administrative or procedural steps
- Forced to make quick decisions without time to think
- Working with people who resist new ideas or improvements
- Roles that require constant maintenance versus innovation
- Tasks that offer no challenge or intellectual stimulation
- Chaotic environments with unclear expectations
- Required to focus on small details for long periods

- Engaging in conversations that lack depth, insight, or meaningful exploration

Innovators feel most fulfilled when they're asked to think deeply, innovate, or bring clarity to confusion. *Innovators* are energized when their day includes opportunities to create, improve, or reimagine. When this happens, they operate with sharpness and ease.

Bankers

Bankers are energized by knowledge, structure, and thoughtful analysis. They thrive when they can gather information, organize details, and bring order to complexity. Activities that fuel *Bankers* include researching, documenting processes, evaluating data, or planning with precision.

Activities that energize *Bankers* include:

- Researching information to gain deeper understanding
- Organizing data, documents, or systems
- Creating structure, order, or clear processes
- Analyzing details to ensure accuracy
- Planning ahead with well-defined steps and timelines
- Reviewing information to verify correctness or completeness
- Documenting procedures or creating reference materials
- Evaluating risks and making thoughtful, informed decisions
- Tracking progress using metrics, lists, or reports
- Managing schedules, logistics, or resource allocation
- Quiet, focused environments with little disruption
- Well-reasoned guidance based on facts and evidence
- Maintaining systems that support consistency and reliability
- Reflecting on information to form clear, logical conclusions

Activities that drain *Bankers* include:

- Working in disorganized or unpredictable environments

- Tasks with unclear instructions or missing information
- Pressured to make quick decisions without time to analyze
- Emotionally charged conversations or conflicts
- Brainstorming sessions with no structure or follow-through
- Dealing with constant interruptions that break focus
- Tasks that require improvisation rather than planning
- Working with people who ignore details or skip steps
- Forced into highly social or relational tasks for long periods
- Responsibilities requiring emotional persuasion versus logic
- Tasks involving ambiguity with no data to guide decisions
- Environments where accuracy is sacrificed for speed

Bankers feel most fulfilled when they're creating clarity, ensuring accuracy, or providing well-reasoned guidance. When their day includes time for reflection, information management, and careful decision-making, they feel grounded, capable, and fully engaged.

Builders

Builders feel most alive when they're taking action and moving things forward. They thrive on momentum, decisiveness, and tangible progress, so activities that let them do rather than just talk will always boost their energy. *Builders* are energized by tasks like tackling a physical project, making quick operational decisions, or stepping in to solve an immediate problem.

Activities that energize *Builders* include:

- Taking decisive action to move a project forward
- Tackling hands-on tasks that produce visible results
- Making quick, confident decisions without overanalyzing
- Leading efforts that require direction and momentum
- Solving immediate, practical problems on the spot
- Jumping into situations that need fast execution
- Managing tasks that involve physical movement or activity
- Taking charge in moments where others hesitate

- Streamlining processes to make things run faster
- Setting goals and knocking them out one by one
- Working in environments where speed and efficiency matter
- Responsibilities requiring strength, courage, or assertiveness
- Driving progress during team projects or group efforts
- Responding to urgent needs or time-sensitive challenges
- Creating order out of chaos through direct action

Activities that drain *Builders* include:

- Sitting through long discussions without clear decisions
- Repetitive tasks that don't lead to visible progress
- Waiting on others to take action or make up their minds
- Environments with excessive rules or bureaucracy
- Tasks that require deep analysis instead of quick execution
- Participating in meetings with no clear purpose or outcome
- Being required to follow slow, methodical processes
- Managing projects where priorities constantly shift
- Work involving heavy documentation or detailed reporting
- Being stuck in planning mode without moving into action
- Navigating group decisions that drag on without resolution
- Tasks that require emotional sensitivity over directness
- Working with people who avoid taking responsibility
- Being micromanaged or restricted from acting independently
- Environments where speed and efficiency aren't valued

Builders gain energy from environments where they can take charge, cut through clutter, and create visible results. When their day includes opportunities to execute, lead, and make things happen, they operate at their highest level.

Squarish CVI™ Profiles

When someone has a squarish CVI™ profile, they tend to find

fulfillment in a wide range of activities, but they also experience a unique kind of energetic drain when their day becomes too lopsided in any one direction. A squarish individual might feel energized by taking decisive action like a *Builder*, connecting deeply like a *Merchant*, solving problems like an *Innovator*, and organizing information like a *Banker*. At the same time, they can feel drained when they're forced to operate exclusively in one mode for too long: too much structure without creativity, too much action without reflection, too much connection without independence, or too much analysis without movement. Keep in mind that their capacity scores are mostly even through all four core values so the amount of time throughout the day spent in each core value is also evenly distributed before they feel their energy waning.

Activities that energize *Squarish CVI™ Profiles* include:

- Switching between different types of tasks
- Solving practical problems and discussing ideas with others
- Working on a project that has creativity, structure, and action
- Collaborating with a team then having time alone to think
- Setting goals and making steady progress toward them
- Learning something new and applying it immediately
- Organizing a system or process then improving it creatively
- Meaningful conversations that lead to tangible outcomes
- Taking action on a task then reflecting on how to refine it
- Balancing hands-on work with strategic planning
- Engaging in group discussions that lead to clear decisions
- Alternating detail-oriented tasks with big-picture thinking
- Helping others while also maintaining personal productivity
- Environments that allow both structure and flexibility
- Tackling a mix of short-term tasks and long-term projects

Activities that drain *Squarish CVI™ Profiles* include:

- Staying locked into one type of task for too long
- Working in environments with no variety or change
  of pace

- Being forced into a single core value mode all day (all action, all analysis, all connection, or all creativity)
- Repetitive tasks with no opportunity to switch gears
- Leaders who expect one consistent style of engagement
- Long meetings with no movement, decision, or interaction
- Tasks that require extreme detail for extended periods
- Being pushed to make rapid decisions without time to think
- Spending too much time alone without collaboration
- Overwhelmed by social interaction with no quiet time
- Navigating chaotic environments with no structure or plan
- Rigid routines that leave no room for creativity or flexibility
- Projects with unclear goals or no sense of progress
- Required to focus on big-picture thinking with no action
- Emotionally charged situations for long stretches

Because their energy is distributed more evenly, Squarish CVI™ profiles thrive when their day includes a blend of doing, thinking, relating, and organizing. This balance allows them to tap into all four core values without burning out in any single one, and keeping this in mind helps them plan their day in a way that honors their natural versatility.

Schedule Your Day and Prepare for Success

Another tip I learned from Justin Erickson from Hardwired Coaching LLC is to start color-coding your work and personal calendars using the four CVI™ colors. By labeling each meeting, task, or event according to the core value it represents, you give yourself a clear preview of the energy required before you ever walk into the room or join the online meeting. This simple habit helps you set expectations, prepare mentally, and show up at your best, even when the activity isn't naturally aligned with your dominant core value. Pair this with the energy management formula, and you'll know exactly when you're likely to hit a drop-off point for each core value throughout the day. With this awareness, you can plan your schedule more intentionally, balance your energy across different types of activities, and avoid pushing yourself past the point where motivation and effectiveness naturally decline.

Closing Thoughts on Energy Management

Energy management is ultimately about understanding that your time, attention, and internal fuel are not limitless and the quality of your day depends on how intentionally you allocate them. Throughout this chapter, you've learned that energy management isn't just about doing less or working harder. It's about aligning your efforts with the activities that naturally fulfill you and minimizing the ones that drain you. The energy management formula gives you a precise way to calculate how many minutes per 24-hours you should spend in each of your CVI™ core values, and once you track it, you'll notice how sharply your motivation drops when you exceed your natural limits. You've also seen that every core value: *Merchant, Innovator, Banker,* and *Builder,* has its own set of energizing activities and draining activities, and recognizing these patterns helps you design your day with intention rather than guesswork.

Whether your profile is strongly weighted toward one core value or more balanced like a squarish profile, the key is the same: your CVI™ wiring tells you exactly where your energy comes from, how it gets depleted, and how to structure your day so you operate at your highest level. When you honor your natural wiring and plan your day around the activities that align with your core values, you don't just get more done, you feel more fulfilled, more effective, and more authentically yourself.

CHAPTER 15
INTERPERSONAL DYNAMICS

nterpersonal dynamics describe the constantly shifting patterns of interaction between people. How we communicate, influence one another, build trust, navigate conflict, and create meaning together. These dynamics are shaped by a combination of internal factors (emotions, beliefs, and personality) and external factors (environment, culture, and power structures). When we understand the components that shape interpersonal dynamics, we gain the ability to interact more intentionally, reduce misunderstandings, and strengthen the quality of our relationships. Below, I'll walk through several major parts that influence interpersonal dynamics, explain how each one works, and offer real-world examples that show what these dynamics look like in everyday life. I will then dive into the CVI™ and how it can help you navigate your relationships based on your CVI™ profile.

Communication Styles

Communication is the backbone of interpersonal dynamics. It includes not only what we say but how we say it: tone, pacing, body language, and even silence. People tend to lean toward certain communication styles: assertive, passive, aggressive, or passive-aggressive. These styles influence how others perceive us and how effectively we get our needs met. Assertive communication generally fosters clarity and respect, while aggressive communication can create defensiveness. Passive communication may avoid conflict but often leads to resentment, and passive-aggressive communication creates confusion and mistrust.

Examples:

- Manager giving clear, respectful feedback that demonstrates assertive communication that builds trust
- Friend who avoids expressing their needs and later feels hurt when others don't meet unspoken expectations
- Coworker using sarcasm to express frustration instead of addressing the issue directly

Emotional Intelligence

Emotional Intelligence (EQ) refers to the ability to recognize, understand, and manage our own emotions while also perceiving and responding to the emotions of others. High EQ helps people navigate conflict, build rapport, and create psychological safety. Low EQ often leads to misinterpretations, impulsive reactions, and strained relationships. EQ includes self-awareness, self-regulation, empathy, and social skills, all of which shape how we show up in interactions.

Examples:

- A team member notices a colleague seems overwhelmed and offers help
- A person chooses to take a moment to decompress before engaging in a sensitive conversation.
- A leader senses tension in a meeting and pauses to ask how everyone is feeling, helping the group reset and communicate more openly.

. . .

Power Dynamics

Power dynamics influence who speaks, who decides, and whose needs are prioritized. Power can come from formal authority (like a boss), expertise, social status, or even personality traits like confidence. Healthy power dynamics allow for shared influence and mutual respect. Unhealthy ones can create fear, resentment, or disengagement. Understanding power dynamics helps people navigate relationships more thoughtfully and avoid unintentionally dominating or silencing others.

Examples:

- A teacher who encourages students to challenge ideas and ask questions creates a balanced power dynamic that supports learning
- A supervisor who dismisses team input because "I'm the one in charge" reinforces an unhealthy power imbalance
- A friend group where one person always chooses the plans without asking others reflects subtle social power that shapes group behavior

Cultural and Social Norms

Culture shapes how people interpret behavior, express emotions, and define respect. Social norms, whether from family, community, or workplace culture, also influence interpersonal dynamics. When people come from different cultural backgrounds, misunderstandings can arise simply because expectations differ. Awareness of cultural norms helps people communicate more sensitively and avoid assumptions.

. . .

Examples:

- In some cultures, direct eye contact signals confidence. In others, it may be seen as disrespectful or confrontational
- A workplace that values fast decision-making may unintentionally frustrate employees from cultures that prioritize consensus
- A family that avoids discussing conflict openly may clash with a partner who believes in addressing issues directly

Conflict Styles

Everyone has a preferred way of handling conflict: avoiding, accommodating, competing, compromising, or collaborating. These styles influence how disagreements unfold and whether they lead to resolution or escalation. Conflict isn't inherently negative. Handled well, it can deepen understanding and strengthen relationships. But mismatched conflict styles often create tension.

Examples:

- One partner wants to talk through an issue immediately (collaborating), while the other needs time to cool down (avoiding), leading to frustration on both sides
- Two coworkers compromise on a project timeline, each adjusting their expectations to meet in the middle
- A team member insists on their solution without considering others' perspectives (competing), causing resentment

Boundaries

Boundaries define what we are comfortable with, emotionally, physically, and mentally. Clear boundaries help maintain respect and prevent burnout. Weak boundaries can lead to overcommitment, resentment, or feeling taken advantage of. Overly rigid boundaries can create distance or isolation. Healthy interpersonal dynamics require boundaries that are communicated clearly and honored consistently.

Examples:

- An employee tells their manager they cannot respond to emails after 7 p.m. to protect personal time
- A friend expresses that they need a day to themselves instead of attending a social event
- A colleague politely declines taking on extra tasks when their workload is already full

Trust and Psychological Safety

Trust is the foundation of strong interpersonal dynamics. It grows through consistency, honesty, and reliability. Psychological safety, the feeling that one can speak up without fear of embarrassment or punishment, allows people to share ideas, admit mistakes, and take interpersonal risks. Without trust, communication becomes guarded and relationships weaken.

Examples:

- A team where members feel safe admitting mistakes tends to innovate more effectively
- A friend who consistently keeps confidences builds deep trust over time

CVI™ and Interpersonal Dynamics

The CVI™ is a powerful lens for navigating relationships because it helps you understand not only your own innate motivations but also the fundamental drivers behind other people's behaviors, decisions, and communication patterns. When you know your personal CVI™ profile, whether you lead with *Merchant, Innovator, Banker,* or *Builder* energy, you gain clarity about why you respond the way you do under stress, what you need to feel respected, and how you naturally approach problem-solving or connection. This self-awareness alone reduces friction, because you can recognize when your reactions are rooted in wiring rather than the situation itself. But the real relational power comes from understanding the CVI™ patterns of others. When you can see that someone is acting from their core value, like a *Builder's* need for action, a *Merchant's* desire for connection, an *Innovator's* drive for solutions, or a *Banker's* need for clarity, you stop taking their behavior personally and start interpreting it through a more compassionate, accurate lens. Instead of assuming someone is being difficult, you can recognize that they're simply operating from their natural core values and stress responses. This allows you to adjust your communication, set expectations more clearly, and collaborate in ways that honor both people's wiring. In personal relationships, this means fewer misunderstandings and more empathy. In professional settings, it leads to smoother teamwork, better conflict resolution, and a deeper appreciation for the diversity of core values and their respective capacities within a group. Ultimately, the CVI™ gives you a roadmap for interacting with others in a way that reduces unnecessary tension and increases mutual respect, making your relationships more intentional, resilient, and fulfilling.

When it comes to communication styles, the CVI™ helps people recognize why they naturally communicate the way they do, whether a *Builder's* directness, a *Merchant's* warmth, an *Innovator's* thoughtfulness, or a *Banker's* precision and how those tendencies may be perceived by others. This awareness allows them to adjust tone, pacing, and delivery to communicate more assertively and effectively. In the realm of emotional intelligence, the CVI™ strengthens self-awareness by highlighting what triggers each core value type and how they tend to react under stress, making it easier to regulate emotions and empathize with others whose wiring differs. Understanding power dynamics becomes easier when individuals can see how each CVI™ type expresses influence. *Builders* through action, *Merchants* through connection, *Innovators* through ideas, and *Bankers* through information allowing them to balance authority, share decision-making, and avoid unintentionally overpowering others. The CVI™ also helps people navigate cultural and social norms by revealing how their internal wiring shapes their expectations of respect, communication, and collaboration, making it easier to recognize when differences stem from CVI™ wiring rather than culture alone. When dealing with conflict styles, the CVI™ clarifies why some individuals confront issues head-on, others seek harmony, others analyze, and others withdraw until they feel informed; insight that helps prevent misinterpretations and supports more productive conflict resolution. In terms of boundaries, the CVI™ helps individuals understand what drains them, what energizes them, and what they need to feel respected, making it easier to set and honor boundaries without guilt or confusion. Finally, the CVI™ strengthens trust and psychological safety by helping people show up more consistently, communicate their needs clearly, and interpret others' behaviors with greater empathy. When individuals understand both their own core values and the values driving the people around them, they can navigate interpersonal dynamics with far more clarity, compassion, and confidence, leading to healthier relationships in every area of life.

Merchant + Merchant

When two *Merchants* interact in their healthy expression, the dynamic is warm, collaborative, and deeply relational. Both individuals' value connection, shared purpose, and emotional resonance, which creates an atmosphere of mutual encouragement and enthusiasm. They naturally uplift one another, communicate openly, and build strong rapport. For example, two *Merchant* coworkers may spend time ensuring the team feels motivated and aligned before diving into tasks. In a personal relationship, they may prioritize quality time, meaningful conversations, and shared experiences that strengthen their bond.

Their mutual optimism and people-centered approach can create a vibrant, supportive partnership.

When both *Merchants* are in their dark expression, the dynamic becomes emotionally volatile and approval-driven. A dark *Merchant* may become manipulative, overly sensitive, or prone to dramatizing situations. When two people with this wiring clash, they may compete for attention, validation, or influence. For example, two *Merchant* coworkers may gossip, form alliances, or become passive-aggressive when they feel unappreciated. In a personal relationship, disagreements may escalate into emotional outbursts, guilt-tripping, or withdrawal. The relationship becomes unstable because both individuals are reacting from insecurity rather than genuine connection.

When two *Merchants* are in a relationship (personal or professional) the key to maintaining healthy interpersonal dynamics is grounding their natural warmth and enthusiasm with intentional communication and emotional regulation. Because *Merchants* are highly attuned to connection, they thrive when they openly express appreciation, check in on each other's feelings, and create space for honest dialogue without slipping into people-pleasing or emotional overextension. To avoid going dark, they need to set gentle but clear boundaries so neither becomes overly dependent on the other's validation. They also benefit from slowing down before reacting, since two *Merchants* can easily amplify each other's emotions if one becomes stressed or insecure. Practically, this might look like agreeing to pause during heated conversations, clarifying expectations instead of assuming, and committing to address concerns directly rather than through hints or triangulation. When both *Merchants* stay grounded, communicate openly, and prioritize authenticity over approval, their natural positive contributions: empathy, enthusiasm, and relational intuition, create a deeply supportive and emotionally rich dynamic.

Merchant + Innovator

A *Merchant* and an *Innovator* in their healthy expression create a dynamic that blends emotional insight with strategic thinking.

Merchants bring warmth, enthusiasm, and relational awareness, while *Innovators* contribute creativity, problem-solving, and thoughtful analysis. Together, they can create solutions that are both people-centered and well-designed. For example, in a workplace setting, the *Merchant* may rally the team around a vision, while the *Innovator* refines the plan to ensure it's effective. In a personal relationship, the *Merchant* brings emotional depth and connection, while the *Innovator* brings curiosity and thoughtful engagement, creating a balanced and stimulating partnership.

When both individuals are in their dark expression, the dynamic becomes a clash between emotional reactivity and intellectual defensiveness. A dark *Merchant* may become dramatic, needy, or manipulative, while a dark *Innovator* may become critical, aloof, or dismissive. For example, the *Merchant* may accuse the *Innovator* of "not caring," while the *Innovator* responds by withdrawing or pointing out flaws in the *Merchant's* reasoning. In a workplace scenario, the *Merchant* may push for consensus or emotional validation, while the *Innovator* becomes frustrated by what they see as irrationality. The relationship becomes strained because both are reacting from fear rather than collaboration.

For a *Merchant* and an *Innovator* to maintain healthy interpersonal dynamics, they need to intentionally blend emotional awareness with thoughtful problem-solving. *Merchants* thrive when they feel connected and understood, while *Innovators* thrive when they have space to think, refine, and explore ideas. To stay in the light, *Merchants* should slow down enough to let the *Innovator* process without feeling pressured for immediate emotional engagement, and *Innovators* should communicate their thought process so the *Merchant* doesn't interpret quiet reflection as disinterest. They both benefit from agreeing to pause before reacting, *Merchants* to regulate emotional intensity, *Innovators* to avoid slipping into detached analysis. In practice, this might look like the *Merchant* checking in with curiosity rather than assumption, and the *Innovator* offering reassurance or clarity before diving into solutions. When both stay grounded, they create a dynamic where ideas are thoughtfully shaped and emotionally supported.

. . .

Merchant + Banker

A *Merchant* paired with a *Banker* creates a dynamic that blends emotional intelligence with structure and clarity. *Merchants* bring enthusiasm, connection, and vision, while *Bankers* contribute stability, accuracy, and thoughtful planning. When both are healthy, this pairing is highly complementary. The *Merchant* inspires and motivates, while the *Banker* ensures that decisions are grounded and well-informed. For example, in a team setting, the *Merchant* may generate excitement around a new initiative, while the *Banker* organizes the details and ensures all necessary information is gathered. In a personal relationship, the *Merchant* brings warmth and spontaneity, while the *Banker* provides consistency and reliability.

When both individuals are in their dark expression, the dynamic becomes a tug-of-war between emotional intensity and emotional withdrawal. A dark *Merchant* may become overly expressive, guilt-driven, or manipulative, while a dark *Banker* may become aloof, rigid, or judgmental. For example, the *Merchant* may accuse the *Banker* of being "uncaring," while the *Banker* retreats into silence or criticism. In a workplace scenario, the *Merchant* may push for decisions based on feelings or group harmony, while the *Banker* resists, insisting on more data or structure. The relationship becomes strained because both individuals feel misunderstood and unappreciated.

For a *Merchant* and a *Banker* to stay in healthy dynamics, they need to honor each other's very different pacing and priorities. *Merchants* bring warmth, enthusiasm, and relational intuition, while *Bankers* bring structure, clarity, and a commitment to accuracy. To avoid going dark, *Merchants* should slow down enough to respect the *Banker's* need for information and predictability, while *Bankers* should communicate their concerns without shutting down or becoming overly rigid. Both benefit from setting clear expectations early: what decisions need emotional alignment, what decisions need data, and how they will navigate differences in communication style. Practically, this might look like the *Merchant* asking, "What information would help you feel comfortable moving forward?" and the *Banker* offering appreciation for the *Merchant's* relational contributions. When both contribute positively, they create a dynamic that feels both emotionally supportive and reliably structured.

Merchant + Builder

When a *Merchant* and a *Builder* interact in their healthy expression, the dynamic blends relational awareness with decisive action. *Merchants* bring emotional intelligence, enthusiasm, and a natural desire for collaboration, while *Builders* contribute clarity, direction, and a strong bias toward execution. Together, they form a balanced partnership in which the *Merchant* ensures people feel valued and aligned, and the *Builder* keeps momentum high and goals clearly defined. In a team environment, the *Merchant* may focus on motivating others, checking in on morale, and fostering connection, while the *Builder* lays out the steps needed to complete the project and drives the group toward action. In a personal relationship, the *Merchant* brings warmth, conversation, and social energy, while the *Builder* handles logistics: planning the route, organizing the schedule, or taking care of practical tasks, creating a dynamic that feels both emotionally rich and efficiently grounded.

When both the *Merchant* and the *Builder* are in their dark expression, the dynamic can quickly become tense, emotionally charged, and unproductive. A dark *Merchant* may become manipulative, overly emotional, or desperate for approval, while a dark *Builder* becomes controlling, impatient, and dismissive of feelings. This often leads to a reactive cycle in which the *Merchant* pushes harder for emotional validation and the *Builder* pushes harder for action, leaving both feeling unheard and misunderstood. For example, during a disagreement, the *Merchant* may accuse the *Builder* of being cold or uncaring, while the *Builder* snaps back with frustration about indecision or emotional intensity. In a workplace setting, the *Builder* may bulldoze ahead without considering individual or team input, while the *Merchant* may gossip, triangulate, or seek alliances to regain influence. The relationship becomes strained because both individuals are operating from insecurity rather than their natural capacities.

For a *Merchant* and a *Builder* to maintain healthy interpersonal dynamics, they need to consciously balance emotional connection with decisive action. *Merchants* thrive when communication feels warm and collaborative, while *Builders* thrive when decisions are clear and progress is tangible. To avoid slipping into their dark expressions, *Merchants* should express their needs directly rather than hinting or seeking approval, and *Builders* should slow down enough to acknowledge feelings and include the *Merchant* in the decision-making process. Both benefit from establishing shared expectations around timing: when to act quickly and when to pause for alignment. In practice, this might look like the *Merchant* saying, "I want to make sure we're on the same page before we move forward," and the *Builder* responding with, "Let's take a moment to talk it through." When both stay grounded, they create a dynamic that is both emotionally attuned and highly productive.

Innovator + Innovator

When two *Innovators* interact in their healthy expression, the dynamic is intellectually rich, creative, and deeply thoughtful. Both individuals enjoy exploring ideas, solving problems, and refining concepts. They appreciate each other's curiosity and ability to see multiple perspectives. For example, two *Innovator* coworkers may spend hours brainstorming solutions, pondering alone, and coming back to brainstorm more, analyzing possibilities, and designing elegant systems. In a personal relationship, they may enjoy deep conversations, shared interests, and collaborative problem-solving. Their mutual appreciation for nuance and creativity creates a stimulating and harmonious partnership.

When both *Innovators* are in their dark expression, the dynamic becomes analytical gridlock. A dark *Innovator* becomes overly critical, indecisive, and prone to overthinking. When two people with this wiring clash, they may endlessly debate possibilities without taking action. For example, two *Innovator* coworkers may spend so much time analyzing risks that they never finalize a decision. In a personal relationship, disagreements may turn into intellectual sparring matches where each person tries to out-analyze the other. The relationship becomes stagnant because both individuals are stuck in fear-based analysis rather than constructive problem-solving.

Two *Innovators* maintain healthy dynamics by embracing their shared love of ideas while also committing to forward movement. *Innovators* thrive when they have space to explore possibilities, analyze patterns, and refine solutions. But two *Innovators* together can easily drift into endless ideation if they're not intentional. To stay productive, they need to set gentle boundaries around decision-making, agree on when "good enough" is truly good enough, and communicate openly about when analysis is helpful versus when it becomes avoidance. They also benefit from checking in emotionally, since *Innovators* can unintentionally stay in their heads and miss subtle relational cues. Practically, this might look like scheduling time for brainstorming followed by a clear decision point, or pausing to ask, "Are we still solving the right problem?" When both stay grounded, they create a dynamic that is intellectually rich, creative, and surprisingly harmonious.

Innovator + Banker

An *Innovator* and a *Banker* in their healthy expression create a dynamic that blends strategic thinking with precision and structure. *Innovators* bring creativity, adaptability, and big-picture problem-solving, while *Bankers* contribute thoroughness, organization, and attention to detail. Together, they can create solutions that are both innovative and reliable. For example, the *Innovator* may design a new workflow, while the *Banker* ensures the process is documented, compliant, and sustainable. In a personal relationship, the *Innovator* brings curiosity and flexibility, while the *Banker* brings stability and thoughtful planning.

When both individuals are in their dark expression, the dynamic becomes a battle between over analysis and rigidity. A dark *Innovator* becomes critical, indecisive, and overly theoretical, while a dark *Banker* becomes inflexible, risk-averse, and aloof. For example, the *Innovator* may criticize the *Banker* for being "too stuck in the rules," while the *Banker* accuses the *Innovator* of being "impractical." In a workplace scenario, the *Innovator* may propose ideas that the *Banker* immediately shuts down, leading to frustration on both sides. The relationship becomes tense because both individuals retreat into their defensive patterns.

For an *Innovator* and a *Banker* to maintain healthy dynamics, they need to intentionally blend creativity with structure. *Innovators* thrive when they can explore ideas and refine solutions, while *Bankers* thrive when decisions are grounded in facts, clarity, and predictability. To avoid going dark, *Innovators* should communicate their ideas in a way that feels concrete enough for the *Banker* to trust, and *Bankers* should share their concerns without shutting down new possibilities prematurely. Both benefit from establishing a shared process: first exploring ideas, then gathering data, then deciding. In practice, this might look like the *Innovator* saying, "Let me walk you through the logic behind this idea," and the *Banker* responding with, "Here's the information we need to make this work." When both work together, they create a dynamic that is both innovative and reliably grounded.

Innovator + Builder

When an *Innovator* and a *Builder* interact in their healthy expression, the dynamic blends thoughtful problem-solving with decisive action. *Innovators* bring creativity, curiosity, and a desire to refine ideas, while *Builders* contribute clarity, direction, and a strong drive to move things forward. Together, they form a powerful partnership in which the *Innovator* ensures quality, strategy, and well-designed solutions, while the *Builder* ensures momentum and execution. For example, the *Innovator* may explore multiple approaches to a new product concept, identifying potential pitfalls or refining the design, while the *Builder* takes those insights and pushes the project into action. In personal relationships, the *Innovator* adds depth, creativity, and intentionality to shared experiences, while the *Builder* initiates plans and handles practical logistics, creating a dynamic that feels both thoughtful and efficient.

When both individuals are in their dark expression, the dynamic becomes a collision between over analysis and impulsiveness. A dark *Innovator* may become critical, indecisive, or overly focused on what could go wrong, while a dark *Builder* becomes forceful, reactive, and unwilling to slow down. This often leads to a frustrating cycle in which the *Builder* accuses the *Innovator* of "dragging things out," and the *Innovator* accuses the *Builder* of "not thinking things through." For example, in a meeting, the *Builder* may push a half-formed plan forward, while the *Innovator* shoots down ideas without offering workable alternatives. In a personal relationship, the *Builder* may make sudden decisions without consulting the *Innovator*, who responds by withdrawing, nitpicking, or pointing out flaws. Both end up feeling misunderstood because each is reacting from fear rather than from their natural positive core values.

For an *Innovator* and a *Builder* to stay in healthy interpersonal dynamics, they need to consciously balance thoughtful analysis with decisive action. *Innovators* thrive when they have time to refine ideas, while *Builders* thrive when they can move quickly and see progress. To avoid slipping into their dark expressions, *Innovators* should communicate their insights clearly and avoid overcomplicating decisions, while *Builders* should slow down enough to consider the *Innovator's* perspective before acting. Both benefit from agreeing on when to explore and when to execute. Practically, this might look like the *Innovator* saying, "Here are the key risks and opportunities," and the *Builder* responding with, "Great...let's choose a direction and move." When both stay grounded, they create a dynamic that is strategic, efficient, and highly effective.

Banker + Banker

When two *Bankers* interact in their healthy expression, the dynamic is calm, structured, and highly organized. Both individuals' value accuracy, clarity, and thoughtful decision-making. They appreciate each other's reliability and commitment to doing things correctly. For example, two *Banker* coworkers may create detailed plans, maintain meticulous records, and ensure that every step of a project is well-documented. In a personal relationship, they may enjoy routines, financial planning, and shared responsibilities that create a sense of stability and predictability.

When both *Bankers* are in their dark expression, the dynamic becomes stagnant and overly cautious. A dark *Banker* becomes rigid, fearful, and resistant to change. When two people with this wiring interact, they may get stuck in endless preparation, risk-avoidance, or criticism. For example, two *Banker* coworkers may delay decisions indefinitely because they feel they never have "enough information." In a personal relationship, they may avoid conflict, resist new experiences, or become overly focused on rules and routines. The relationship becomes constricted because both individuals are operating from fear rather than stability.

Two *Bankers* maintain healthy dynamics by grounding their shared love of structure with intentional openness and flexibility. *Bankers* thrive when decisions are well-informed, predictable, and low-risk but two *Bankers* together can easily become overly cautious or slow to act. To stay productive, they need to agree on when "enough information" is truly enough, communicate openly about concerns without letting fear drive decisions, and intentionally build in moments of spontaneity or experimentation. They also benefit from checking in emotionally, since *Bankers* can default to logic and miss relational cues. Practically, this might look like setting deadlines for decisions, dividing research responsibilities, or intentionally celebrating progress to avoid stagnation. When both stay grounded, they create a dynamic that is steady, reliable, and deeply supportive.

Banker + Builder

When a *Banker* and a *Builder* interact in their healthy expression, the dynamic blends accuracy with action, creating a partnership that is both steady and productive. *Bankers* bring structure, thoroughness, and a commitment to well-informed, low-risk decisions, while *Builders* contribute clarity, direction, and a drive to move things forward quickly. Together, they strike a powerful balance. The *Banker* ensures decisions are grounded and sustainable, and the *Builder* ensures progress doesn't stall. For example, the *Banker* may carefully review compliance requirements or gather essential data before a new system is implemented, while the *Builder* pushes the project into motion once the foundational details are in place. In personal relationships, the *Banker* often handles planning, budgeting, and long-term organization, while the *Builder* takes charge of immediate tasks and practical execution, creating a dynamic that feels both secure and efficient.

When both individuals are in their dark expression, the dynamic becomes a standoff between urgency and resistance. A dark *Banker* may become rigid, fearful, or overly cautious, while a dark *Builder* becomes domineering, impatient, and dismissive of details. This often leads to gridlock. The *Builder* pushes harder for immediate action, and the *Banker* digs in deeper, insisting that nothing can move forward without more information or certainty. For example, the *Builder* may demand, "We need to do this now," while the *Banker* counters with, "We can't do anything until we know more," bringing progress to a halt. In a personal relationship, the *Builder* may make impulsive decisions or purchases, while the *Banker* responds with criticism, withdrawal, or withholding of any resources they control. Both end up feeling unheard and disrespected, and the relationship becomes strained because each person is reacting from fear rather than from their natural positive core values.

For a *Banker* and a *Builder* to maintain healthy interpersonal dynamics, they need to intentionally balance accuracy with momentum. *Bankers* thrive when decisions are well-informed and low-risk, while *Builders* thrive when progress is fast and clear. To avoid going dark, *Bankers* should communicate their concerns without shutting down action, and *Builders* should slow down enough to respect the *Banker's* need for clarity and structure. Both benefit from agreeing on what decisions require thorough analysis and which ones can move quickly. In practice, this might look like the *Banker* saying, "Here's the information we need before moving forward," and the *Builder* responding with, "Great...let's gather that and then act." When both stay grounded, they create a dynamic that is both stable and highly productive.

Builder + Builder

When two *Builders* interact in their healthy expression, the dynamic is fast-paced, direct, and highly productive. Both value decisiveness, autonomy, and results, which can create a strong sense of mutual respect. They appreciate each other's clarity and efficiency, and they often work well together when roles are clearly defined. For example, two *Builder* coworkers may divide responsibilities quickly and execute a project with minimal friction. In a personal relationship, two *Builders* may enjoy shared activities that involve action, problem-solving, or physical engagement, appreciating each other's straightforward communication style.

When both *Builders* are in their dark expression, the dynamic can become explosive. A dark *Builder* becomes controlling, confrontational, and unwilling to compromise. When two people with this wiring clash, power struggles are almost inevitable. Each wants to lead, each believes their way is the right way, and neither naturally backs down. For example, two *Builder* coworkers may argue over who gets to make the final decision, escalating into a battle of wills. In a personal relationship, disagreements can turn into shouting matches or cold standoffs because both individuals react quickly and intensely. The relationship becomes volatile because both are operating from force rather than collaboration.

When two *Builders* work to maintain healthy interpersonal dynamics, they need to be intentional about balancing their shared drive for action with patience, collaboration, and mutual respect. *Builders* naturally move fast, make decisions quickly, and prefer to take charge, which means the healthiest version of this pairing requires conscious effort to slow down, listen, and share leadership. To achieve great results, both *Builders* should practice checking in before acting, clarifying who is leading which part of a project, and acknowledging each other's contributions rather than competing for control. They also benefit from building in brief pauses before reacting, since two fast-moving personalities can escalate tension if neither takes a moment to breathe. In practice, this might look like agreeing on roles upfront, asking "How do you want to approach this together," or intentionally dividing responsibilities so both feel empowered. When both *Builders* stay grounded and collaborative, they create a dynamic that is decisive, efficient, and highly productive without tipping into power struggles or impatience.

"I Have You Covered"

Overlaying two CVI™ profiles is one of the most powerful ways to illuminate the natural dynamics between two people, because it turns abstract personality differences into a clear, visual map of how their core values interact. When you place one profile directly on top of the other, it becomes immediately obvious how much of each quadrant: Vision (*Merchant*), Strategy (*Innovator*), Structure (*Banker*), and Action (*Builder*) are covered by the pairing. You can literally see where the partnership is strong, where it's balanced, and where it may need intentional support. The real insight comes from comparing the capacity scores in each quadrant. Instead of guessing who should take the lead in a particular phase of a project or moment of decision-making, both individuals can look at the overlay and understand, without ego or emotion, who has more natural energy for that part of the process. This doesn't mean one person is "better" or that the one with the higher capacity score must always lead, it simply shows where each person has more innate *fuel*. Because every effort naturally flows through *Vision, Strategy, Structure,* and *Action*, the overlay helps both people anticipate when one may need to carry the other for a stretch, and when it's time to switch roles. This visual removes the personal charge from the dynamic. Instead of interpreting differences as resistance, conflict, or disinterest, both individuals can *read the moment*, understand each other's wiring, and intentionally let the person with the stronger capacity shine while the other supports. Remember: you don't need a larger capacity to lead someone. You just need humility, awareness, respect for each other's core values, and the willingness to move fluidly between supporting and being supported.

Balanced and Aligned Team

In the past, I have overlaid CVI™ profiles for high-ranking senior leaders alongside the profiles of their past, current, and potential staffs. The comparison revealed striking patterns in how these senior leaders naturally operate and how well their immediate support staffs either aligned with what they needed or where it didn't work out. In some cases, the support staff either had too much of a core value that wasn't needed and therefore the work partnership did not work out or the individual covered areas that were lacking in the senior leader so the partnership was positively beneficial to the leader. This made my feedback to these senior leaders almost psychic or prophetic as I could predict the type of partnership they either had in the past or will have with individuals they were looking to hire. The insights were genuinely eye-opening for them, prompting requests for additional overlays to help inform the best fit and composition for future staff.

Final Thoughts on Interpersonal Dynamics

Interpersonal dynamics are shaped by a rich blend of communication styles, emotional intelligence, power balance, cultural norms, conflict tendencies, boundaries, and trust so understanding these elements gives us a powerful roadmap for building healthier, more resilient relationships. When we recognize how our tone, pacing, and communication patterns affect others, we become more intentional and less reactive. Relationships are healthier when we strengthen emotional intelligence and navigate conflict with empathy instead of defensiveness. When we understand power dynamics, we avoid unintentionally overpowering or silencing others. When we stay aware of cultural and social norms, we reduce assumptions and increase sensitivity. When we understand conflict styles, we stop misinterpreting differences as disrespect and instead see them as natural variations in how people process tension. When we set and honor boundaries, we protect our energy and show others how to treat us. And when we cultivate trust and psychological safety, we create relationships where honesty, vulnerability, and collaboration can thrive. Remembering these key points and using the knowledge of the individual's CVI™ wiring doesn't just help us avoid misunderstandings, it helps us show up with clarity, compassion, and confidence, allowing every relationship in our personal and professional lives to grow stronger, healthier, and more deeply connected.

CHAPTER 16
TEAM DYNAMICS

Team dynamics describe the ways people interact, communicate, and collaborate within a group, shaping whether a team becomes productive and cohesive or tense and ineffective. Healthy team dynamics grow when members trust one another, communicate openly, and share a clear sense of purpose. Successful project teams thrive because individuals feel comfortable voicing concerns, offering ideas, and asking questions without fear of being dismissed. Clear roles, mutual accountability, and leadership that encourages participation rather than control also strengthen a team's ability to work smoothly. In contrast, unhealthy team dynamics often develop when communication breaks down, conflicts are ignored, or certain voices dominate while others are sidelined. When a workplace team becomes competitive to the point of secrecy or when a manager consistently dismisses feedback, causing team members to disengage or stop contributing altogether, the team's dynamic becomes unhealthy and loses its effectiveness. These patterns show that team dynamics are shaped not only by individual personalities but also by the environment, expectations, and norms that guide how people work together.

The CVI™ helps improve team dynamics by giving every individual a clearer understanding of their innate core values, motivations, and preferred ways of contributing. When people know whether they naturally lead with *Builder* energy (action and results), *Merchant* energy (relationships and vision), *Innovator* energy (problem-solving and systems thinking), or *Banker* energy (knowledge and precision), they can approach their work with greater confidence and authenticity. This self-awareness reduces internal friction because individuals stop trying to force themselves into roles that drain them and instead lean into the areas where they naturally excel. For example, someone with strong *Innovator* energy may realize that their tendency to analyze before acting isn't hesitation, it's an ability that helps the team avoid costly mistakes. Meanwhile, a *Builder* may recognize that their drive to move quickly is valuable but needs to be balanced with input from others. When each person understands their core wiring, they communicate more clearly, set healthier boundaries, and collaborate with less tension, ultimately improving both personal performance and the overall team dynamics.

Improve Communication and Reduce Misunderstandings

As mentioned previously in this book, the CVI™ also enhances team dynamics by helping people understand how their teammates lead, communicate, deal with conflict, and make decisions. Many workplace conflicts stem not from actual disagreement but from differences in communication styles. A *Merchant*-heavy teammate may express ideas enthusiastically and focus on relationships, while a *Banker*-heavy teammate may communicate in a more structured, detail-oriented way. Without a shared framework, these differences can lead to frustration or misinterpretation. The CVI™ gives teams a common language to explain these patterns, reducing the likelihood of taking things personally or assuming negative intent. When team members understand that a colleague's directness, caution, or enthusiasm is simply part of their core value set (not a criticism or challenge), they respond with more patience and empathy. This shift dramatically reduces unnecessary conflict and creates a more psychologically safe environment where people feel comfortable speaking up. Over time, communication becomes more efficient, respectful, and aligned with each person's natural positive contributions.

Merchants

A *Merchant* naturally elevates team communication because they are deeply attuned to people, relationships, and emotional undercurrents. They create an atmosphere where individuals feel heard, valued, and safe expressing their thoughts, which encourages open dialogue and reduces misunderstandings. Their instinct to connect helps them bridge gaps between teammates who might otherwise struggle to relate to one another, and they often act as the emotional glue that keeps conversations respectful and collaborative. *Merchants* excel at drawing out quieter voices, validating diverse perspectives, and framing discussions in ways that build trust rather than tension. Their warmth and empathy make it easier for teams to navigate difficult topics, resolve conflicts constructively, and maintain a sense of unity even during stressful moments. Because they communicate with sincerity and a genuine desire to understand others, they help teams stay aligned not just on tasks, but on shared purpose and motivation.

However, a *Merchant's* communication style can also hinder team dynamics when their desire for harmony outweighs the need for clarity or directness. They may soften messages to avoid hurting feelings, which can lead to confusion, mixed signals, or unresolved issues that linger beneath the surface. When conflict arises, a *Merchant* might prioritize keeping the peace over addressing the root problem, allowing tension to build quietly instead of guiding the team toward a firm resolution. Their tendency to focus on emotional impact can make it difficult for them to deliver tough feedback or set boundaries, especially if they fear damaging relationships. In fast-paced or high-stakes situations, this reluctance to be direct may slow decision-making or prevent the team from confronting performance challenges. Because they are so attuned to how others feel, *Merchants* can unintentionally over-accommodate certain personalities, creating imbalances in communication where more assertive voices dominate and quieter frustrations go unspoken.

Innovators

An *Innovator* strengthens team communication by encouraging deeper thinking, thoughtful dialogue, and a more strategic exchange of ideas. They naturally ask insightful questions that help the group explore possibilities, clarify assumptions, and uncover connections that others may overlook. Their calm, reflective style creates space for more measured conversations, especially in situations where the team risks rushing to conclusions. *Innovators* often act as intellectual bridges, translating complex concepts into clearer language and helping teammates understand the "why" behind decisions. Because they value ideas over ego, they promote an environment where people feel comfortable sharing unconventional thoughts or proposing new approaches. Their ability to see multiple angles also helps them mediate misunderstandings, reframing issues in ways that reduce tension and guide the team toward more thoughtful, collaborative communication.

However, an *Innovator's* communication style can also hinder team dynamics when their natural tendencies lean too far toward analysis or exploration. They may take longer to articulate their thoughts, which can frustrate teammates who prefer quick, direct exchanges. Their desire to consider every angle can make conversations feel slow or overly complex, especially for action-oriented individuals who want clear direction. *Innovators* may also unintentionally derail discussions by introducing new ideas before the team has finished addressing the current topic, creating confusion or a sense of scattered focus. When they are still processing internally, they can appear distant or disengaged, leading others to misinterpret their silence as lack of interest or agreement. In high-pressure situations that require fast, decisive communication, their thoughtful, exploratory style may be seen as hesitation, which can disrupt momentum and create friction within the group.

. . .

Bankers

A *Banker* strengthens team communication by bringing clarity, structure, and consistency to every interaction. They excel at organizing information, documenting decisions, and ensuring that everyone has access to accurate, reliable details. This helps reduce confusion and prevents misunderstandings that can derail collaboration. *Bankers* communicate in a steady, methodical way that keeps discussions grounded and focused, especially when conversations start to drift or become emotionally charged. Their commitment to precision ensures that expectations are clearly stated, processes are well understood, and follow-through is dependable. Because they value thoroughness, they often ask the questions others overlook, helping the team address gaps before they become problems. Their calm, detail-oriented communication style creates a sense of stability that helps teams feel secure and aligned.

However, a *Banker's* communication style can also hinder team dynamics when their need for certainty and structure becomes too rigid. They may struggle in conversations that require quick decisions, improvisation, or emotional nuance, often slowing the group down while they seek more information or clarification. Their preference for detailed explanations can overwhelm teammates who want concise, high-level communication, leading to frustration or disengagement. *Bankers* may also come across as overly cautious or resistant to new ideas, especially when discussions involve change or ambiguity. Because they prioritize accuracy over emotional connection, they may unintentionally dismiss feelings or relational cues that are important to others. In fast-moving or highly collaborative environments, their communication can feel overly formal or inflexible, creating tension with teammates who value spontaneity, creativity, or rapid dialogue.

. . .

Builders

A *Builder* strengthens team communication by bringing directness, clarity, and a strong sense of purpose to every conversation. They cut through ambiguity quickly, helping the group stay focused on what matters most and preventing discussions from drifting into unproductive territory. Their confidence encourages others to speak plainly and commit to decisions, which can speed up alignment and reduce confusion. *Builders* are skilled at rallying people around a goal, using straightforward language that energizes the team and keeps momentum high. In moments of uncertainty, their decisive communication style provides stability and direction, helping teammates feel grounded and ready to act. Because they value efficiency, they often streamline communication channels, ensuring that information flows cleanly and that everyone understands expectations, responsibilities, and next steps.

However, a *Builder's* communication style can also hinder team dynamics when their drive for speed and action overshadows the need for patience or deeper dialogue. Their directness may come across as blunt or dismissive, especially to teammates who prefer more context, emotional nuance, or collaborative discussion. *Builders* can unintentionally dominate conversations, leaving less assertive voices unheard or causing others to feel rushed into decisions before they are ready. When the team needs to explore ideas, process emotions, or build consensus, a *Builder's* urgency may create tension or shut down valuable contributions. They may also become frustrated with what they perceive as unnecessary discussion, which can lead to curt responses or a tone that discourages open communication. In these moments, their strength in driving action becomes a barrier to the relational and reflective communication that some situations require.

Squarish CVI™ Profile

A squarish individual improves team communication by acting as a natural integrator who can understand and relate to all four core value energies. Their balanced wiring allows them to translate between different communication styles, helping teammates who think, speak, or process information in very different ways find common ground. They can shift from analytical to relational, from strategic to action-oriented, depending on what the moment requires, which makes them a stabilizing presence in discussions. Because they appreciate the strengths of every CVI™ profile, they tend to validate diverse viewpoints and encourage more inclusive dialogue. This helps reduce misunderstandings, soften conflict, and create an environment where people feel comfortable contributing. Their ability to see multiple sides of an issue also allows them to reframe conversations in ways that promote clarity and shared understanding, strengthening the overall communication flow within the team.

However, a squarish individual may hinder team communication when their versatility leads to mixed signals or a lack of clear direction. Because they can empathize with every perspective, they may hesitate to take a firm stance, which can leave the team unsure about priorities or next steps. Their ability to shift between communication styles can also make them appear inconsistent, especially to teammates who prefer a more predictable or decisive approach. In emotionally charged or high-pressure situations, they may struggle to choose which core value to lean into, causing delays or overly diplomatic responses that fail to address the core issue. Their desire to maintain balance can lead them to over-explain, over-accommodate, or avoid necessary confrontation, which may allow misunderstandings to linger. When the team needs strong direction or a clear communication anchor, their broad adaptability can unintentionally create ambiguity rather than alignment.

Core Value	How They Thrive	Why They Struggle
Builder	Excels with clear, direct communication; delegates and decides efficiently	Can appear blunt or impatient; may overlook emotional nuance
Merchant	Builds rapport easily; reads emotional cues; fosters open dialogue	Avoids conflict; may soften messages too much or overinterpret tone
Innovator	Communicates well when exploring ideas; offers balanced, thoughtful insights	Explanations may be too complex; struggles with fast-paced or emotional conversations
Banker	Provides clarity, detail, and accuracy; reduces ambiguity	May overwhelm with detail; hesitates when unprepared; struggles with spontaneous dialogue
Squarish	Adapts communication style to match the situation; bridges gaps between different personalities	May seem inconsistent or unclear; can hesitate because they see multiple perspectives at once

Figure 11. Core Values Communication Overview.

Build Balanced Teams and Assign Roles Strategically

Another powerful way the CVI™ improves team dynamics is by helping leaders and HR offices build balanced teams and assign responsibilities in ways that maximize innate CVI™ wiring. Teams often struggle not because of a lack of talent but because the distribution of core values is uneven or misaligned with the work. For example, a team overloaded with *Builders* may move quickly but overlook important details, while a team dominated by *Bankers* may gather excellent information but struggle to make timely decisions. By mapping out the CVI™ profiles of the group, leaders can identify gaps, overlaps, and opportunities to create a more harmonious blend of energies. This allows for smarter role assignments such as giving *Innovators* the lead on complex problem-solving, *Merchants* the lead on client relationships, *Builders* the lead on execution, and *Bankers* the lead on documentation or quality control. When people are placed in roles by their HR Department that match their natural core values, they perform better, feel more fulfilled, and collaborate more effectively. The entire team benefits from a more intentional, core values-based structure.

Taylor Protocols™ has a program called the *Top Performer Profile™* that provides this level of insight. This system is used to evaluate job roles using the CVI™ to analyze job roles, create a *Top Performer Profile™*, and then match candidates in order to improve hiring and support organizational design. You can learn more about this system by going to the *Taylor Protocols* web site.

When evaluating team fit, it's important to remember that an individual's dominant core value (*Chapter 2*) or CVI™ Contribution Type™ (*Chapter 4*) is only one part of the picture. Every person has capacities in all four core values (*Chapter 3*), and those capacities influence how strongly they express certain behaviors, contributions, and challenges. The descriptions below focus on more targeted patterns that become increasingly accurate as a person's capacity in a given core value grows. To get a truly holistic understanding of how someone will function within a team, it's essential to consider their dominant core value, Contribution Type™, and the full range of their core value capacities, rather than relying on a single label or profile slice.

Merchants

A *Merchant* can dramatically improve team dynamics when placed in roles that allow them to build relationships, foster trust, and strengthen the emotional fabric of the group. Their natural empathy and ability to read people make them exceptional at creating an environment where individuals feel valued, supported, and connected. This helps reduce conflict, encourages open communication, and boosts morale across the team. *Merchants* excel at bringing people together around shared purpose, smoothing over interpersonal friction, and ensuring that everyone feels included in the conversation. They thrive in roles such as team lead, culture champion, onboarding mentor, client-facing liaison, or any position that requires building rapport and maintaining strong relational ties. In these roles, their warmth and intuitive understanding of others help the team collaborate more effectively and maintain a positive, cohesive atmosphere.

However, team dynamics can suffer when a *Merchant* is placed in roles that require emotional detachment, strict objectivity, or difficult decision-making that may disappoint or upset others. Their deep concern for harmony can make it challenging for them to enforce boundaries, deliver tough feedback, or make choices that prioritize performance over relationships. In roles that demand firm accountability or rapid, decisive action, a *Merchant* may hesitate or soften messages to avoid conflict, which can lead to confusion, unresolved issues, or uneven expectations within the team. They may struggle in positions such as performance manager, disciplinarian, operations enforcer, or roles that require frequent confrontation or resource allocation that feels "unfair." In these situations, their strengths become constraints, and their desire to protect relationships can unintentionally hinder clarity, momentum, and the team's ability to address problems directly.

Innovators

An *Innovator* can significantly improve team dynamics when placed in roles that allow them to elevate thinking, introduce fresh perspectives, and help the group navigate complexity with clarity. Their natural strengths in pattern recognition, strategic insight, and creative problem-solving make them invaluable in discussions where the team needs to explore possibilities, refine ideas, or challenge assumptions. *Innovators* help teams communicate more thoughtfully by asking insightful questions, reframing issues, and encouraging deeper analysis before decisions are made. They bring calm, reflective energy that balances more reactive personalities and helps prevent rushed or poorly considered choices. *Innovators* flourish in roles such as strategic advisor, process designer, innovation lead, systems thinker, or any position where the team benefits from someone who can see multiple angles and guide conversations toward smarter, more holistic solutions. In these roles, they strengthen communication by helping the team think more clearly, collaborate more intentionally, and align around well-reasoned strategies.

However, team dynamics can suffer when an *Innovator* is placed in roles that demand rapid execution, constant multitasking, or strict adherence to predefined processes. Their natural desire to explore options and analyze possibilities can slow momentum in environments where quick decisions are essential. In roles that require heavy structure or repetitive tasks, they may become disengaged or frustrated, which can create communication gaps or tension with teammates who rely on fast, direct responses. *Innovators* may also struggle in positions such as operations enforcer, production manager, accounting, or any role that prioritizes speed, routine, or rigid compliance over thoughtful exploration. In these situations, their tendency to think broadly rather than act quickly can be misinterpreted as indecision or lack of urgency, which may hinder team cohesion and disrupt the flow of communication.

Bankers

A *Banker* can greatly improve team dynamics when placed in roles that rely on clarity, consistency, and well-structured communication. Their natural strengths in accuracy, documentation, and process management help teams stay organized and aligned, reducing confusion and preventing small issues from turning into larger problems. *Bankers* excel at creating systems that keep information flowing smoothly, ensuring that everyone knows what has been decided, what needs to happen next, and how progress will be tracked. Their calm, methodical communication style brings stability to group interactions, especially when discussions become chaotic or overly emotional. They ask the practical questions others may overlook, helping the team think through details that support stronger execution. *Bankers* flourish in roles such as project coordinator, quality assurance lead, compliance manager, documentation specialist, or any position that requires maintaining order, tracking commitments, and ensuring that the team operates with precision and reliability.

However, team dynamics can suffer when a *Banker* is placed in roles that demand rapid improvisation, high emotional engagement, or constant adaptation to shifting priorities. Their preference for structure and complete information can slow momentum in environments where quick decisions are essential. In roles that require intuitive people-reading, spontaneous communication, or navigating interpersonal conflict, a *Banker* may feel uncomfortable or overwhelmed, which can create tension or communication gaps within the team. They may struggle in positions such as crisis manager, high-velocity operations lead, culture-building facilitator, or any role that requires fast pivots, emotional sensitivity, or flexible decision-making. In these situations, their need for certainty and order may be misinterpreted as rigidity or resistance, potentially hindering collaboration and slowing the team's ability to respond effectively to dynamic challenges.

Builders

A *Builder* can significantly elevate team dynamics when placed in roles that harness their natural drive, decisiveness, and ability to create forward momentum. They thrive in environments where clarity, action, and accountability are essential, and they help teams avoid stagnation by cutting through ambiguity and pushing conversations toward concrete outcomes. *Builders* bring a sense of urgency that energizes others, and their direct communication style helps eliminate confusion about priorities or expectations. They excel at rallying people around a goal, keeping the group focused, and ensuring that commitments turn into results. *Builders* flourish in roles such as project lead, operations manager, task-force captain, crisis coordinator, or any position where the team needs someone to take charge, make quick decisions, and maintain steady progress. In these roles, they strengthen team dynamics by providing structure, direction, and the confidence that the work will move forward no matter the obstacles.

However, team dynamics can suffer when a *Builder* is placed in roles that require patience, deep listening, or a highly collaborative and exploratory approach. Their instinct to move quickly can unintentionally shut down discussion, overshadow quieter voices, or create pressure that makes teammates feel rushed or unheard. *Builders* may struggle in roles that demand emotional sensitivity, consensus-building, or extended periods of reflection, as these environments can feel slow or inefficient to them. They may also become frustrated when others need time to process ideas or when decisions require broad input rather than swift action. *Builders* often struggle in roles such as team mediator, culture facilitator, strategic analyst, or positions that require nurturing long-term relational harmony. In these situations, their strengths can become liabilities, and their push for speed or decisiveness may disrupt communication, create tension, or hinder the team's ability to explore ideas fully before committing to a direction.

Squarish CVI™ Profile

A squarish individual can greatly improve team dynamics because they naturally understand and appreciate all four core value energies, allowing them to act as a bridge between teammates who communicate, think, and work very differently. Their balanced wiring helps them translate perspectives, mediate misunderstandings, and create an environment where everyone feels seen and included. They can shift fluidly between relational support, creative problem-solving, structured planning, and decisive action, depending on what the team needs in the moment. This adaptability makes them especially valuable in roles such as team facilitator, cross-functional coordinator, project integrator, culture ambassador, or any position that requires harmonizing diverse personalities and keeping communication flowing smoothly. In these roles, they elevate team dynamics by promoting understanding, reducing friction, and ensuring that no single core value dominates at the expense of others.

However, team dynamics can suffer when a squarish individual is placed in roles that demand strong specialization, rigid consistency, or unwavering commitment to a single core energy. Because they can see the validity of multiple viewpoints, they may hesitate to take firm stances or struggle to enforce boundaries when clarity is needed. Their flexibility can become a liability in roles that require strict decisiveness, deep technical focus, or sustained emotional intensity. They may struggle in positions such as high-pressure crisis lead, strict compliance enforcer, specialized technical expert, or roles that require long periods of operating in one dominant core value without room to shift. In these situations, their broad adaptability can create ambiguity, slow decision-making, or lead to internal conflict as they try to balance competing priorities. This can unintentionally hinder team dynamics by making direction unclear or by causing teammates to rely too heavily on them to fill gaps that should be addressed through clearer role definition.

Core Value	How They Thrive	Why They Struggle
Builder	Takes charge, drives momentum, and ensures execution	May dominate decisions; becomes frustrated with slow or indecisive teammates
Merchant	Understands people deeply; builds cohesion and morale	Avoids tough decisions; may prioritize harmony over performance alignment
Innovator	Designs solutions, improves systems, and sees strategic patterns	Struggles with repetitive tasks or rigid roles; may seem indecisive
Banker	Ensures accuracy, structure, and consistency; stabilizes the team	Resists change; slows down when information is incomplete or unclear
Squarish	Sees the value of all four energies; can flex into multiple roles and identify team gaps	May be overused as a "utility player"; struggles to define a clear specialty or advocate for one role

Figure 12. Building Teams and Assigning Roles Overview.

Reduce Burnout and Increase Engagement

The CVI™ also contributes to healthier team dynamics by reducing burnout and increasing engagement. When individuals consistently work outside their core value contributions, they experience stress, frustration, and fatigue (*Reference Chapter 14 on Energy Management*).

Over time, this leads to disengagement and even turnover. The CVI™ helps leaders identify when someone is being asked to operate too far outside their natural zone for too long. For instance, a *Merchant* who thrives on connection may feel drained if isolated in data-heavy tasks, while a *Banker* may feel overwhelmed if forced into constant improvisation or rapid-fire decision-making. By understanding these dynamics, leaders can adjust workloads, redistribute responsibilities, or provide support that keeps people energized rather than depleted. This not only improves individual well-being but also stabilizes the team as a whole. When people feel seen, valued, and aligned with their core values, they show up with more enthusiasm, creativity, and resilience. Qualities that elevate the entire group's performance.

Merchants

Merchants can play a powerful role in minimizing burnout on a team because they naturally tune in to emotional well-being, relational health, and the subtle signs of stress that others might overlook. Their instinct to check in, offer encouragement, and create a sense of belonging helps teammates feel supported rather than isolated during demanding periods. *Merchants* often notice when someone is overwhelmed and can intervene early by redistributing workload, initiating honest conversations, or simply providing the empathy that helps people reset. They also excel at celebrating wins (big or small) which boosts morale and keeps motivation alive. For example, a *Merchant* might organize informal team touch points to maintain connection, pair teammates thoughtfully so no one feels alone in a challenge, or advocate for breaks and realistic timelines when they sense the group is stretched thin. Their ability to foster trust and emotional safety creates an environment where people feel comfortable asking for help, which is one of the strongest buffers against burnout.

However, *Merchants* themselves are highly vulnerable to burnout when placed in roles or team dynamics that demand emotional detachment, constant conflict management, or decisions that may disappoint others. Because they care deeply about harmony and connection, situations where they must enforce strict accountability, deliver tough feedback, or prioritize performance over relationships can drain them quickly. They may also burn out in environments where team members are disengaged, unresponsive, or resistant to connection, as this undermines the very strengths they rely on. Roles such as disciplinarian, crisis enforcer, or positions requiring frequent confrontation can be especially taxing. To prevent burnout, *Merchants* need clear boundaries, shared responsibility for emotional labor, and leaders who recognize that they cannot be the team's sole source of relational support. Giving them space to recharge, pairing them with teammates who can handle tough conversations, and ensuring they have permission to say no when emotional demands become too heavy helps preserve their energy and allows them to continue contributing in the relationally rich ways that make them so valuable.

Innovators

An *Innovator* can play a major role in minimizing burnout on a team because they naturally bring clarity, creativity, and thoughtful problem-solving to situations that might otherwise feel overwhelming. Their ability to step back, analyze patterns, and identify smarter ways of working helps reduce unnecessary stress and inefficiency. *Innovators* often spot bottlenecks before they escalate, propose streamlined processes, and introduce tools or strategies that make workloads more manageable. For example, they might redesign a workflow to eliminate redundant steps, create a decision-making framework that reduces confusion, or help teammates reframe challenges in ways that feel less emotionally draining. Their calm, reflective presence also helps stabilize team energy during high-pressure moments, encouraging others to slow down, think clearly, and avoid reactive decision-making. By offering thoughtful solutions and helping the team operate more intelligently rather than more intensely, *Innovators* create an environment where burnout is less likely to take root.

However, *Innovators* themselves are prone to burnout when placed in roles or team dynamics that demand constant urgency, rapid-fire decisions, or rigid adherence to processes that leave no room for exploration. Environments where they are pressured to act quickly without time to think, or where their ideas are dismissed in favor of speed, can drain them quickly. Roles such as crisis responder, high-velocity operations lead, or positions requiring repetitive, detail-heavy tasks can feel suffocating because they limit the *Innovator's* ability to think broadly and creatively. Team dynamics that involve constant interruptions, emotional volatility, or unclear expectations can also overwhelm them, as these conditions disrupt their natural need for space to process and reflect. To prevent burnout, *Innovators* benefit from having protected thinking time, clear priorities, and the autonomy to explore solutions before committing to action. Pairing them with teammates who can handle rapid execution, giving them opportunities to contribute strategically rather than reactively, and ensuring they are not overloaded with repetitive tasks helps preserve their energy and allows them to contribute at their highest level.

Bankers

A *Banker* can minimize burnout on a team by bringing structure, predictability, and clarity to environments that might otherwise feel chaotic or overwhelming. Their natural strengths in organization, documentation, and process management help reduce the mental load on teammates who struggle with ambiguity or shifting expectations. *Bankers* create systems that keep information accessible and responsibilities clearly defined, which prevents confusion and reduces the stress that comes from constantly trying to "figure things out." For example, a *Banker* might build a shared tracking system that keeps deadlines visible, maintain detailed notes so the team doesn't waste energy rehashing decisions, or establish routines that make workloads more manageable. Their calm, steady communication style also helps stabilize team morale during high-pressure periods, giving others a sense of reliability and grounding. By ensuring that processes run smoothly and that people know what to expect, *Bankers* help the entire team conserve emotional and cognitive energy...one of the most effective ways to prevent burnout.

However, *Bankers* themselves are highly susceptible to burnout when placed in roles or team dynamics that demand constant improvisation, rapid pivots, or emotionally charged interactions. Environments where expectations change frequently, information is incomplete, or decisions must be made quickly without time for analysis can drain them quickly. Roles such as crisis responder, high-velocity operations lead, or positions requiring heavy emotional labor, like conflict mediator or morale manager, can overwhelm a *Banker* because they pull them away from the structure and clarity they rely on. Team dynamics that involve disorganization, inconsistent communication, or teammates who ignore established processes can also be exhausting, as *Bankers* often feel responsible for holding everything together. To prevent burnout, they need stable routines, clear expectations, and the authority to maintain the systems they create. Pairing them with teammates who can handle fast-paced improvisation, giving them time to prepare before major decisions, and ensuring they are not the sole keeper of organizational order helps protect their energy and allows them to contribute at their highest level.

Builders

A *Builder* can minimize burnout on a team by injecting clarity, momentum, and a strong sense of direction into the group's daily rhythm. Their natural drive to take action helps prevent the kind of stagnation that often leads to frustration and emotional fatigue. *Builders* cut through ambiguity quickly, which reduces the mental load on teammates who struggle when expectations are unclear or constantly shifting. They keep projects moving forward, ensuring that tasks don't pile up or linger unresolved, one of the biggest contributors to burnout. For example, a *Builder* might step in to break a large, overwhelming project into manageable steps, make quick decisions that remove bottlenecks, or rally the team with a clear plan when morale is dipping. Their confidence and decisiveness create a sense of stability, helping others feel supported and less anxious about what comes next. By providing structure, momentum, and a bias toward action, *Builders* help the entire team conserve emotional energy and maintain a healthier, more sustainable pace.

However, *Builders* themselves are prone to burnout when placed in roles or team dynamics that require constant patience, emotional sensitivity, in-depth research, or prolonged deliberation without clear outcomes. Situations where decisions drag on, where people avoid taking responsibility, or where the team repeatedly revisits the same issues can drain them quickly. Roles such as team mediator, culture facilitator, or positions requiring extensive consensus-building can feel suffocating because they force *Builders* to slow down in ways that conflict with their natural wiring. They may also burn out in environments where others resist taking action, leaving the *Builder* to carry the weight of momentum alone. To prevent burnout, *Builders* need clear authority to make decisions, teammates who share responsibility for execution, and environments where progress is visible and celebrated. Giving them defined goals, reducing unnecessary meetings, and pairing them with colleagues who can handle relational or reflective tasks helps preserve their energy and allows them to operate at their best without becoming overwhelmed by dynamics that clash with their core strengths.

Squarish CVI™ Profile

A squarish individual can minimize burnout on a team because their balanced access to all four core value energies allows them to sense what the group needs at any given moment and adjust accordingly. They can shift into relational support when the team is emotionally strained, step into structured *Banker*-style organization when processes feel chaotic, bring in *Innovator*-style reframing when people are stuck, or adopt *Builder*-style decisiveness when momentum is lagging. This versatility helps prevent pressure from accumulating in any one area, which is a major contributor to burnout. For example, a squarish teammate might notice rising tension and initiate a grounding conversation, reorganize a workflow to reduce overwhelm, or help the group rethink a problem in a way that feels more manageable. They often act as a stabilizing force, smoothing communication, redistributing emotional load, and helping teammates feel both supported and understood. Their ability to flex into whatever role the moment requires makes them a natural buffer against stress and fatigue across the team.

However, squarish individuals are at high risk of burnout when placed in roles or team dynamics that demand constant shape-shifting without clear boundaries or support. Because they can do a bit of everything, teams may unintentionally over-rely on them to fill gaps, mediate conflicts, or adapt to dysfunction that others are unwilling to address. Environments with unclear expectations, chronic interpersonal tension, or constant switching between priorities can drain them quickly, as they feel compelled to meet everyone's needs simultaneously. As a leader, they have to resist the urge to take on everything that comes their way. Delegation is very hard for them to do because they can just pass all of the tasks to themselves in all four areas (*Merchant, Innovator, Banker,* and *Builder*). They can also end up being the choke point if in charge because they sometimes need to be able and *reach out and touch* the areas, they are responsible for which means their areas of responsibility can only go as far as their capacity allows them to.

To prevent burnout, they need clearly defined responsibilities, shared ownership of relational and operational tasks, and permission to say no when demands exceed their capacity. Giving them structured support, predictable rhythms, and teammates who can take on specialized responsibilities helps preserve their energy and allows them to use their versatility as a strength rather than a burden.

Core Value	How They Thrive	Why They Struggle
Builder	Stays energized by action and progress; thrives with clear goals	Overcommits; ignores fatigue; becomes drained when progress stalls
Merchant	Gains energy from connection and meaningful relationships	Absorbs others' stress; overextends emotionally; avoids boundaries
Innovator	Stays engaged when given space to think and solve problems	Burns out when rushed, restricted, or stuck in repetitive tasks
Banker	Thrives with predictable workloads and clear expectations	Overwhelmed by chaos, rapid change, or unclear direction
Squarish	Avoids burnout by shifting between energies; stays engaged through variety	Flexibility leads others to overload them; may not notice burnout until all energies are depleted

Figure 13. Maintaining Energy and Burn-Out Overview.

Strengthen Trust and Collaboration

The CVI™ improves team dynamics by fostering deeper trust and collaboration. When team members understand each other's core values, they develop a greater appreciation for the unique contributions each person brings. Instead of viewing differences as obstacles, they begin to see them as complementary contributions. This shift encourages more inclusive decision-making, where diverse perspectives are welcomed rather than dismissed. It also builds trust because people feel understood at a deeper level, not just for what they do, but for who they are. Teams that use the CVI™ often report that conversations become more honest, feedback becomes easier to give and receive, and collaboration becomes more fluid. The shared understanding created by the CVI™ acts as a foundation for stronger relationships, more effective teamwork, and a culture where people feel safe to contribute their best ideas. Over time, this trust becomes a competitive advantage, enabling the team to navigate challenges with unity and confidence.

. . .

Merchant

A *Merchant* strengthens trust and collaboration on a team by creating an environment where people feel genuinely valued, heard, and emotionally connected. Their natural empathy allows them to sense when someone is struggling or feeling overlooked, and they step in to build bridges before tension escalates. *Merchants* excel at fostering open dialogue, encouraging teammates to share ideas without fear of judgment, and celebrating contributions in ways that make people feel appreciated. They often initiate relationship-building moments such as informal check-ins, team-bonding conversations, or thoughtful recognition that deepen trust and strengthen the social fabric of the group. For example, a *Merchant* might mediate a misunderstanding between two teammates by helping each person feel understood, or they might bring the team together around a shared purpose during a stressful project. Their ability to create psychological safety helps collaboration flourish because people are more willing to take risks, ask for help, and support one another when they feel connected.

However, a *Merchant* can unintentionally weaken trust and collaboration when they go dark, a state where emotional overload or relational stress causes them to withdraw, avoid difficult conversations, or become inconsistent in their communication. When overwhelmed, they may retreat inward and stop offering the warmth and connection the team relies on, leaving others confused about what they are thinking or feeling. For example, a *Merchant* who feels unappreciated might quietly disengage from discussions, offer vague agreements instead of honest input, or avoid addressing a brewing conflict because they fear upsetting someone. They may also promise support to multiple teammates in an effort to keep everyone happy, only to fall short because they overextended themselves, which can create frustration or a sense of unreliability. In more intense moments, a *Merchant* might triangulate and build alliances against those who have hurt or wronged them on the team. These behaviors can erode trust because teammates sense the frustration but they do not want to take sides.

When a *Merchant* goes dark, the relational glue they normally provide weakens, and the team may struggle with mixed signals, unresolved tension, or a lack of emotional clarity.

Innovator

An *Innovator* strengthens trust and collaboration on a team by helping people think more clearly, communicate more thoughtfully, and work together with a shared sense of purpose. Their natural ability to analyze situations from multiple angles allows them to bring clarity to complex conversations, which helps teammates feel more confident and aligned. *Innovators* often ask insightful questions that draw out deeper thinking and encourage others to articulate their ideas more fully. This creates an environment where people feel intellectually respected and safe to contribute. They also excel at reframing problems in ways that reduce tension and open up new possibilities. For example, an *Innovator* might help two teammates stuck in a disagreement see the underlying assumptions driving their conflict, or they might propose a creative solution that integrates everyone's concerns. Their calm, reflective presence helps stabilize group dynamics, making collaboration smoother and more grounded.

However, an *Innovator* can weaken trust and collaboration when they go dark, which happens when they feel dismissed, rushed, or pressured to act without adequate time to think. In this state, they may withdraw into analysis, become overly detached, or stop sharing their insights altogether. For example, an *Innovator* who feels their ideas are repeatedly ignored might retreat into silence during meetings, offering minimal input even when their perspective is needed. They may also become overly critical or skeptical, questioning others without offering constructive alternatives. In more intense moments, they might disengage from collaboration entirely, focusing on independent work while avoiding team discussions that feel chaotic or emotionally charged. This withdrawal can create confusion, as teammates sense the *Innovator* pulling away but do not understand why. When an *Innovator* goes dark, the team loses the clarity, thoughtful dialogue, and integrative problem-solving they normally provide, which can lead to misunderstandings, stalled progress, and a breakdown in collaborative trust.

Banker

A *Banker* strengthens trust and collaboration on a team by bringing consistency, clarity, and reliability to every interaction. Their steady presence helps teammates feel grounded because they know the *Banker* will follow through, document decisions accurately, and keep information organized. This reduces misunderstandings and creates a shared sense of stability that makes collaboration easier. *Bankers* help teams trust one another by ensuring that expectations are clear and that everyone has access to the same facts. For example, a *Banker* might maintain detailed meeting notes so no one feels left out of the loop, create a transparent tracking system that keeps responsibilities visible, or clarify ambiguous instructions before they cause confusion. Their calm, methodical communication style also helps de-escalate tense moments, allowing the team to stay focused on solutions rather than conflict. By providing structure and dependability, *Bankers* help the team operate with confidence and mutual respect.

However, a *Banker* can weaken trust and collaboration when they go dark, which happens when they feel overwhelmed by chaos, pressured to act without enough information, or frustrated by teammates who ignore established processes. In this state, they may withdraw into rigid routines, become overly critical, or shut down communication altogether. For example, a *Banker* who feels the team is being careless might stop sharing updates, retreat into solo work, or insist on rules without explaining their reasoning. They may also become passive and avoid contributing if they believe their need for clarity will be dismissed. In more intense moments, a *Banker* might quietly disengage from collaboration, offering minimal input while privately feeling resentful or anxious about the lack of structure. This withdrawal can create confusion because teammates rely on the *Banker* for stability and may not realize why they have pulled back. When a *Banker* goes dark, the team loses the clarity, organization, and steady communication that normally support trust, which can lead to misalignment, frustration, and a breakdown in collaborative flow.

Builders

A *Builder* strengthens trust and collaboration on a team by providing clarity, direction, and a sense of dependable momentum that others can rally around. Their straightforward communication style helps eliminate ambiguity, which makes teammates feel secure about what needs to happen and how to move forward together. *Builders* are often the ones who step in when a project is stalling, turning vague intentions into concrete actions and ensuring that commitments are honored. For example, a *Builder* might take charge of organizing a scattered project plan, set clear deadlines that everyone can align with, or step into a leadership role during a stressful moment to keep the group focused and unified. Their willingness to make decisions and take responsibility builds confidence within the team, and their action-oriented nature helps people trust that progress will continue even when challenges arise. By creating structure and driving execution, *Builders* help the team collaborate more effectively and feel supported by a strong, reliable presence.

However, a *Builder* can weaken trust and collaboration when they go dark, which happens when they feel ignored, undermined, or forced into prolonged indecision. In this state, their usual decisiveness can flip into aggression, impatience, or dismissive. For example, a *Builder* who feels the team is overthinking or avoiding action might stop participating in discussions, offer only curt responses, or push ahead independently without coordinating with others. They may also become overly controlling or dismissive if they believe others are slowing things down, which can create tension and make teammates feel unheard. In more intense moments, a *Builder* might shut down emotionally, retreat from collaboration, or express frustration in ways that feel abrupt or harsh. This shift can erode trust because the team relies on the *Builder's* stability and clarity, and their sudden withdrawal or rigidity creates uncertainty. When a *Builder* goes dark, the group may experience fractured communication, reduced psychological safety, and a breakdown in the collaborative rhythm that normally benefits from the *Builder's* strong, steady leadership.

Squarish CVI™ Profile

A squarish individual strengthens trust and collaboration on a team by naturally bridging gaps between different personalities and work styles. Because they have relatively balanced access to all four core value energies, they can understand and validate a wide range of perspectives, which helps teammates feel seen and respected. Their ability to shift between relational support, structured organization, creative problem solving, and decisive action allows them to meet people where they are and keep communication flowing smoothly. For example, a squarish teammate might help a *Merchant* and a *Builder* understand each other during a tense moment, or they might translate an *Innovator's* abstract idea into a concrete plan that a *Banker* can execute. They often serve as informal mediators, connectors, and integrators, helping the team stay aligned even when pressures rise. Their flexibility and empathy create an atmosphere of psychological safety, making it easier for people to collaborate openly and trust that their contributions will be understood in context.

However, a squarish individual can weaken trust and collaboration when they go dark, which happens when the constant pressure to adapt, mediate, and fill gaps becomes overwhelming. Because they can do a little of everything, teams may unintentionally rely on them too heavily, and when that burden becomes too much, they may withdraw, become indecisive, or shut down emotionally. For example, a squarish person who feels pulled in too many directions might stop offering their usual support, avoid taking a stance to prevent disappointing anyone, or quietly disengage from conversations where they once played a stabilizing role. They may also become overly agreeable on the surface while privately feeling resentful or exhausted, which creates mixed signals that confuse the team. In more intense moments, they might retreat into silence, delay decisions, or distance themselves from collaboration altogether because they no longer have the energy to balance competing needs. When a squarish individual goes dark, the team loses a key source of cohesion and translation, and the sudden absence of their integrative presence can lead to misunderstandings, fractured communication, and a noticeable drop in collaborative trust.

Core Value	How They Thrive	Why They Struggle
Builder	Builds trust through decisive action and reliability	May overshadow others; struggles when collaboration slows momentum
Merchant	Creates emotional safety; unifies the team; fosters openness	Takes breaches of trust personally; avoids conflict; may over-accommodate
Innovator	Integrates diverse perspectives; collaborates through thoughtful problem-solving	Withdraws when ideas are dismissed; struggles with emotional intensity
Banker	Builds trust through consistency, accuracy, and dependability	Withdraws in chaotic or unstructured environments; distrusts fast decisions
Squarish	Connects easily with all four energies; acts as a bridge that strengthens team unity	May appear unpredictable; internal conflict between energies can create hesitation or mixed signals

Figure 14. Core Values Trust and Collaboration Overview.

Team Dynamic Placemat

A lot of information has just been shared about how the core values shape, strengthen, and sometimes complicate team dynamics, and it is completely normal not to remember every detail. The expectation is not perfect recall but rather knowing where to look when you need clarity. Keeping *The Human Cheat Code*™ nearby as a quick reference guide will help you revisit key concepts whenever questions arise or team situations shift. Another powerful way to visualize and understand team dynamics is to create a *team dynamic placemat,* which gives you a clear, at-a-glance snapshot of how each person contributes and how the group functions as a whole.

Creating a single placemat that displays everyone's CVI™ profiles is an incredibly powerful way to visually see the areas of capacity and possible tension on a team. When I was first introduced to the CVI™, my immediate instinct was to build exactly this kind of placemat. Something visual, simple, and always accessible because the CVI™ isn't meant to be a one-and-done experience. I've built placemats for teams as small as 4-people up to 18-people, creating extra placemats to capture the whole team breaking them out if necessary (front office team, division leadership, etc.).

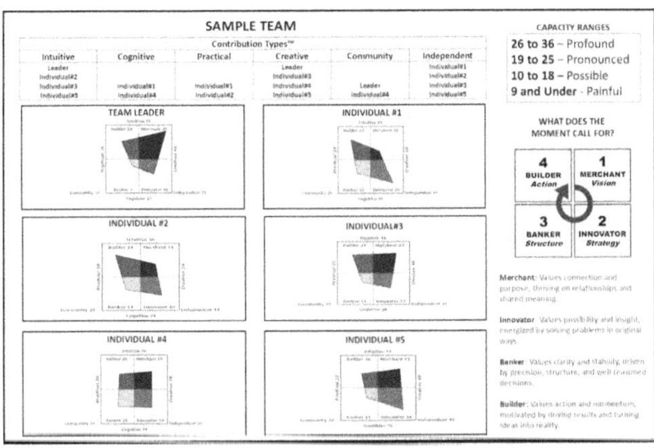

Figure 15. Sample Team Dynamic Placemat

The CVI™ is a framework for effective living, a lens through which people can understand themselves and others with more clarity and compassion. A team placemat makes those lessons visible every day. I have actually laminated these placemats to extend its life and utility. The team dynamic placemat helps people remember each other's capacities, anticipate how teammates naturally operate, and normalize the idea that different energies bring different contributions. It also reinforces the idea that diversity of wiring is an asset, not a barrier. With everyone's core values laid out on one-page, the team gains a shared understanding and a shared map for navigating collaboration, communication, and conflict more intentionally.

For a leader, seeing the entire team on one placemat is like having a strategic dashboard for human dynamics. It allows them to instantly recognize where the team is strong, where it may be unbalanced, and where certain energies might be overextended or underutilized. A leader can use this insight to assign roles more thoughtfully, anticipate friction points before they escalate, and ensure that each person is working in alignment with their natural core values. It also helps leaders avoid the common trap of expecting everyone to think or behave like they do. Instead, they can tailor their coaching, communication, and expectations to match each person's core wiring. This kind of visibility transforms leadership from guesswork into intentional, core values-based guidance.

When everyone on the team has access to the placemat, the benefits multiply. Team members can quickly understand how to approach one another, who to go to for certain types of support, and how to structure collaboration in a way that honors everyone's core values. During projects, the placemat becomes a practical tool for assembling balanced working groups, distributing responsibilities, and preventing misunderstandings. In day-to-day interactions, it helps people interpret behaviors through a values-based lens rather than through frustration or assumption. It encourages empathy, reduces unnecessary conflict, and builds a culture where differences are understood rather than judged. Ultimately, a shared placemat becomes a living resource that keeps the team aligned, self-aware, and connected.

Closing Thoughts on Team Dynamics

As a kid I used to watch a cartoon comprised of all my favorite superheroes. Every episode showed how each super power contributed to the team and overcame the enemy. Likewise, individuals with *profound* and *pronounced* CVI™ capacities are like those super heroes that can contribute to the team's success when they use their core values to full capacity in positive ways.

Individuals with squarish CVI™ profiles are like those leaders who can do it all but their power is evident when they participate in all four quadrants, guide the team through the process and transitions, and call on those whose moment it is. ***Important Point: Individuals don't have to be well-rounded but teams should be.***

For this reason, having all core values represented on a team and then leveraging each core value appropriately and at the right time allows a leader to get the most out of their team. Team dynamics thrive when people understand themselves, understand each other, and have a shared framework for how to work together and that's exactly what the CVI™ brings to a team. Across all the core values: *Merchants, Innovators, Bankers, Builders,* and even *Squarish* profiles, the CVI™ highlights how each person naturally communicates, collaborates, solves problems, and responds to stress. Healthy team dynamics emerge when these differences are recognized as positive contributions rather than friction points. *Builders* drive action, *Merchants* build connection, *Innovators* create solutions, *Bankers* ensure accuracy, and *Squarish* profiles bridge gaps between everyone.

When teams use tools like a shared core values placemat, they keep these insights visible and actionable, preventing the CVI™ from becoming a one-time experience and instead turning it into a living framework for effective teamwork. Leaders gain clarity on how to assign roles, anticipate challenges, and support each person's core values, while team members gain empathy, reduce misunderstandings, and collaborate more intentionally. The big takeaway is simple: when a team understands the natural wiring of its people, communication improves, trust deepens, burnout decreases, and performance rises because everyone is finally working in alignment with who they truly are.

CHAPTER 17
FRAMEWORK OVERLAY

he CVI™ isn't the kind of assessment you take once, get a bit of feedback on, attend a training session, and then forget about and put on a shelf. It's a living framework, something you can overlay onto any person, group, situation, or action to understand what's really happening beneath the surface. I call it *The Human Cheat Code™* because you can walk into any environment, sense the natural flow of what should be happening, and recognize immediately when things are out of alignment so you can help guide individuals and situations back on track. When you understand the forces that drive each core value, you begin to see them expressed in people long before they ever take the assessment themselves. The CVI™ was designed to be used constantly, dozens, even hundreds of times a day because it becomes a lens through which you interpret behavior, communication, conflict, and collaboration. And because it's a framework rather than a judgment, it strips away bias and allows you to respond from a place of humility, clarity, and genuine understanding. When you embrace the CVI™ as a daily tool, not a one-time event, it becomes a powerful ally in strengthening relationships, elevating your work, and navigating every corner of life with greater wisdom and intention.

We'll now explore several scenarios that show just how versatile the CVI™ framework truly is. These scenarios demonstrate how the CVI™ can be applied across a wide array of challenges, helping people navigate situations with clarity, confidence, and purpose.

SECTION I: Leaders

Leadership is rarely about having all the answers. More often, it's about walking into rooms filled with tension, uncertainty, or pressure and finding a way to bring clarity where confusion reigns. Leaders must navigate personalities, motivations, and emotional undercurrents that aren't always visible on the surface.

The CVI™ gives leaders a powerful lens to understand what drives people at their core. When leaders know their own values, and can recognize the values in others, they gain the ability to respond with precision, empathy, and confidence.

The following stories place you inside leadership moments. You'll see how leaders with different CVI™ combinations use their innate core values to transform conflict, decision paralysis, team dysfunction, resistance, and crisis into opportunities for alignment and growth.

The Conflict in the Conference Room (Merchant/Innovator)

The storm outside rattled the windows, but the real thunder was happening inside the conference room. Sarah paused in the doorway, taking in the scene. Two team members leaning across the table, voices sharp and overlapping, papers scattered like debris from an explosion. The tension was so thick it felt like humidity in the air.

"Are you kidding me?" one of them snapped. "You completely ignored the timeline!"

"Oh, please," the other shot back. "You dumped half the work on me at the last minute!"

Sarah felt her stomach tighten. She was the project lead and this was the last thing she needed. For a split second, she felt the urge to slam her notebook on the table and demand silence. But she caught herself.

This wasn't about the deadline. This was about values colliding.

She stepped forward, her voice calm but firm. "Alright, let's pause. I want to hear both of you, but one at a time."

Her *Merchant* energy softened her tone, creating a sense of emotional safety. She could feel the room exhale as she acknowledged both perspectives.

Then her *Innovator* value took over. She scanned the situation.

One teammate was a *Builder* (direct, urgent, ready to act).

The other was a *Banker* (cautious, detail-oriented).

They weren't fighting each other.

They were fighting for their values.

"Here's what I'm hearing," Sarah said, drawing two columns on the whiteboard. "You need clarity and structure. And you need momentum and action. Both are valid."

The room shifted. Shoulders dropped. Arms uncrossed.

She mapped out a plan that honored both needs. A timeline with clear checkpoints (for the *Banker*) and flexible action windows (for the *Builder*). The argument dissolved not because she forced peace, but because she understood the values beneath the conflict.

Later, one of them approached her. "I don't know how you do that," he said. "You always know what we actually mean, even when we're yelling."

Sarah smiled. She said to herself, "It's not magic. It's the CVI™."

A Blueprint for Victory (Banker/Builder)

Erin was known for her steady, practical leadership. As a *Banker/Builder*, she worked on empowering her team versus doing things herself. She relied on structure, clarity, and long-term thinking rather than charisma. When HarborWorks Construction fell behind on its largest project, the team panicked. Subcontractors were frustrated, the client was losing trust, and blame was spreading through the halls.

During a tense meeting with the client, people argued and

defended themselves. Erin's *Builder* resisted the urge to take over and instead stayed quiet, absorbing every detail. Her *Banker* mind naturally sorted the chaos into priorities. Later that day, she gathered the team and presented a new plan. Her *Banker*-side ensured there was a realistic timeline, a clear communication system, and a risk-management approach that anticipated obstacles before they appeared.

Her *Builder* confidence steadied everyone. The team left the room relieved. They finally had a structure they could trust.

Over the next two months, Erin's plan brought the project back to life. Subcontractors felt supported, the client received consistent updates, and the team moved in sync. When the client returned for a scheduled visit, they saw a project not only recovered but ahead of the revised schedule.

"You saved this project," the client said. Erin simply nodded. Her victory came from doing what her wiring made her best at: building systems that last and protecting the mission from falling apart.

The Team on the Brink (Builder/Merchant)

The office felt like a pressure cooker. Deadlines loomed, tempers flared, and productivity slipped through the cracks. Allison watched her team unravel. People snapping at each other, emails dripping with passive aggression, meetings filled with tension instead of progress.

She could feel the weight of it pressing on her chest.

During a particularly tense meeting, two team members argued over who was responsible for a missed deliverable. Another rolled her eyes dramatically. Someone else muttered under his breath.

Allison closed her notebook. "Everyone, take a breath," she said. "We're not doing this."

As a *Builder/Merchant*, she knew she had to intervene before the team collapsed.

Her *Builder* value kicked in first. She spent the afternoon creating a clear, structured plan with deadlines, responsibilities, and checkpoints. The team needed direction, and she provided it.

But structure alone wouldn't fix the emotional fractures.

So, she shifted into her *Merchant* energy. She walked from desk to desk, reconnecting with each person, listening to their frustrations, and reminding them of their contributions.

"You're not alone in this," she told one teammate. "We're going to get through this together," she told another.

The next morning, the team entered the office with a different energy. Meetings became productive again. People collaborated instead of competing. The tension dissolved.

One teammate approached her privately. "I don't know what changed," he said, "but it feels like we're a team again."

Allison smiled. "We just needed to be understood and valued."

The Leader Facing Resistance (Innovator/Banker)

When Margaret introduced a new workflow system, she expected excitement. Instead, she got crossed arms, skeptical glances, and whispered complaints.

"This is going to slow us down."

"Why are we changing something that works?"

"I don't get it."

The resistance was palpable.

But Margaret didn't take it personally.

She took it as data.

As an *Innovator/Banker*, she understood that people weren't rejecting the system, they were reacting from their core values.

Builders felt slowed down.

Merchants felt disconnected from the decision.

Bankers felt uncertain about the details.

So, she adjusted her approach.

She used her *Innovator* clarity to break the workflow into simple, digestible steps. She anticipated questions before they were asked. Then she used her *Banker* value to provide documentation, FAQs, and predictable structure.

She held a meeting and said, "I want you to see exactly how this helps each of you."

By the end of the week, the resistance had faded. People were using the system confidently. Productivity increased.

One team member said, "I didn't think I'd like this, but it actually makes sense."

Margaret smiled and said to herself, "That's the power of understanding what people value."

The Leader Navigating a Crisis (Merchant/Builder)

The moment the system crashed, chaos erupted. Phones rang nonstop, customers demanded answers, and the team spiraled into panic. John felt the weight of leadership settle on his shoulders.

"Everything's down!" someone shouted.

"We're losing clients!" another cried.

John raised his hands. "Everyone, breathe."

As a *Merchant/Builder*, he used his *Merchant* energy to calm the room, reassure his team, and keep communication open. People needed emotional grounding, and he provided it.

Then he activated his *Builder* value: assigning roles, prioritizing tasks, and driving action with confidence.

"You handle customer communication."

"You work with IT."

"You document everything."

The team snapped into motion.

Within hours, the system restored, clients updated, crisis passed.

Later, a teammate said, "I don't know how you stayed so calm."

John replied, "I wasn't calm. I was aligned."

Closing Thoughts on Leaders

Leadership becomes exponentially more effective when leaders understand the core values driving human behavior. The CVI™ gives leaders a lens that cuts through confusion and reveals the motivations beneath actions. Whether navigating conflict, guiding teams through change, or making high-stakes decisions, leaders who use the CVI™ lead with clarity, empathy, and purpose.

Reflection Questions

- How does your dominant core value influence your leadership style?
- When you face conflict, which value do you naturally lead with? Ignore?
- Where do you see misalignment between your core values and your daily leadership actions?
- Which of your secondary values do you underuse in leadership moments?
- How could understanding the CVI™ reduce stress or conflict on your team?
- What leadership situation are you currently facing where the CVI™ could help?

SECTION II: Couples

Relationships are where our core values show up most vividly and sometimes most painfully. When two people come together, they bring not only their histories and hopes, but also their natural ways of thinking, feeling, and responding to the world. The CVI™ gives couples a shared language to understand these differences, not as flaws or incompatibilities, but as essential parts of who each person is.

In the following stories, you'll step into the intimate spaces where couples struggle, misunderstand, reconnect, and grow. Each narrative shows how two people use their CVI™ core values to bridge emotional gaps, resolve recurring conflicts, and build deeper connection. These stories are not about perfection, they're about awareness, compassion, and the courage to understand one another at a deeper level.

· · ·

The Kitchen Table Conversation (Banker/Builder)

The morning sunlight spilled across the kitchen table, catching the steam rising from two untouched mugs of coffee. Estelita sat across from her husband, arms folded, jaw tight. They had been here before. The same argument, the same tension, the same feeling of talking past each other.

"I just don't feel heard," her husband said quietly, staring at the table instead of at her.

Estelita exhaled, long and slow. She wasn't trying to ignore him. She wasn't trying to be dismissive. But every time emotions ran high, she felt herself shutting down, scrambling for solutions instead of connection.

As a *Banker/Builder*, Estelita's natural instinct was to evaluate, but under stress, her *Builder* value took over, pushing her toward action instead of empathy. She realized that her husband, an *Innovator/Merchant*, needed clarity and connection in conversations, not intensity.

She leaned forward. "Okay," she said softly. "Help me understand what I'm missing."

Her husband looked up, surprised by the shift in tone.

Estelita let her *Banker* energy lead. She listened, took in all his concerns, without interrupting, without defending, without trying to fix anything. She nodded, asked gentle questions, and reflected back what she heard.

Then, once the emotional fog cleared, she activated her *Builder* value. "Here's what I can do differently," she said. "And here's what I need from you so we don't keep looping."

For the first time in months, the conversation didn't end in frustration. It ended in understanding.

Later, her husband said, "That felt different. It felt like you were actually with me."

Estelita smiled. "I was. And humility helped me get there."

. . .

The Planner and the Spontaneous One (Banker/Merchant)

David sat on the couch with his laptop open, spreadsheets neatly organized, color-coded tabs lining the top of the screen. He had spent hours planning their upcoming vacation: flights, hotels, activities, backup plans for weather, even restaurant reservations.

He turned the screen toward his wife with a proud smile. "What do you think?"

His wife blinked. "It's… a lot."

Her tone wasn't unkind, but David felt his stomach drop. He had poured his heart into this. Planning was how he showed love. As a *Banker/Merchant*, structure and preparation made him feel safe and he wanted his wife to feel that safety too.

But his wife, a *Builder/Innovator*, felt suffocated by too much structure. She needed freedom, flexibility, room to explore.

David closed the laptop slowly. "You don't like it."

"It's not that," his wife said, sitting beside him. "I love that you care this much. But I also want space to just… wander."

He took a breath. She is a *Builder/Innovator*, he reminded himself.

His *Banker* value helped him articulate his needs clearly. "I need some structure so I don't feel anxious," he said. "But I also want you to enjoy the trip."

Then he let his *Merchant* energy soften the moment. "What if we build a loose plan? A few anchors each day, and the rest is open?"

His wife's face lit up. "That actually sounds perfect."

Together, they created a hybrid itinerary. Enough structure for him, enough freedom for her. And for the first time, planning felt like a shared experience instead of a tug-of-war.

The Emotional Disconnect (Innovator/Builder)

Nora sat on the edge of the bed, hands clasped, staring at the floor. Her husband paced the room, voice trembling with emotion.

"I just feel like you don't care," he said. "You shut down every time I try to talk to you."

Nora's chest tightened. She cared deeply, more than she could express. But as an *Innovator/Builder*, emotional intensity overwhelmed her. Her mind raced to find solutions, to fix the problem, to make the feelings stop.

But that wasn't what her husband needed. He was a *Merchant/Banker*, he needed connection, reassurance, presence.

She took a slow breath. "Stay with him," she told herself.

She used her *Innovator* clarity to stay grounded, listening without trying to solve anything. She repeated back what she heard, making sure she understood.

Then she used her *Builder* value to take meaningful action. She sat beside him, placed a hand on his back, and said, "I'm here. I'm not going anywhere. Tell me what you need."

Her husband's shoulders relaxed. The pacing stopped. He sat beside her, leaning into the moment.

For the first time, Nora wasn't trying to fix the emotion, she was meeting it.

And that changed everything.

The Recurring Argument About Responsibilities (Builder/Banker)

Every Sunday afternoon, the same argument erupted. Chores weren't done, expectations weren't met, and both partners felt misunderstood. Jamie stood in the kitchen, arms crossed, frustration radiating off her.

"I asked you three times to take out the trash," she said.

Her husband, a *Merchant/Innovator*, sighed. "I just forgot. I wasn't trying to ignore you."

As a *Builder/Banker*, Jamie valued action and structure. When tasks weren't done, it felt like disrespect. But her husband wasn't being careless, he simply didn't operate from the same value set.

Jaime paused. This isn't about the trash, she realized. This is about values.

She used her *Banker* value to create a simple, predictable system. A shared checklist on the fridge, with clear responsibilities and deadlines. Then she used her *Builder* energy to take the lead on tasks requiring speed and decisiveness.

Her husband felt supported instead of criticized. The arguments faded. The house ran smoothly. And Jamie felt the relief of structure without the resentment of carrying everything alone.

The Couple Facing a Life Transition (Merchant/Innovator)

Moving to a new city had shaken everything: routines, friendships, comfort. Esther sat on the balcony of their new apartment, staring at the unfamiliar skyline. Her husband unpacked boxes inside, trying to stay busy.

"I feel lost," Esther whispered when he joined her outside.

As a *Merchant/Innovator*, she felt disconnected and uncertain. Her husband, a *Builder/Banker*, coped by diving into logistics: setting up utilities, organizing the kitchen, assembling furniture.

They weren't misaligned. They were grieving differently.

Esther used her *Merchant* energy to initiate a conversation about their feelings, fears, and hopes. Then she used her *Innovator* value to create a shared plan for adjusting: exploring the city, finding community groups, setting new routines.

Her husband softened. "I didn't realize you needed this," he said.

"I didn't either," Esther replied.

Together, they stepped into their new life, not perfectly, but united.

Closing Thoughts on Couples

Relationships thrive not because partners are the same, but because they learn to honor each other's differences. The CVI™ gives couples a framework to understand the deeper motivations behind behavior, turning conflict into clarity and disconnection into connection.

The stories above show that love grows strongest when partners see each other fully and respond with intention, compassion, and alignment.

. . .

Reflective Questions

- Which story felt most familiar to your own relationship experiences?
- How do your core values influence the way you communicate with your partner?
- What recurring conflict in your relationship might actually be a values mismatch?
- How does your partner's core value shape the way they express love or stress?
- Which of your values do you lean on most during emotional conversations?
- Which value do you underuse with your partner?
- How could the CVI™ help you navigate your next disagreement with more clarity?
- What is one small change you can make today to honor your partner's core values?

SECTION III: Teams

Teams are living systems. Complex, dynamic, and deeply influenced by the personalities and values of the people within them. When teams thrive, it's rarely by accident. It happens when individuals understand not only their own positive contributions but also the motivations and needs of those around them.

The CVI™ gives teams a shared framework that removes guesswork and reveals the deeper drivers behind behavior. When team members understand each other's core values, communication becomes clearer, collaboration becomes smoother, and conflict becomes easier to navigate.

The following stories place you inside team environments: project rooms buzzing with tension, cross-department groups struggling to communicate, teams on the brink of burnout, and organizations navigating change. Each narrative shows how the CVI™ helps teams realign, reconnect, and regain momentum.

The Misaligned Project Team (Innovator/Merchant)

The project room felt like a battlefield. Sticky notes covered the walls, laptops were open on every surface, and the air buzzed with frustration. Rich stepped inside and immediately sensed the tension. Team members talked over each other, priorities clashed, and progress had stalled.

"We can't keep changing the plan every day," one person snapped.

"Well, we can't keep ignoring new information," another shot back.

Rich closed the door behind him, taking in the chaos. As an *Innovator/Merchant*, he naturally saw patterns where others saw noise. He watched the interactions closely. The *Builder* pushing for action, the *Banker* demanding structure, the *Merchant* seeking connection, the *Innovator* craving clarity.

They weren't misaligned because they lacked skill. They were misaligned because they didn't understand each other's values.

"Alright," Rich said, stepping forward. "Let's reset."

He used his *Innovator* clarity to map out the core issue. Everyone was working from their own value lens, not a shared one. He drew four quadrants on the whiteboard and labeled them with the core values.

"Here's what's happening," he said. "We're not wrong, we're just speaking different languages."

The room quieted.

Then he used his *Merchant* energy to bring everyone together. He facilitated a conversation where each person shared what they needed to feel effective. *Builders* wanted momentum. *Bankers* wanted predictability. *Merchants* wanted connection. *Innovators* wanted logic.

By the end of the meeting, the team had a new plan, one that honored every value.

The tension dissolved.

The energy shifted.

The team moved forward with renewed cohesion.

The Team Struggling with Communication (Banker/Innovator)

Deadlines were slipping, and no one could agree on why. Emails were vague, meetings were rushed, and tasks fell through the cracks. Margie sat in the conference room reviewing the latest missed deliverable, feeling the weight of the team's frustration.

"This isn't working," someone muttered.

"No one knows what anyone else is doing," another added.

As a *Banker/Innovator*, Margie approached the problem differently than most. Instead of blaming people, she looked for patterns. She noticed that *Builders* were acting before information was complete, *Merchants* were improvising, and *Bankers* were waiting for clarity that never came.

The issue wasn't effort.

It was communication.

She gathered the team and said, "We're not failing because we're unskilled. We're failing because we're misaligned."

She used her *Banker* value to create a structured communication system: clear expectations, defined channels, and predictable updates. Then she used her *Innovator* energy to refine the system so it worked for all value types.

Builders got quick action steps.

Bankers got detailed documentation.

Merchants got collaborative check-ins.

Innovators got logical workflows.

Within two weeks, deadlines were met consistently. The team felt lighter, more connected, more confident.

One teammate said, "It's like we finally understand each other."

Margie smiled. "That's the CVI™ in action."

. . .

The Team Facing Burnout (Merchant/Banker)

The exhaustion was visible. Slumped shoulders, short tempers, and a sense of dread hanging over the office. Jayden watched his team drag themselves through another meeting, their energy drained, their creativity gone.

"We're drowning," someone whispered.

Jayden felt it too. As a *Merchant/Banker*, he was deeply attuned to the emotional climate of the team. He sensed the burnout long before anyone said it out loud.

As a *Merchant*, he called a meeting. Not to discuss tasks, but to discuss people.

"Talk to me," he said gently. "What's going on?"

At first, no one spoke. Then the floodgates opened. People shared their stress, their overwhelm, their fear of failing. Jayden listened with his *Merchant* heart, validating their experiences, acknowledging their exhaustion.

Then he shifted into his *Banker* value. He created predictable routines, clearer expectations, and manageable workloads. He removed unnecessary meetings, clarified priorities, and built in recovery time.

Within days, the team's energy began to return.

Within weeks, they were performing better than ever.

One teammate approached him privately. "Thank you," they said. "I didn't realize how much I needed someone to see us."

Jayden smiled. "That's what the CVI™ helps me do."

The Team with Conflicting Work Styles (Builder/Innovator)

Some team members moved at lightning speed, while others needed time to think. The result? Frustration on both sides. Monica watched the tension build during a planning session.

"Are we still talking about this" a *Builder* snapped. "Just do it."

"We haven't thought it through," an *Innovator* replied, exasperated.

Monica stepped in. As a *Builder/Innovator*, she understood both sides intimately. She knew *Builders* needed action to feel productive, while *Innovators* needed clarity to feel confident.

"You are both right," she said. "We need a process that honors both."

She used her *Builder* value to set clear action steps and timelines, giving the fast-paced workers the structure they needed. Then she used her *Innovator* clarity to create space for thoughtful input before decisions were finalized.

The team relaxed.

The tension eased.

The work flowed.

One teammate said, "I didn't realize how much our values were clashing."

Monica nodded. "Once you see it, you can fix it."

The Team Navigating Change (Banker/Merchant)

When the company announced a major restructuring, uncertainty rippled through the team. People whispered in hallways, productivity dipped, and anxiety spread like wildfire. Joel watched his team struggle, their confidence shaken.

"What does this mean for us?" someone asked.

"Are our roles changing?" another whispered.

As a *Banker/Merchant*, Joel knew he had to steady the ship.

He used his *Banker* value to gather accurate information, not rumors, not guesses, but facts. He created a clear summary of what was known, what was unknown, and what the next steps would be.

Then he used his *Merchant* energy to communicate openly and compassionately. He held space for questions, acknowledged fears, and reassured the team that they would navigate the transition together.

The panic faded.

The team regained focus.

Trust was restored.

One teammate said, "I feel like we can handle anything as long as you're leading us."

Joel smiled. "It's not me. It's the values we're honoring."

Closing Thoughts on Teams

Teams thrive when they understand each other's abilities, needs, and motivations. The CVI™ provides a framework that removes bias, reduces friction, and creates alignment. These stories show how teams can use the CVI™ to communicate better, collaborate more effectively, and navigate challenges with confidence.

When teams operate with CVI™ awareness, they don't just work together, they thrive together.

Reflective Questions

- Which story reminded you of a team you've been part of? How would you handle that situation?
- How do your core values influence how you collaborate with others?
- What team conflict might actually be a values mismatch rather than a personal issue?
- Which value do you rely on most when under pressure?
- Which value do you underuse when collaborating?
- How could the CVI™ help your team communicate better?
- What is one change you could make today to better honor the values of your teammates?

Final Thoughts on Using the CVI™ Framework Daily

Take a moment to look back at the world you've just walked through: boardrooms filled with tension, kitchen tables layered with emotion, teams navigating pressure, and individuals discovering the deeper motivations behind their actions. Across every story and every scenario, one truth has echoed again and again:

When you understand core values, you understand people.

The CVI™ is not simply a tool for leaders, couples, or teams. It is a framework for life. A way of seeing the world that brings clarity and understanding. It reveals the invisible forces that shape how we communicate, how we decide, how we love, how we lead, and how we respond to stress.

And once you see those forces, you can't unsee them.

You begin to notice the *Builder's* urgency in a heated conversation.

You recognize the *Banker's* need for structure and certainty.

You appreciate the *Merchant's* desire for connection.

You value the *Innovator's* search for clarity when things feel chaotic.

You start to understand people aren't difficult, they're different.

They're not resisting you. They're protecting their values.

They're not ignoring you. They're responding from their wiring.

And you, too, are responding from yours.

Throughout this chapter, you've seen how leaders use the CVI™ to guide teams through conflict and crisis. You've watched couples bridge emotional gaps and build deeper connection. You've witnessed teams transform misalignment into momentum. And woven through every story is a reminder that the CVI™ is not a one-time assessment. It's a daily practice.

A lens.
A compass.
A powerful guide.

It helps you understand yourself with honesty and others with humility. It removes the guesswork from human behavior and replaces it with insight. It turns reactive moments into intentional ones. It transforms relationships (professional and personal) by giving you the language to honor the core values and needs of the people around you. *But the most powerful transformation happens within you.*

Because when you understand your core values, you understand your purpose. You begin to see why certain tasks energize you while others drain you. Why certain environments bring out your best while others suppress your positive contributions. Why certain conflicts feel personal even when they're not. *You begin to see the blueprint of who you were created to be.*

And when you align your actions with that blueprint, when you combine your inner design with intentional choices, you step into a life marked by clarity, confidence, and contribution.

This is the real gift of the CVI™…it helps you live a fulfilling life. Not by trying to become someone else. Not by forcing yourself into roles that don't fit. Not by guessing at what others need. But by honoring the values that make you uniquely equipped to impact the world.

So, as we close this chapter, remember this: You now carry a framework that can guide you through any situation. Leadership challenges, relationship struggles, team dynamics, personal decisions, and moments of uncertainty. You have a tool that helps you see people clearly, respond with intention, and act with purpose.

The CVI™ is not the end of your journey. It is the beginning of a new way of living.

Where you understand others compassionately.
Where you contribute meaningfully.
Where you lead authentically.
Where you love intentionally.
Where you grow continuously.

And where you step boldly into the purpose that has been waiting for you all along.

Your next chapter isn't written yet, but now, you have the clarity to write it well.

CHAPTER 18
THE JOURNEY AHEAD: LIVING WITH PURPOSE

You've reached the end of this book, but you're standing at the beginning of something far more important, the beginning of a new way of living, leading, relating, and contributing. The CVI™ is no longer just a concept you've read about. It's a framework you can carry into every conversation, every decision, and every moment of your life.

Now is the time to put it into motion.

Start noticing your values in action.

Pay attention to the moments when your core values come alive, when you feel energized, aligned, and fully yourself. Those moments are clues pointing toward your purpose.

Start recognizing the values in others.

Watch how people communicate, decide, react, and connect. When you see their core values, you stop taking things personally and start responding with understanding.

Start using the CVI™ daily.

Not once a week. Not when things go wrong.

Every day. Throughout your day.

In the small moments that shape the big ones.

Use it when you're making decisions.

Use it when you're resolving conflict.

Use it when you're leading, loving your partner, navigating change.

Use it when you're unsure what to do next.

Start living with intention.

Your values are not random. They are the blueprint of how you were designed to contribute to the world. When you align your actions with your core values, you unlock clarity, confidence, and momentum.

Start becoming the person you were created to be.

Not by trying harder. Not by becoming someone else. But by stepping fully into who you already are.

The CVI™ is a powerful guide.
Your values are a compass.
Your purpose is waiting.
Now is the moment to act.

Take what you've learned and bring it to life. In your leadership approach, your relationships, your teams, and your own personal journey. The world needs what only you can offer. Your next step begins now.

Final Thoughts

The end of a book is never really an ending. It's a doorway. A threshold between what you've learned and what you choose to do with it. As you close these pages, you're not stepping away from the CVI™. You're stepping into a new way of seeing yourself, others, and the world.

Throughout this book, you've walked beside leaders navigating conflict and crisis, couples learning to understand each other more deeply, and teams discovering how to collaborate with clarity and trust. You've seen how the CVI™ framework reveals the motivations beneath behavior, the patterns beneath tension, and the potential contribution beneath struggle. But the true power of the CVI™ isn't just found in the stories of others. It's found in what you choose to do next.

The CVI™ is not a test. It's not a label. It's not a box to fit into or a certificate to hang on a wall. **It's a lens.** One you can carry with you into every conversation, every decision, every relationship, and every challenge. It's a way of seeing the world that removes judgment and replaces it with understanding. It takes the guesswork out of human behavior and replaces it with clarity. It transforms frustration into curiosity, conflict into alignment, and confusion into purpose.

And perhaps most importantly, it reminds you that you were created with intention. Your core values are not random. They are not accidental. They are not flaws to fix or traits to hide.

They are the blueprint of how you were designed to contribute to the world. When you understand your values, you understand your purpose. When you understand the values of others, you understand your path forward.

The CVI™ becomes a compass, one that points you toward the work you're meant to do, the relationships you're meant to build, and the impact you're meant to make. It helps you see where you naturally thrive, where you naturally struggle, and where you naturally bring value. It shows you how to lead with authenticity, love with intention, and collaborate with humility.

And as you've seen throughout these chapters, the CVI™ is not something you use once in a while. It's something you can use **dozens of times a day**. In the quick decisions, the subtle interactions, the moments of tension, and the opportunities for connection. It becomes a quiet guide, shaping how you show up in the world.

But the journey doesn't end here.

The real transformation begins when you truly start applying the CVI™ to your own life, not just in the big moments, but in the small ones. When you pause before reacting. When you choose curiosity over assumption. When you recognize the value in someone else's perspective. When you honor your own values instead of apologizing for them.

This is where purpose takes root. This is where growth begins. This is where alignment becomes possible.

You are a unique combination of values, experiences, and gifts. No one else in the world has your exact blend of core values. No one else sees the world the way you do. No one else can contribute what you can contribute.

And when you combine that inner design with intentional action, when you align your values with your choices, you step into the purpose that has been waiting for you all along. So, as you close this book, remember this:

You are not meant to fit into someone else's mold. You are not meant to dim your abilities to match the room. You are not meant to navigate life blindly, guessing at what people need or what you're capable of.

You are meant to live with clarity. You are meant to lead with confidence. You are meant to love with understanding. You are meant to contribute with purpose.

The CVI™ is a powerful guide. Your values are your compass. Your life is your canvas. And the journey ahead is yours to shape.

COMPLETING THE CVI™

If you want to complete the CVI™ assessment, set up an individual feedback session, or a training event, visit www.1012solutions.com.

ACKNOWLEDGMENTS

I would like to personally thank Justin Erickson who is the Founder of Hardwired Coaching LLC. He introduced me to the CVI™ and I learned a lot from him as I began my journey using the CVI™. I also want to thank Travis Stovall who is CEO of eREP, Inc. whose platform hosts the CVI™. He trained me as a Value Added Reseller and expanded my understanding of the CVI™ . I am truly grateful to these two gentlemen for shaping my understanding of the CVI™.

ABOUT THE AUTHOR

Rodney Lee Mills is the Founder of 1012 Solutions LLC™ and is a Value-Added Reseller (VAR) for the CVI™. He received his CVI™ certification through eRep™. Rodney is a retired Lieutenant Colonel (Lt Col) from the United States Air Force and served over 20 years in the military and almost 20 years in the United States federal civil service.

www.ingramcontent.com/pod-product-compliance
Lightning Source LLC
Chambersburg PA
CBHW050905260726

48660CB00001B/34